DATE DUE

FEB 1 0 2009

Developing Alternative Media Traditions in Nepal

Developing Alternative Media Traditions in Nepal

MICHAEL WILMORE

LEXINGTON BOOKS

A division of
ROWMAN & LITTLEFIELD PUBLISHERS, INC.
Lanham • Boulder • New York • Toronto • Plymouth, UK

LEXINGTON BOOKS

A division of Rowman & Littlefield Publishers, Inc.
A wholly owned subsidiary of The Rowman & Littlefield Publishing Group, Inc.
4501 Forbes Boulevard, Suite 200
Lanham, MD 20706

Estover Road
Plymouth PL6 7PY
United Kingdom

British Library Cataloguing in Publication Information Available

Library of Congress Cataloging-in-Publication Data

Wilmore, Michael, 1969–
  Developing alternative media traditions in Nepal / Michael Wilmore.
      p. cm.
  Includes bibliographical references and index.
  ISBN-13: 978-0-7391-2525-0 (cloth : alk. paper)
  ISBN-10: 0-7391-2525-7 (cloth : alk. paper)
  eISBN 13: 978-0-7391-3052-0
  eISBN 10: 0-7391-3052-8
1. Alternative mass media—Nepal. I. Title.
  P96.A442N359 2008
  302.23095496—dc22

2008015432

Printed in the United States of America

♾™ The paper used in this publication meets the minimum requirements of American
National Standard for Information Sciences—Permanence of Paper for Printed Library
Materials, ANSI/NISO Z39.48–1992.

In memory of
Buddha Ratna Shakya

Contents

Tables

Abbreviations

CDO	Chief District Officer
CDP	Communication for Development Palpa
CPN (Maoist)	Communist Party of Nepal (Maoist)
DD	*Doordarshan*
DFID	Department for International Development, UK
GBS	*Gãu Bikãs Samiti* (see 'VDC')
GTZ	*Gesellschaft für Technische Zusammenarbeit* (German Organization for Technological Cooperation)
Helvetas	*Schweizer Gesellschaft für Internationale Zusammenarbeit* (Swiss Organization for International Cooperation)
HMG	His Majesty's Government
ICT	Information and Communication Technology
INGO	international non-governmental organization
INHURED	International Institute for Human Rights, Environment and Development
JCs	Junior Chamber of Commerce
LISP	Local Initiative Support Program (Helvetas)
MSN	*Mellemfolkeligt Samvirke Nepal* (Danish Association for International Cooperation, Nepal)
NC	Nepal Congress Party
NEFEJ	Nepal Forum for Environmental Journalists
NRs	Nepali Rupees
NTV	Nepal Television
PDP	Palpa Development Project (GTZ/Helvetas)
RCTV	Ratna Cable Television
RDP	Rural Development Palpa
RONAST	Royal Nepal Academy of Science and Technology
RPP	*Rastriya Prajatantra Party* (National Democratic Party)
RSRDC	Rural Self Reliance Development Center (*Swambalamban*)

RSS	*Rastriya Samachar Samiti* (National News Agency)
SLC	School Leaving Certificate
TWP	Tinau Watershed Project (GTZ/Helvetas)
UDLE	Urban Developments through Local Efforts (GTZ project)
UML	Communist Party of Nepal (United Marxist-Leninist)
UMN	United Mission to Nepal
UNDP	United Nations Development Program
UNESCO	United Nations Educational, Scientific and Cultural Organization
USAID	United States Agency for International Development
VDC	Village Development Committee (see 'GBS')

.

Preface

This book is based on doctoral research that began in 1994. At that time Nepal was less than four years into what has been a turbulent period of political transformation and violent civil war following the People's Movement (*Jana Andolan*) for the restoration of democracy in 1990. The revolution of April that year brought long suppressed anger regarding the lack of political freedom into the open, but it did not prove to be a conclusive moment of transformation. A simple list of the most important events of the past eighteen years indicates how dramatic have been the ongoing upheavals experienced by Nepal's people: the so-called People's War was initiated in 1996 by the Communist Party of Nepal (Maoist); King Birendra and his immediate family were murdered by his eldest son, Crown Prince Dipendra, in 2001; the short-lived direct rule of King Gyanendra that started in February 2005 was ended by a second Jana Andolan in April 2006; most recently the creation of an interim coalition government comprising the seven largest mainstream political parties and the Maoists brought overt political violence to an end and declared Nepal to be a republic. These events have, of course, been accompanied by continuing conditions of chronic poverty experienced by the great majority of Nepal's population.

However, amidst this situation of almost perpetual crisis there has been a remarkable transformation in Nepal's media. Whereas in 1990 almost all media were state controlled and access to modern forms of mass communication was extremely limited, by the decade's end new forms of media, spearheaded by the rapid growth of independent newspapers and FM radio broadcasting were proliferating at an incredible rate. As the Nepali media researcher Pratyoush Onta has written in relation to the rise of the independent radio sector, "its achievements constitute a slap in the face to those who make it their business to repeat the cliché that 'nothing happened during the era of multiparty democracy'" (2006: 119). It may also be the case that the crises of the past two decades have contributed to the conditions of looser state control and popular demand that were exactly what was required for Nepal's mediascape to be radically transformed (Hutt 2006).

My own experience of Nepal's media revolution began, as anthropological research often does, serendipitously, through an almost-by-chance encounter with a Nepali academic, Dipak Gyawali, of the *Royal Nepal Academy of Science and Technology* (RONAST), who in 1993 was conducting research in the UK.

During my postgraduate studies, I had become greatly interested in examples of what had come to be called 'indigenous media'. These were defined by the anthropologist Faye Ginsburg as media "produced by indigenous peoples, sometimes called the 'Fourth World,' whose societies have been dominated by encompassing states, such as the United States, Canada, and Australia" (1991: 107). I had previously worked in student journalism and publishing as an undergraduate and wanted to combine this with my growing academic interest in how people were taking advantage of new technologies, such as video and desktop publishing, to become the producers of their own media. I did not at that point have any firm idea about where I would go to learn more, but after discussing these ideas with a possible research supervisor, I was put in contact with Dipak. It was he who first told me about the work that was happening in community television in the town of Tansen in the western hills of Nepal that is described in this book. Although it was immediately apparent that this organization and their work did not conform to classic definitions of indigenous media, the possibilities for learning more about how people were confronting what Daya Kishan Thussu (1998) has called "the electronic empires" of global media were evident. This study has subsequently developed into a wide ranging analysis of the ways that media are adopted and adapted in the particular circumstances of a locality, and of the wider anthropology of Nepal.

Following a short scoping trip in 1994, I was able to return to Tansen to conduct a year of fieldwork between September 1995 and September 1996. It was an immense privilege to be given access to the work of the many people in this beautiful town who were (and still are) devoting their lives to developing different media to serve the needs of their community. I was also given huge assistance by the many dozens of other people who I met throughout my stay in Tansen and who helped me to understand more about their lives and culture. An anthropologist's greatest debt is owed to the people who take the time to answer questions, often with immense patience, and are willing to let a stranger enter their lives as a researcher. I cannot thank all these people by name, but I would like to say here how immensely grateful I am to all those who helped me in this work. Whenever possible I have avoided using the names of informants or employed pseudonyms in this work. The exceptions to this rule relate to people who may be clearly identified from their work and whose involvements in community media make them well known figures in Tansen and Nepal.

A number of people must, however, be thanked individually for their contributions to this work, although I alone bear full responsibility for what is included here. First, I would like to offer warm thanks to those who work for or on behalf of *Ratna Cable Television* and *Communication for Development Palpa*. Foremost amongst this remarkable group of people must be the late Buddha Ratna Shakya and his son Mahesh Shakya, Bharat Sharma, and Vinaya Kasajoo. Buddha Ratna died just over a year before this book was published and it is dedicated to his memory. Siddhartha Shrestha, his wife Renuka, and son Sijan adopted us into their family in Tansen. Their friendship sustained us whilst we were far from home and I cannot imagine being able to have completed this work without them. I also received great help and friendship from Nirmal

Shrestha, Madhav Pandey, Basanta Gahat Raj, and the members of their families.

During my fieldwork, I was greatly assisted by representatives of the following organisations in Tansen: *Redd Barna* (Norwegian Save the Children Fund), *Mellemfolkeligt Samvirke* (Danish Association for International Co-operation), the *US Peace Corp*, the *United Mission to Nepal Hospital[UMN] (Tansen)*, *UMN Community Health Development Project*, *Helvetas*, the *East Palpa Children's Committee*, *Swambalamban* (the Rural Self Reliance Development Centre), *Reyukai Nepal*, and *Nepal Red Cross Palpa*. Representatives of *Palpa District Administration* and *Tansen Municipality* were also of great assistance. I would particularly like to thank Direndra Prasad Shrestha, who was mayor of Tansen during my stay in Nepal, for his time and patience during my questioning. Ram Sharan Simkada and all the staff of the *Himalayan Computer and Language Institute* in Tansen gave me great help during my time in Nepal.

Many people in Kathmandu gave me assistance and useful information. My fieldwork was only possible due to the kind help of the *Centre for Nepal and Asian Studies* at *Tribhuvan University*, who sponsored my research visa application. Nirmal Tulhadar, Damini Vaidya, and Bijay Kumar Arjyal were unfailingly helpful throughout this process. I would also like to acknowledge the assistance of the *Higher Education Section of HMG Nepal Ministry of Education and Culture* who facilitated my visa application.

Members of the following organisations based in Kathmandu also gave me help: the *Nepal Forum for Environmental Journalists*, *Himal South Asia*, *Urban Development Through Local Efforts (GTZ)*, the *Nepal Foundation for Advanced Studies*, and the *Asia Foundation*. I have already mentioned the contribution made by Dipak Gyawali when this work was in its earliest stages, but I would like to thank him again for all his kind help and advice when I was in Nepal. I will always be very grateful for the encouragement he gave me during this project.

I am indebted to many people in the UK for their support and guidance. Foremost amongst these is my research supervisor, Dr Allen Abramson, of the *Dept. of Anthropology, University College London*. Allen has been an inspirational teacher, supervisor and friend during my studies. I also learned a great deal from the staff and students of UCL, who are too numerous to be mentioned by name. I would like to thank the examiners of the thesis upon which this book is based, Professor David Morley of *Goldsmiths College, University of London* and Professor David Gellner of the *Institute of Social and Cultural Anthropology, Oxford University*, for their kind and helpful comments. Three friends, Ian Harper, Radha Harper, and Damian Walter, must be thanked in particular for the help and hope they have given me from the outset of this work. My colleagues Andrew Skuse and Jo Fildes have been unfailingly supportive since I came to work at the *University of Adelaide*. Claire Smith and Gary Jackson have also provided me with many great opportunities to learn and develop as a researcher during the past few years in Australia. I am continuing to learn about Nepal's mediascape through collaborative work with Jo Tacchi and June Lennie of *Queensland University of Technology*, and with the *Equal Access* organization based in San Francisco and Patan, Nepal. Although these collaborations have begun only recently, I know that this work has greatly benefited from their ongoing contributions to my knowledge and experience.

The award of grants by the *Royal Anthropological Institute* (Emslie Horniman Scholarship and Radcliffe-Brown Fund) and the *University of London* (Irwin Fund) made my research possible. I would like to thank them for their generous financial support.

Material used in chapter 1 appeared in the journal *Anthropology Matters* (2001, 3; http://www.anthropologymatters.com/). An early version of chapter 6 was published in *Studies in Nepali History and Society* (2001, 6:2; http://www.asianstudies.emory.edu/sinhas/). A version of chapter 7 appeared in the journal *Ethnos* (2006, 71:3; http://www.informaworld.com). I am very grateful to the publishers of these journals for their permission to use this material and to the anonymous reviewers of these original works, whose comments were of great assistance.

Finally, this project would never have been completed without the wonderful support of Harriet and our two sons, Albie and Olie. I offer this work to them with my love.

Transliteration

The system of transliteration used in this study is derived from Ralph Turner's (1980 [1931]) *A Comparative and Etymological Dictionary of the Nepali Language*. Commonly used proper nouns, however, have been written in their more familiar forms.

Chapter 1
Introduction:
How Television Came to Tansen

Men make their own history, but they do not make it just as they please; they do not make it under circumstances chosen by themselves, but under circumstances directly encountered, given and transmitted from the past.

Karl Marx (1972 [1869]: 10)

Citizens' media are vital social phenomena. As such, I suggest that our attempts to understand them should be more dynamic and should be able to follow the subject of study in its historical movements, rather than remaining trapped in static formulas that freeze citizens' media, blinding us from their mobility through time, space and the live texture of culture and power.

Clemencia Rodriguez (2001: 165)

Introduction

This book is a study of what Molnar and Meadows (2001: 122) refer to as "the possibilities of 'small' television." It examines how a group of entrepreneurs and activists living in Tansen, a provincial town in the hills of western Nepal, came together in the early years of the 1990s to create their own television station. Taking advantage of what were then newly accessible technologies of video, cable and satellite, *Ratna Cable Television* (RCTV) and its sister organization, *Communication for Development Palpa* (CDP), became one of the first producers of community media in Nepal and, quite possibly, the first community television station in South Asia. Since their inception in the early 1990s, RCTV and CDP have grown, faced setbacks and been transformed into a hub for local, community-based multi-media production.

1

A detailed study of the origins and early work of RCTV/CDP enables us to appreciate the circumstances under which the possibilities of small-scale media production can be successfully realized in places such as Nepal. However, the purpose of this work is not to identify any simplistic formula for success in small-scale media organizations. Indeed, the central argument pursued here is that any such formula will inevitably be condemned to failure due to the evident role that local circumstances played in both the origins and subsequent survival of any particular initiative. As we shall see in the following chapters, the names of these organizations point to the crucial roles played by individuals (such as the founder of RCTV, Buddha Ratna Shakya) and localities (that is, Palpa district, of which Tansen is the headquarters) played in the development of this example of 'small' television. This concern with the careful contextualization of our understanding of RCTV/CDP is also reflected in the key questions that informed the conduct of the ethnographic research upon which this study is based. How did a small-scale, cable television organization making its own original programming come into being at this time and in this place? How did it come to take on its particular social and cultural characteristics in the course of its work? In other words, we are concerned here with an attempt to understand why this small-scale television organization began in Tansen and not some other part of Nepal (or South Asia for that matter), why it took on the particular characteristics that it did and how the organization changed over the course of the first years of its existence.

Although the approach to understanding advocated here is one that emphasizes the need for detailed ethnographic research into the particularity of a place and the people that live there, this does not mean that we are not simultaneously attempting to draw more general conclusions from what we learn. Daniel Miller (2003: 76) advocates "radical empiricism" as a means to avoid simplistic interpretations of complex realities. He insists that it is the *uncritical* application of a priori models of social and cultural practice which inevitably leads to some things being overlooked or discounted as relevant to the matters at hand. I emphasize *uncritical* here in order to avoid the assumption that this study is based upon a naïve concern with 'the facts of the matter', unmediated by any theoretical presuppositions. Any research and any researcher will inevitably miss much that could have been relevant to their work, but the crucial task is to let the situation as it is found provide the means to judge whether any prior theoretical formulation or experience of a related situation provides an adequate basis upon which to understand the matters at hand.

This work, therefore, presents *a* case study of the possibilities of a 'small' television organization, but it cannot be considered as *the* definitive example of how such organizations come into being and develop over time. The experiences of RCTV/CDP in Tansen cannot provide a blueprint for success in small-scale, non-mainstream media production. There is no chance that the factors that led to the creation and ultimate success of RCTV/CDP could ever be replicated elsewhere, either in Nepal or in another country. Rather, the general point that I will work to establish in this study is that the circumstances under which some form of small-scale, non-mainstream media can be established are not necessarily those that we might expect given the social, cultural, political, or economic circumstances prevailing in a place. At the same time, we should also not expect that small-scale or non-mainstream media organizations will always adopt a radical, progressive, or oppositional position, either in their organization of production process or in the content of the media that they produce.

The approach adopted here helps us to eschew the sorts of binary oppositions that are often characteristic of analyses of media (Rodriguez 2001; Deger 2006), although as the discussions of non-mainstream media in the following chapter illustrate, such oppositional discourse is difficult to avoid. It also seeks to present a more subtle appreciation of the motivations and actions of those who are the creators of non-mainstream media. As we shall see, the creation of what appear to be non-mainstream media can originate from circumstances and actions that occur in a complex relationship to supposedly mainstream factors, such as the operation of commercial media markets or the institutions of the nation-state. As Mark Peterson (2003: 214–5) observes,

> What seems straightforward when looking at certain examples becomes murky and ambiguous as our scrutiny takes us inevitably to border zones, such as the ethnic, minority and indigenous television produced in the United States, with various degrees of state and private involvement. Indigenous films, activist media, independent filmmaking, home movies and other such terms all simply point to a key aspect of contemporary media production: the technologies of production are not monopolies of states and capital-intensive corporate entities but involve a wide variety of networks, communities and social groups, which coexist alongside and define themselves dialogically against, state and private dream factories.

To adopt a phrase of Eric Michaels (1986), who was one of the most influential advocates and researchers of small-scale television, the Palpali "invention of television" in the early years of the 1990s demonstrates both the possibilities for production and the ways in which these arise in the midst of the inevitably entangled "modes of cultural production" (Michaels 1994: 121) that prevail in such a complex environment. Rodriguez's (2001: 165) warning regarding the dangers of becoming trapped in "static formulas" is one that must be heeded in any analysis of media.

New Media in Nepal

The mass media in Nepal have experienced unprecedented growth since 1990 when the late King Birendra finally gave in to the demands of protesters and lifted a three-decade-long ban on political parties. A new constitution initiated a system of parliamentary democracy and gave people hope that they would see a significant increase in living standards built upon the new political freedoms arising from the People's Movement (*Jana Andolan*) for the restoration of democracy. At the start of the 1990s virtually all national media, including newspapers, radio and television were state owned and controlled, but less than two decades later independent mass media flourish in Nepal and provide a model for media development towards which other peoples in the South Asian region look for inspiration (Page and Crawley 2001). We have already noted Pratyoush Onta's comment that the achievements of independent media, especially radio "constitute a slap in the face to those who make it their business to repeat the cliché that 'nothing happened during the era of multiparty democracy'" (Onta 2006: 119). Despite endemic poverty that can in part account for the terrible ten years of civil conflict initiated by the Communist Party of Nepal (Maoist)'s declaration of the 'People's War' in 1996 (Dixit 2006; Hutt 2004), the mass media provide one sector of industry, culture and society where life in Nepal has been undeniably transformed for the better.

Yet, this transformation in media has not been matched by a correspondingly dramatic improvement in the livelihoods of the great majority of people in Nepal. Equally, the growth of independent mass media does not appear to have had any directly observable or unequivocal catalyzing effects that have led to improvements in other areas of life. Whilst the transformation of mass media is itself an index of development, it also dramatically contrasts to the relatively poor performance of democratic era Nepal according to many other criteria of development and provides a cautionary note to those who see independent media as capable of bringing about wider positive changes in their own right. It is surely correct to view the media and information and communication technologies (ICTs) more broadly, as an integral component of social, political and economic transformation, but at the same time we must be cautious in our estimation of how and to what ends such influences occur. As Ernest Wilson notes, "so far, there is little evidence that ICTs act as an independent variable to influence significantly the balance of power between the powerful and the weak" (2004: 167).

Lacking in much research into the relationship between changing media on the one hand and wider social transformation and development on the other is an appreciation of "the precise mechanisms explaining the appropriation and division of the technology concerned in everyday life" (van Dijk 2006: 232). Such an appreciation requires the application of qualitative research methodologies that complement the existing and ongoing quantification and measurement that characterizes the great majority of studies of media change and development. To quote Wilson again, in order to understand the dynamic relationship between media and society "social scientists should start their investigations by reviewing deeply rooted indigenous practices and institutions. They should study the way in which local social forces that grow from those practices and institutions selectively restructure local conditions to take advantage of some aspects of imported knowledge, even while resisting others" (2004: 399). This is not to deny the validity of quantitative studies of media and development, but to argue that these studies can only be used to understand how such complex phenomena are related if they are combined with qualitative investigations that take the 'local' circumstances of the relationship into account.

This study of media in Nepal follows the spirit of Wilson's advice, if not his precise theoretical or methodological pathway by examining in detail how television and other media came to be incorporated into the lives of the inhabitants of Tansen. Although the state-owned broadcaster, *Nepal Television* (NTV), had begun broadcasting in the Kathmandu Valley region in 1985, it took almost a decade for its transmissions to reach the district of Palpa of which Tansen is the headquarters. Nevertheless, television had already been part of people's lives in the town for some time with satellite dishes, video recorder technologies and televisions capable of receiving broadcasts from Indian television stations in relatively common use. Uniquely amongst the towns of Nepal, Tansen's mediascape (Appadurai 1990) also came to include an organization that from 1992 produced original programs broadcast through the cable system of a private, family-owned business. Although seemingly far removed from the hub of modernization and development in the capital, Tansen has been at the forefront of media development in Nepal and the South Asian region more broadly in the past two decades with community newspapers and radio broadcasting now adding to its mediascape (Pringle, Bajracharya and Bajracharya 2004). Nepal's media revolution cannot be traced back to Tansen in the early 1990s in any simplistic sense of its being a point of origin; many other people, places and factors contributed to these changes, as we shall see in the course of this work. However, we can look to Tansen and the work of RCTV/CDP in order to understand what influences affected the early stages of Nepal's development of new media, especially as this was experienced outside the Kathmandu Valley, which has tended to attract the most investment and comment. Just as this early development of media was constructed out of material, social and cultural circumstances inherited from the past, so too does the present mediascape of Nepal build upon the foundations laid down by organizations such as RCTV/CDP. Marx's enduring statement about the weight of history is chosen as one of the epigraphs for this chapter to indicate the continuing influence that his crucial insight has upon my own and many other researchers' attempts to understand the influences of the past upon the present.

As even this brief introduction indicates, this work presents a study in the "tension between cultural homogenization and cultural heterogenization" (Appadurai 1990: 295) in the development of media in Nepal. How television and other mass media technologies came to be used in Tansen serves as an example of the ways in which people one might expect to be marginalized within both national and global mediascapes attempt to assert control over the means through which their lives are represented within their own community and to outsiders. As this study shows, however, these processes of empowerment through media development take place within local social and cultural contexts that are both complex and frequently marked by deep differences in their cultural and socio-economic characteristics. The questions of exactly who counts as one of 'our people', *aphno manche* in Nepali, and what the local community actually consists of that it might be represented in the media are ones that have been of great concern to many people involved in Tansen's remarkable mediascape. Examining how these tensions have arisen and how different people within the community have tried to resolve them provides an example that forces us to look again and reevaluate events in the countless other places where people find their lives are being transformed by rapid developments and innovations in mass media.

As previously noted, arguments about the relationship of media transformations to wider social change are often united by shared assumptions about how such media impacts are generated or even determined by the qualities of different technological or material characteristics of media. However, as anthropologist Mark Liechty (1998) has observed, the history of television in Nepal, for example, does not follow the historical trajectories mapped out in other locales, especially the metropolitan centers of Europe and North America within which many mass media technologies were first developed. Liechty's observation has been increasingly replicated by other researchers who are skeptical of modernist narratives of media development and of developmental discourses more generally (Scannell 2002; Escobar 1995). Indeed, we should be prepared in our analyses to stop viewing cultural and historical differences in the use of media technologies as simply the result of the local variations in the application of otherwise uniform processes of cultural adaptation and behavior, because such an argument simply reasserts the uniformity of the modernist narrative of social process in the last instance. As Stacy Pigg argues in her studies of AIDS and development communication in Nepal, we must move "beyond discussions of systems of knowledge that tend to come to rest in an overly static, binary and implicitly hierarchical vocabulary of difference...If we merely envision different knowledge systems bumping into each other, or supplanting one another, we risk oversimplifying the already syncretic, hybrid, polyglot conditions with which most people contend" (Pigg 2001: 482–3). It is not the case that variations in local cultural practices and social institutions influence the ways in which media are taken up and put to use in any given community in any straightforward way, but that the self-same local social forces referred to by Wilson in the above quotation are themselves constituted and transformed through particular mediations of communications. Anthropologist Terence Turner notes that the act of representing culture through media is one that "contributes to the material social reality of the thing represented rather than merely reflecting a pre-existing objective reality separate from the act of representation" (quoted in Deger 2006: 43). I examine this point in greater detail in chapter 7.

The difference this makes to analysis is subtle but has profound consequences. Rather than reifying modern, mass media as cultural entities that have universal characteristics transcending any given context of use, they are seen as the tools and techniques through which social actors make their agency manifest in practice. Local context does not then just provide a limiting framework within which actors are able only to accept those elements of mass media that are deemed by either community insiders or outsiders to be appropriate. Instead, mass media are one means amongst many other facets of culture through which local contexts of action are constituted. Media are potentially empowering to the extent that they can be used to bring about such definitions of locality that are recognized as legitimate by members of the producer's community.

This point was brought home to me by an initial problem in my research. When conducting a brief survey of the media available to people living in Tansen I asked people whether they watched local television in the pilot questionnaire, meaning did they watch the programs made by the town's cable television operators. But for many people the concept of 'local television' (istaniya telebhijan) stood for Nepal Television (NTV) as opposed to Indian television, especially its national broadcaster Doordarshan. In a television environment in which state-run broadcasters were dominant, the notion of local broadcasting operated on the scale of national comparison. The subsequent question in the survey itself was amended to avoid this confusion by referring to 'Tansen's local television program' (tansenko istaniya telebhijan karykram). I learnt much through the survey, but nothing as useful as this initial mistaken assumption that my respondents would understand my reference to local television to be confined to that produced in the immediate urban locale where people lived and worked. This illustrates very well, I think, the ways in which our systems of knowledge are built up using elements such as media. It is not just that television serves as a means through which information about localities are disseminated, but that what we come to think of as the basic ontological properties of locality itself are built up out of the media (Silverstone 1999). As Mazzarella (2004: 353) explains,

> Accounts and analyses often imply that media are something that happen to or are imposed on already-constituted local worlds. The local, in this view, is composed of a certain set of cultural values and practices to which media must then adapt, in order to find an audience. The media are then commonly understood to 'impact' the local world in a number of beneficial and/or deleterious ways. But rarely is it acknowledged that mediation, and its attendant cultural politics, necessarily precedes the arrival of what we commonly recognize as 'media': that, in fact, local worlds are necessarily already the outcome of more or less stable, more or less local, social technologies of mediation.

For me, a British-born anthropologist who had lived all his life with television in the UK, the organization of knowledge of local regions via the broadcast footprint of terrestrial television stations seemed quite natural. When Tansen's cable television program was unique within the electronic mediascape of Nepal it did not fit into any comparable framework for envisioning locality. The existence today of many dozens of independent radio broadcasters, each with their own unique, if frequently overlapping, signal area makes it more likely that this way of conceptualizing space in terms of the places served by particular broadcasters will become more common. Although this case study describes a very different situation and outcomes, it does demonstrate Eric Michaels' (1986) claim following his path breaking studies of indigenous media in Australia, that when we look at the arrival of a new element of culture in a community (television, for example), we see potential not just for it to change the community but also for notions of community itself to be reinvented in the process. This claim will be examined in greater detail in chapter 2.

At the same time, as has already been noted in passing, media are only one amongst many facets of culture that are available to and utilized by people to create such localized worlds of value and practice. In modern, industrialized

societies, media and communication technologies as they are typically understood do, of course, play a leading role in the process of mediation to which
Mazzarella refers. However, he goes on to emphasize and this study bears out
the fact that they are only one amongst the total range of cultural materials and
practices utilized in any given context.

I emphasize this point because one of the most important things we can
learn from what happened when television came to Tansen is that the reasons for
its introduction lie as much *within* the life and history of that community as they
do with factors outside. The question of whether television *would ever* come to
Tansen could only ever be answered in the affirmative and in that respect it is an
irresistible cultural force. But the question of *how* television came to Tansen
could never be determined in advance and would always be contingent upon the
particular circumstances of the community itself, the most important, of course,
being the abilities of the people living in this place to have an influence over this
history. Whilst there were many factors that 'pushed' television into the fabric of
life in Tansen, there were also many factors that worked to 'pull' television into
the town in ways that led to a distinctive "invention of television" (Michaels
1986).

A brief moment from my fieldwork serves, I think, to illustrate the importance of these points with great clarity. In 1995, Keshab, a middle-aged member
of the untouchable Sunar caste of goldsmiths, accepted from me a small copper
coin—a British two penny piece—and added it to his collection then displayed
between us. Dozens of coins, old and new from around the world, along with
various medals and other tokens, lay on a small cloth spread out to protect them
from the dust of the floor. In purely economic terms, my coin was almost worth-
less, but then Keshab began to teach me another way of valuing the coins in his
collection. One by one he picked up the foreign coins and asked the simple question, "King?" I carefully examined each coin to work out which country it came
from and if I replied, "No king", Keshab responded with satisfaction and delight
in his voice, "Freedom!"

Material objects, as Keshab demonstrated, do not maintain fixed meanings;
rather they have an almost limitless capacity for attaining meaning given the
shifting social contexts within which they may be used. Whilst the most stable
meaning of my coin might have been derived from its economic value when
used within the boundary of the monetary system of the United Kingdom, beyond that boundary this meaning as a token of economic exchange was lost. It
gained new value and new meaning when it became a small gift, the token of a
developing friendship. In part a symbol of the imagined freedoms to be found in
the states that issued these coins, I felt that his collection of foreign coins served
as a poignant reminder of the continuing disparity between the freedoms that
some, including myself, had to travel to Keshab's country and the near impossibility of his ever being to make the opposite journey. Nevertheless, they gained
further meanings after becoming part of Keshab's collection and, through his
unique approach to categorization, were used to teach me a lesson about the differing political circumstances within which we lived our lives.

As the example of Keshab's coin collection indicates, even those elements of culture, such as money, which might appear to be most indicative of techno-cultural systems shared on a global scale can be subject to creative re-appropriation by people to suit their own, local situation. The forces of international trade, tourism and development—in short, globalization—that bring or push foreign currency or commodities into a national economy are undoubtedly powerful, but are paralleled (if not balanced) by the countervailing tendencies that 'pull' such commodities into circulation in localities in unexpected ways (Thomas 1991; Miller 1992). This study examines a technology, television, which is frequently regarded as the harbinger of global cultural uniformity. It looks at how in the town of Tansen certain people and agencies worked to invent their own way of making television in their community and in so doing reinvented their community itself. In particular, I examine the processes of inclusion and exclusion that lead to the identification of exactly who 'our people' (*aphno manche*) are in the context of community media.

Chapter Outline

The remainder of this opening chapter is taken up with three sections. The first presents a general introduction to Nepal that provides an overview of the physical and human geography of the country, as well as a brief account of political history up to the time at which fieldwork for this study was undertaken. The aim of this account is less to provide a comprehensive overview of Nepal—for which there are a number of excellent existing sources (Gellner et al. 1997; Hutt 1994 and 2004; Stiller 1993; Whelpton 2005)—than to set the scene for the more detailed accounts of the history and ethnography of Tansen that follow in later chapters. The second section, which introduces Tansen and the work of *Ratna Cable Television/Communication for Development Palpa* (RCTV/CDP), is also designed as a prelude to what comes latter in this study, particularly in the next chapter before the more detailed contextual information is encountered in chapters 4 and 5. Finally, the chapter ends with a discussion of methodology that explores the potential limitations of this study through a self-reflexive account of the fieldwork process.

Chapter 2 provides an account of the origins and early work of RCTV/CDP. This account is framed by a discussion of the various ways in which alternative and indigenous media organizations have been conceptualized and described in previous analyses. The description of RCTV/CDP in this chapter makes it clear that many of the characteristics of these types of media organization are present in this case. However, it also highlights the continuing difficulty in isolating any single definition or conceptualization as the most appropriate in this instance. Descriptions of RCTV/CDP using terms such as non-mainstream, alternative, local, radical, indigenous, community, citizen, or other similar terms, help us to explore their work, but don't exhaust the range of possibilities. Even the term 'small' television that has been used up to this point in the chapter could potentially mislead us when we attempt to understand the scale of the working relationships—and indeed the scale of the ambitions—of those who continue to produce the RCTV program.

Chapter 3 examines the broader mediascape of Nepal and considers how this was influenced by both the material conditions in which the uses of various media were developed in Nepal and the discourses surrounding media as a component of development. Since the 1950s and up to the time of RCTV/CDPs creation in the early 1990s, development (*bikās*) has served as a key element of the imagining of the nation (Anderson 1991). This chapter argues that how media were utilized in Nepal and how they were limited to some uses and not others can only be understood within the context of a pervasive and often aggressively asserted ideology of development (Pigg 1992). A later chapter (6) discusses how this national ideology could be seen to influence the local characteristics and working of media in Tansen in the 1990s.

Chapter 4 is the first of two chapters that present the local context for our analysis of RCTV/CDP; it examines the history of Tansen and Palpa district. Tansen rose to prominence in the early years of the Nineteenth Century as the unification of the modern nation-state of Nepal was completed by the House of Gorkha. The last independent kingdom to be absorbed into modern Nepal, the region continued to play a key strategic and political role throughout the next hundred years. Today, even after this role has been lost and the region sidelined by more economically and politically important places, the memory of past glories continues to inform a deeply held sense of local identity.

Chapter 5 examines the contemporary social, economic and cultural characteristics of Tansen's population. The predominantly quantitative description included in the first part of the chapter enables us to understand how Tansen was rapidly changing in the early years of the 1990s. Migration to and from the town, as well as intergenerational differences led to a population that was in flux. From being a predominantly Newar bazaar since its foundation, Tansen was becoming a more ethnically, religiously and culturally diverse community. The latter part of the chapter examines some of the attitudes to these changes, the ways that historical memory inflected such attitudes and people's aspirations for the future of the town.

As mentioned above, chapter 6 continues the discussion of development discourses and ideology in relation to the particular case of RCTV/CDP. Just as the earlier chapter examined how this ideology was given form and substance in the national media of Nepal, this chapter considers how the work of RCTV/CDP was both enabled and constrained by notions of development. The chapter considers both the process of media production work and the works produced (the content or text of the television broadcasts) in order to examine development as a concrete reality affecting the day-to-day organization of local media. Of particular importance is the creation of strong bonds between those who have taken it upon themselves to lead the struggle for development in Palpa district and Tansen. The importance of these relationships is assessed in terms of the creation of social capital (Putnam 2000), although this case study provides empirical material that is useful in the critical reevaluation of this contentious concept.

Chapter 7 places the work of RCTV/CDP into a quite different comparative context through an examination of the local television program's coverage (or lack thereof) of religious festivals. The fact that the programs made by this organization feature only some of these festivals is significant if we consider the complex role that mass media play in the mediation of socio-political relations between different sections of the town's diverse population. Nevertheless, it is argued that the examination of other processes of cultural mediation, including the festivals themselves, enables a better understanding of how mass media are incorporated into the construction of community and social identity in the public arena.

The final chapter briefly considers some of the subsequent changes that have occurred in the mediascape of Nepal over the past ten years, in particular the struggle to assert the right to freedom of speech in the face of opposition from both the state and the forces of the Maoist insurgency. The conclusion identifies some of the ways in which this case study of the possibilities of so-called 'small' television has relevance for those who seek to explore these possibilities in other places and those who wish to understand how people's lives are increasingly mediated through technologies like television in contemporary Nepal and globally. Understanding processes of audience formation is identified as an area of crucial importance needing further work in order to understand the bases upon which alternative media producers seek legitimacy for their work.

Introducing Nepal and Tansen

Situated along the central spine of the Himalayan mountain range, Nepal is approximately eight hundred kilometers long from east to west and one hundred and sixty kilometers wide from north to south. The country covers an area of about one hundred and forty seven thousand square kilometers and in the early 1990s had a population of eighteen and a half million people. So, whilst her neighbors India and China dwarf Nepal, it is useful to be reminded by Rishikesh Shah (1992: 1) that she is by no means a small country, with "70% of member nations of the United Nations . . . smaller than Nepal in terms of population and over 40% . . . smaller in terms of area." The spectacular facts of Nepal's mountainous geography serve to increase the sense of the country's size on the ground. It is the case, however, that the common designation of the country as "tiny" (Raj 1985) sometimes appears more appropriate due to the contrast with Nepal's two massive neighbors. As the unifier of Nepal, King Prithvi Narayan Shah, observed with regard to the political relations of the Himalayan region, Nepal is like a yam stuck between two rocks.

The Himalaya is a collection of massive mountain ranges and many of the world's highest peaks, including the world's highest mountain, Mount Everest (*Sagarmatha* in Nepali or *Chomalongmo* in Tibetan), are located within the borders of Nepal. The Himalayas dominate the geography, climate and ecology of the region. First, we may divide the country into five bands that run roughly parallel along an east-west axis. The area in which the mountain ranges rise above two thousand metres above sea level is a sparsely occupied zone of alpine and arctic desert vegetation. To the north of this zone is the inner-Himalayan zone comprised of a mixture of alpine, glacial and peri-glacial vegetation, which rises towards the Chinese border and the high Tibetan Plateau. South of the high Himalayas, between altitudes of two thousand to one hundred metres above sea level are the central hill ranges where a considerable proportion of the population of Nepal lives (see Table 1.1 *Population Distribution of Nepal by Development and Ecological Regions, 1991*). Two hill ranges, the Mahabharat Lekh and Churia Siwalik, which are considerably lower than the Himalayas but still formidable obstacles, extend along the southern extent of this zone of temperate and tropical forest, a great deal of which has been cleared for agricultural use.

Table 1.1. Population Distribution of Nepal by Development and Ecological Regions, 1991

Development Region		Ecological Region			
		Mountain	Hill	Tarai	Total
Eastern	No.	359,156	1,429,138	2,658,455	4,446,749
	%	1.94	7.72	14.37	24.04
Central	No.	471,005	2,679,599	3,033,351	6,183,955
	%	2.54	14.49	16.40	33.44
Western	No.	19,655	2,420,878	1,330,145	3,790,333
	%	0.11	13.09	7.19	20.39
Mid-Western	No.	260,529	1,217,555	930,330	2,408,414
	%	1.41	6.59	5.03	13.03
Far-Western	No.	332,785	670,719	675,797	1,679,301
	%	1.80	3.63	3.65	9.08
Total	No.	1,443,130	8,417,889	8,628,078	18,491,097
	%	7.80	45.53	46.66	100.00

Source: HMG, Nepal (1994)

To the south of these ranges, running along the border with India is the Tarai, the northern-most extent of the Gangetic flood plain, which comprises about 15% of Nepal's total surface area. Since the eradication of endemic malaria in the late-1950s, this tropical forested zone has seen extensive forest clearance. By the early 1990s it was home to just under 50% of Nepal's population and the site of the country's most productive agricultural land. Finally, the Inner Tarai comprise of a series of separate, long, flat valleys known as *dun*, which lie between the Mahabharat and Siwalik ranges. Again, this is valuable agricultural land and often supports a high density of population.

The town of Tansen (population approximately sixteen thousand in 1994) is situated on Srinagar Hill, which is part of the Mahabharat Lekh overlooking two such *duns* (the Madi and Parbas Valleys) which were formed by the watershed of the Tinua River. On a clear day from the summit of Srinagar Hill at approximately sixteen hundred meters above sea level one can turn north to face the incredible spectacle of the Annapurna and Daulagiri mountain ranges or look south to see the Tarai stretching out into the distance between the peaks of the Siwalik range. The summit of Srinagar has been landscaped by the municipal government into a park and pleasure gardens that are a popular spot with picnickers from as far away as Gorakhpur in Uttar Pradesh, India. During the damp winter months and the monsoon, the town is shrouded in cloud, a fact that has led some to refer romantically to Tansen as "a city in the mist" (de Folo 1994).[1] The middle of the town lies at a height of about thirteen hundred meters, but the steeply inclined streets that form the central spine of the settlement, leading from the bus station at one end to the upper most residential areas at the summit of the hill, cover a variation in altitude of almost five hundred meters.

The second major aspect of Nepal's geography, a concomitant of the Himalayan range, is the presence of innumerable river systems both large and small, which generally run from the high mountains to the north down to the Tarai and thence on to the Gangetic flood plain in the south. So, whilst the mountains and hills divide the country into areas aligned east to west, the rivers systems such as the Seta, Karnali, Kali Gandaki, Sun Kosi, Dudh Kosi and Arun, divide the country into areas that run north to south.

The overall effect of this geography, as Ludwig Stiller notes (1993), is to create geographical and ecological pockets between which contact and communication is difficult if not impossible. Stiller maintains that these brutal facts of geography have been major factors influencing the history of Nepal and the ways of life practiced in the Himalayas.

Tansen itself is situated above the watershed of the Tinua River to the south, which provides water to irrigate many of the fields of the Madi and Parbas valleys. During the monsoon, the Tinau watershed provides either vital irrigation or disastrous floods that affect the livelihood of the villagers in this area. To the north of Srinagar Hill flows the mighty Kali Gandaki, forming the northern boundary of Palpa District. This river is of great sacred importance to the people of Nepal (Kasajoo 1988; Messerschmidt 1992). It plays an important role in the life of Tansen, because it is to the banks of the Kali Gandaki at nearby Ramdi Ghat in the northeast of the district that the deceased of the town are brought to be cremated. Previously the site of cremations had been Rani Ghat, the location of an abandoned palace that was once the residence of a Rana Governor of Palpa and the closest accessible site on the river by foot. The construction of a road, the Siddhartha Highway (*rajmarg*), linking Tansen to the city of Pokhara in the centre of Nepal has today made Ramdi easier to reach.

The geographic factors recounted above have affected the growth and pattern of communication systems in Nepal. Even today, the basis of almost all transport in the vast majority of the hill and mountain areas is still portering by people or, less commonly, by mule (Dixit 1995). This will be the case until at least the near future, because, as Dixit notes, the topography of the hills makes the construction of roads prohibitively expensive or simply impossible for even the most sophisticated engineer. Perhaps more importantly, chronic poverty also means that labor for portering is cheap and plentiful. The roads that do exist are mainly confined to the Tarai, which now has a continuous stretch of highway running east to west, and to a roughly rectangular area in the centre of Nepal. This rectangle of roads is defined by the cities of Kathmandu at the north-eastern corner, Pokhara at the north-western corner, Hetauda to the southeast, and finally Butwal in the south-western corner. Additional roads, generally without metalled surfaces, do reach out into the hill areas, but their impact on the lives of the majority of hill people is still at most indirect. What has occurred with the construction of this road system is the refocusing of trade in the hills onto the newer, roadside settlement that have grown at important road-heads or intersections.

Table 1.2. Population Size of Administrative Regions of Nepal in 1991, including Selected Districts and Municipalities

Development Region	Number of Districts	Average District Population	Total District Population
Eastern Mountain	3	119,719	359,156
Eastern Hill	8	178,642	1,429,138
Eastern Tarai	5	531,691	2,658,455
Central Mountain	3	157,002	471,005
Central Hill	9	297,733	2,679,599
Kathmandu District	—	—	675,341
Kathmandu Municipality	—	—	421,258
Central Tarai	7	433,336	3,033,351
Western Mountain	2	9,828	19,655
Western Hill	11	220,080	2,420,878
Palpa District	—	—	236,313
Tansen Municipality	—	—	13,599
Kaski District	—	—	292,945
Pokhara Municipality	—	—	95,286
Western Tarai	3	443,382	1,330,145
Rupendehi District	—	—	522,150
Butwal Municipality	—	—	44,272
Mid-Western Mountain	5	52,106	260,529
Mid-Western Hill	7	173,936	1,217,555
Mid-Western Tarai	3	310,110	930,330
Far-Western Mountain	3	110,928	332,785
Far-Western Hill	4	167,680	670,719
Far-Western Tarai	2	337,899	675,797

Source: HMG, Nepal (1994) and HMG, Nepal (1995)

The geographical divisions of the country discussed above were reflected in and formed the basis of the division of Nepal into a series of political and administrative regions that continue to be used by the government through the work of the National Planning Commission to organize and coordinate national development plans (Martinussen 1993). Each of these Development Regions was further sub-divided into Development Zones (*Anchal*) and each Zone into a number of Districts (see Table 1.2 *Population size of Administrative Regions of Nepal, including Selected Districts and Municipalities, 1991*). This political and administrative hierarchy continued at District level through the division of the area into Village Development Committees (VDCs) (*gãu bikās samiti, GBS*) for rural areas and Municipalities (*nagarpālikā*) for urban areas. The situation was further complicated by the fact that a number of VDCs are grouped for adminis-trative purposes into larger units called *Ilākā* and subdivided into wards, which are the smallest unit at which political representation occurs. Tansen Municipal-ity, for example, was made up of fifteen wards in Palpa District of Lumbini Zone, which is the southern-most Zone of the Western Development Region.

Districts were also divided up into a number of constituencies for the pur-poses of electing members of the lower house of the National Parliament (*prati-nidhi sabhā*) (Borre, Panday and Tiwari 1994).[2] Palpa District was divided into three constituencies and the People of Tansen voted in the elections held for the central constituency (Palpa-2).

This hierarchical organization of administration and political representation was, roughly speaking, identical to that of the previous system (the *Panchāyat*), which existed for thirty years prior to 1990. The fundamental difference brought about by the events of the People's Movement (*jana āndolan*) of that year was that the elected representatives of the people were allowed to openly express affiliation to political parties and campaign for election using party funds and support. At the time of my research, Tansen Municipality was controlled by the Nepali Congress Party following their electoral victory in ten out of the town's fifteen wards. Each of Palpa's three MPs, however, were members of the Com-munist Party of Nepal (United Marxist-Leninist), which had just lost power na-tionally.

The geography of the Himalayas was described above in terms of the com-munication difficulties that it imposes on the human population, but, as the late Harka Gurung (Salter and Gurung 1996: 1) has pointed out, it is equally the case that "the Himalaya, interposed between the centers of two major Asiatic civiliza-tions, is no more an ethnic barrier than it is a major water divide. It has been both a frontier and region of refuge." A rough approximation of the result of this ethnic interface is that peoples, such as the Limbu, Rai, Newar, Tamang, Magar and Gurung, who trace their ultimate origins to the northern regions of the Hi-malayas, have come to predominate in the east of the kingdom, whilst the west of the kingdom is dominated by groups collectively known in the anthropologi-cal literature as the Hill (*Parbatiya*) Castes.[3] The ethnic and caste composition of Palpa District in 1991 is outlined in Table 1.3 (*Population of Palpa District by Ethnicity and Caste, 1991*).

Peoples who have their physical, cultural and linguistic origins in the Ti-betan border region inhabit the extreme northern, high Himalayan, areas of Ne-pal. These include the Sherpa, Thakali and various other groups known in Nepal by the collective term *Bhotia* (that is Tibetans).[4] A wide mixture of peoples inhabit the Tarai at the southern extreme of the country, as one might expect in an area rich in agricultural resources and rapidly growing towns. Indigenous to the Tarai are a variety of communities who do not trace their origins or direct ethnic connection directly to either the Himalayan or Hill peoples, the most numerous being the Tharu who made up approximately 6.5% of Nepal's total population in the early 1990s. Since the eradication of malaria in the region in the late 1950s and early 1960s, migration from both the hills of Nepal and the neighboring Indian states of Uttar Pradesh and Bihar has led to massive population increase in the Tarai. The region has been a frequent location of political and social tension in recent decades due to communal tensions caused by these population pressures (Chitrakar 1990; Dogra 1990; Gaige 1975; Gellner et al. 1997; Krauskopff 2003).[5]

Table 1.3. Population of Palpa District by Ethnicity and Caste, 1991

Ethnicity	Caste	Number	Percentage
Parbatiya	Bahun (Brahmin)	47,911	20.3
	Chetri (Kshatriya)	20,150	8.5
	Occupational (Dalit)	29,192	12.4
	All	97,253	41.2
Magar		116,694	49.4
Newar		8,967	3.8
Kumal[a]		5,060	2.1
Thakuri		2,928	1.2
Others[b]		5,411	2.3
Total		236,313	100.0

Source: HMG, Nepal (1994)
[a] The Kumal are a small ethnic group that is concentrated in Palpa District. They specialize in pottery production and portering as a means of livelihood.
[b] 'Others' includes groups from Nepal and elsewhere who are below 1,000 in number.

Given these circumstances of both physical and human geography in the Himalayan region, the unification of Nepal by the Shah monarchy of Gorkha in the middle of the Eighteenth Century is little short of miraculous. Within the lifetime of one man, King Prithvi Narayan Shah (AD 1723 to 1775), the geographical extent of the unified state became recognizably, if not precisely, that seen today. The conquest of the Newar Kingdoms of the Kathmandu Valley in 1769 and the appropriation of their wealth, which was accumulated through the Valley's position as an entrepôt for trade between Tibet and India, was clearly the major event in what Stiller (1995) refers to as "the rise of the house of Gorkha."

This expansion which eventually encompassed an area extending between what are today the Indian states of Darjeeling in the east and Himchal Pradesh in the west, inevitably brought Nepal into conflict with the other growing power on the sub-continent, the British East India Company. By 1816, the era of Nepali expansion had been brought to an end with defeat at the hands of the British. Deprived of large tracts of territory and the possibility of further expansion, Nepal's ruling aristocracy was plunged into a period of bitter and violent internecine conflict, out of which one family, headed by Jang Bahadur Rana, the second of the country's renowned leaders, emerged victorious following a bloody coup d'état in 1846 (Stiller 1981). The dynasty founded by Jang Bahadur Rana ruled as hereditary 'Prime Ministers' until 1950 and reduced the Shah monarchy to little more than the figurehead of the state.

The Rana family may have presided over a period of relative political stability, but their autocratic regime led to economic and social stagnation through the systematic exploitation of the country's resources by favored elements of the aristocracy (Regmi 1978; Seddon 1987). Not the least amongst the instances of this exploitation was the promulgation of laws, the Muluki Ain of 1854, which reconfirmed in law the hierarchical system of social distinction based on caste, indeed extending this system to ethnic groups to whom caste was an alien custom (Höfer 1979). The Ranas also attempted to isolate the people of Nepal from the influence of the surrounding states, particularly British-ruled India, believing that such isolationism would help to preserve their own hegemony in Nepal.[6]

A century of Rana rule was brought to an end in 1950 when a revolution, precipitated by the flight to India of King Tribhuvan (1913–1955), forced the Rana government to accept political reform.[7] After a period of political experiment in the 1950s, Nepal's first democratic parliamentary elections were finally held in 1960. These resulted in the formation of a government led by B.P. Koirala of the Nepali Congress Party (Joshi and Rose 1966). By 1961, however, the parliament had been dissolved and political parties banned by King Mahendra (1955–1972) using the monarch's emergency powers enshrined in the new constitution, under the pretext of restoring political stability. In place of the previous constitutional arrangements, Mahendra instituted a system of 'non-party democracy' known as the *Panchayat*, after the Sanskrit name for the assemblies through which the country was theoretically governed. In practice, however, the country entered into a period of government by absolute monarchy. It is during this period of Panchayat rule that Nepal first began to receive large-scale donations of foreign aid, through which the country's modern physical infrastructure (communication, health and educational facilities in the main) began to be constructed on a scale hitherto unseen.

By the narrowest of margins, the Panchayat survived a referendum on its future in 1980 that had been granted by King Birendra (1972–2001) after widespread public unrest. However, this unrest and general dissatisfaction with the Panchayat system was not quelled by this gesture (Borre, Panday and Tiwari 1994; Hoftun and Raeper 1994). Further protest in 1990, predominantly in the cities of Patan, Bhaktapur and Kathmandu in the Kathmandu Valley, led to bloodshed and the capitulation of the King and his allies amongst the Panchayat elite. Since 1990, then, Nepal has entered its second period of parliamentary democracy, a period characterized by extreme political instability exacerbated by the violence of the Maoist 'People's War'.[8]

Writing in 1928, the diplomat and historian Percival Landon could count barely ten urban centers of any size outside the Kathmandu Valley and noted that Tansen was amongst the three or four most important (the others included Pokhara, Hetauda and possibly Butwal; see Landon 1993). Since the late 1960s, however, Tansen has declined in importance, both administratively, due to the reduction in size of Palpa District to only a rump surrounding the town, and economically, as new industrial and trading towns have grown-up along the border with India following the eradication of endemic malaria in the Tarai. The town enjoyed a brief heyday following the opening of the road connecting Butwal to Pokhara in the early 1970s, when it became an entrepôt for Indian-manufactured commodities that began to flow into the country at this time. However, this role has been usurped as branch roads into the surrounding districts of Gulmi, Agra-khanchi, Parbat and Syngja have siphoned off this trade (Gyawali et al. 1993). It is now possible to travel to Kathmandu by bus in less than 12 hours and the cities of Gorakhpur and Lucknow in Uttar Pradesh in less than a day. This improved communication has facilitated the flight of both people and capital from the town and one could be justified in claiming that location, once a blessing, is today the town's curse. As Sharma (1994: 229) observes, for most of the hill towns of Nepal "the stress on road development has proved to be their complete undoing." Nevertheless, recent attempts to stimulate tourism tend to make a positive feature of Tansen's relative isolation from the commercial and population pressures that have dramatically altered the landscape of the towns of the Kathmandu Valley and the Tarai (Shrestha 1994).

Recent changes in the demographic and ethnic composition of the community are related to these developments. Although the overall population of the town continues to rise, the new inhabitants are increasingly from the Magar, Brahmin and Chetri population of the rural areas of Palpa and adjacent districts and this contrasts with the inter-urban character of much previous migration to and from Tansen.[9] These families and individuals have come to the town to take advantage of the opportunities for consumption that the urban environment offers, in particular electricity, education for their children and the health facilities offered by the two hospitals located in the municipality.

Just as the history of Tansen prior to 1950 is reflected in the town's architecture, more recent changes have lead to a municipality area divided between the densely packed redbrick housing of the old town area inhabited by the Newar population and the rapidly spreading ribbons of concrete buildings that reach out along the sides of the roads leading into the bazaar, where new immigrants tend to live.[10] Another feature of the town's contemporary landscape, as with all the towns and cities of Nepal, is the infrastructure of terrestrial, satellite and cable television. However, media in Tansen includes something that would have been unimaginable under the Panchayat regime and is not seen in other Nepali towns; a community television station. Not only does this offer compelling evidence of the new freedom of political expression and democracy that has existed since the 1990 revolution, but it also demonstrates how the people of this town have responded to "the autodynamics of the new market forces now operative in Nepal, which everywhere disfavors the hill towns as new economic and urban centers" (Sharma 1994: 229).

Living in Tansen: Some Notes on Fieldwork

The first and most obvious point about conducting fieldwork in a complex urban context is that it is impossible for any one person, be they a citizen of the town or a foreign researcher, to get to know even a fraction of those resident in a town with any degree of intimacy. This is even the case in a relatively small town like Tansen.[11] I decided, therefore, to administer a concise survey in the first months of my research to familiarize myself with the different peoples who lived in the municipal area and to give me some systematic data through which these differences could be described. This survey was carried out between 19th November and 7th December 1995. In addition to its more general sociological focus, the survey sought to answer some basic questions about the availability and use of media in the town and correlate this with information on such things as household composition, income, education, literacy and ethnicity or caste. The survey had two ancillary results. The first was the provision of a sample of town citizens that I had contact with and from whom I was able to select a group at a later date in my research to be questioned in greater detail on the subjects that this preliminary survey had touched upon. The second benefit was that my Nepali language skills improved greatly through the constant repetition of the questions and answers provoked in this survey, although throughout the administration of the survey I was accompanied by a Nepali friend who helped with the translation of people's responses.

Detailed commentary on this preliminary survey is given in chapter 5, which provides a statistical description of the social and cultural characteristics of the town. As the above comments indicated, the aim of this survey was primarily to provide a description Tansen in a simple statistical form and at no point was any precisely formulated and statistically testable hypothesis intended as part of this exercise. Although the survey had a quantifiable result, it was always envisaged as an adjunct to the qualitative aspects of this research and an aid to describing the diversity of the town's population.

The same was true of the more detailed follow-up survey mentioned above. I was aware from the very first moment of my arrival in Tansen that my day-to-day contacts in Tansen would be limited to a restricted circle of people. Perhaps inevitably, as my language skills were initially relatively restricted, I tended to associate with people who could speak some English. As my survey results show, many of Tansen's people are highly educated and English is widely spoken. Nevertheless, it is also apparent that the benefits of this education are not evenly distributed throughout the community and again my preliminary survey showed this in sharper detail. Other factors, of which gender was by far the most important, led to similar sorts of problems. The detailed follow-up survey was, therefore, a limited attempt to rectify this imbalance in my own contacts with the people of Tansen. A survey, even though it is relatively unstructured in its administration and exhaustive in its coverage, can never take the place of the knowledge of another person that is built up through long-term familiarity and friendship. This aspect of the research is, therefore, a compromise between the recognition of the need for this sort of breadth of knowledge of the people of Tansen in my research and the acknowledgement that, given the resources available to me and the vagaries of my own person, such knowledge would never be gained solely through participant observation. I was also able to check the veracity of the responses to my first survey by returning to my respondents to ask the same questions in more detail and was relieved to find that in very few cases was there any disagreement between the two.

I have said little up to this point about the use of participant observation, the usual source of most ethnographic (qualitative) data in anthropological fieldwork. The character, if not the actual purpose, of ethnography is, as I have pointed out above, quite different in the culturally complex and diverse setting of an urban environment than in the 'village' settings in which the techniques of participant observation were first formulated. Whilst the essential skills of observation and recording remain the same, any attempt to use participant observation to generate a holistic and exhaustive ethnographic record of town life would be doomed to failure. I was content to let my use of participant observation be as unstructured as my surveys were structured or systematic in their formulation and execution. Such an approach provided a fascinating counterpoint to the results of the survey. Whereas the former presented a neatly subdivided and categorized view of the urban population, the ethnography emphasizes the tangled and agglomerated nature of urban life. Whereas the survey was administered with a strict eye on the questions of the representative nature of the sample chosen (that as many women as men be interviewed, for example), I was content to let the network and patterns of my everyday associations dictate the content of my ethnography. The effects of this approach are discussed below.

Participant observation included trips beyond the geographical boundaries of the municipality. Initially, I had been concerned that my experience in Tansen would be rather limited and I had considered extending my research to other communities, either rural or urban, in order to provide a comparative dimension to my study. Recognition of the enormity of such a task quickly led me to revise this plan and I decided to make a virtue out of this problem. Rather than select places to visit myself I let my informants choose where we should go and, apart from necessary trips to Kathmandu to renew visas or the odd trip to Pokhara for a break from research, I only left Tansen when invited to do so by the people I knew. These trips included a visit to a student's family home in the Tarai, a visit with a Red Cross worker to a drinking water project in a near-by village, a visit to the home village of an informant's wife with their children, amongst many more. In this way, I grew to understand the ways in which the lives and livelihoods of Tansen's citizens spread beyond the limits of the municipal space, a factor that I explored in other ways through the two surveys, which included questions on travel, residence and work in other places.

The final major element of my research methodology was the use of open ended or unstructured interviews to develop a better understanding of several important areas of life in Tansen. Apart from my contacts with those involved in the production of local media in the town, I also concentrated on the three topics that have frequently been identified by citizens of the town as the core elements of its economy both now and into the future; these being health care provision, education and tourism (Kasajoo 1994; see chapters 3 and 6). Throughout the year of my fieldwork, I met with people involved in these aspects of town life, often returning to re-interview certain individuals on several occasions as my knowledge of the town changed and new facts came to my attention. My understanding of the educational institutions of the town was greatly aided by the fact that Harriet, my wife, lived with me in Tansen for all but the last month of fieldwork, and was employed as a teacher in one of the town's English medium boarding schools. Indeed, by the time she left Tansen, Harriet was considerably better known than I was by the children of the bazaar who she taught and their parents. Through her work, I came to know of aspects of life in the town that would otherwise have passed me by.

This by no means exhausts the range of data and sources used in this study. Photographs, videotaped copies of local television broadcasts, music cassettes, copies of books and articles on the cultural life and history of Tansen from the private collections of citizens and various organizations, leaflets on tourism and development work in Palpa; all these things have helped me come to know this place and its people in greater detail. I have collected information from whatever places and in whatever form that were accessible. Inevitably, only a fraction of this material will ever be used as research data, but simply recognizing the huge range of sources available helped me to understand in some limited way the complexities of this urban community and the challenge confronting me in trying to analyze the role that media play in the lives of its people.

Concern with methodology should not and cannot end when one leaves the field. Rather in the process of writing and reflecting on the fieldwork experience one becomes aware of the various interests that guided the selection of the 'facts' that were recorded during what in most cases is only one brief moment of the research process. Recognition of the interested nature of one's analysis does not mean that such analysis is invalid; on the contrary, I would argue that this might be what makes valid analysis possible at all. According to Bourdieu, the validity of one's analysis rests not upon an ability to place oneself in a position of lofty objectivity, nor is it obtained through the fantasy of total empathy. Rather, it comes about through the recognition that the problems we have sought to answer in a particular social situation are structured by the social situation of which we are ourselves a part.

> One cannot avoid having to objectify the objectifying subject. It is by turning to study the historical conditions of his own production, rather than by some form or other of transcendental reflection, that the scientific subject can gain a theoretical control over his own structures and inclinations as well as over the determinants whose products they are, and can thereby gain the concrete means of reinforcing his capacity for objectification. Only a sociological self analysis of this kind, which owes and concedes nothing to self indulgent narcissism, can really help to place the scholar in a position where he is able to bring to bear on

> his familiar world the detached scrutiny which, with no special vigilance, the
> ethnologist brings to bear on any world to which he is not linked by the inher-
> ent complicity of being involved in its social game, its *illusio*, which creates the
> very value of the objectives of the game, as it does the value of the game itself
> (Bourdieu 1988: xii).

One's own subject position is likely to place limits upon understanding that may
be difficult to discern. However, it is out of recognition that such limits exist that
the true nature of our participation during ethnographic fieldwork becomes apparent to us.

This point can be appreciated by considering the fact that I was a native
speaker of English living in a community where the ability to speak English was
frequently regarded as a marker of privilege. Tansen, like most towns, was built
upon trade and, during my time there, I found that one of the few things I could
offer in the market was my ability to speak English. I had no qualifications as a
teacher, but at various times during the year I taught classes at a local computer
and language institute, with a group from a Dalit (Untouchable) organization and
sometimes on a one-to-one basis. Many people seemed eager to learn English
and I was able to barter my command of what one friend and learner called
"sweet words" for knowledge of their local community. I hoped it was a fair
exchange, but I often seemed to learn more than my pupils did.

This was especially the case with one of the older students, Dev Rana, the
head of the district office of an International non-governmental organization in
Palpa. I first met Dev at the language institute and we agreed to carry on our
conversations outside of school hours. Dev's English was already very good
because two years prior to coming to Palpa he had studied Development Administration at a Canadian university, studies that were jointly paid for by his
INGO and the university. He had recently arrived in Tansen to work as senior
co-coordinator for the INGO's work in the east of the district. Prior to this, he
had been their coordinator at one of their project sites in the east of Palpa. Dev
was a member of the Magar ethnic group, as were the majority of those in the
area he worked, although he was originally from another district and clearly
from an entirely different socio-economic class.

Apart from often expressing sentiments about the general problems of development in Nepal, Dev's comments were perhaps most revealing of both his
own attitudes and of the actual practical dynamic of development work when he
discussed the specific characteristics of the areas in which the INGO worked in
Palpa district. In response to a question about why these areas of Palpa were
chosen as the project sites, he said that every one was an isolated and backward
area. He mentioned the continuing use of swidden (slash & burn) agriculture as a
key indicator of this backwardness. He added that the most appropriate word for
these areas is that they are *kaccā* meaning backward and undeveloped (literally
translated either as crude, inexperienced, or irresponsible). There was, he alleged, a lack of toilets in these areas, the farm animals roamed free and were not
caged, the children were not sent to school, and the adults were ignorant of politics. He developed this last point by saying in English that "they have very 'indigenous knowledge'", meaning, I believe, that they were concerned with tradi-

tional rather than modern things and not aware of matters outside of their own community. Clearly he was using the word 'indigenous' in a negative, even pejorative way.

During his time in east Palpa, Dev initiated a meeting for the chairs of the VDCs in the project area. The project office was also being built on land donated to the INGO by a wealthy Magar man, an ex-sergeant in the British Army. To honor this man, Dev employed a painter from Tansen to travel to the project area to create a mural portrait of the sergeant and his wife. He showed me a photograph of this portrait from amongst a set of pictures in several albums. He wanted to use the photos to back up his characterization of the area and pointed out how dirty the living conditions were, with women washing pots near the animals and open cooking fires in the round houses of the villages. In contrast to all this, the new project office, rectangular with decorated awning, window frames and a garden, was very different. There were also pictures of another two wall murals in the project office, one of the Hindu god Ram and the other of the Buddha. He said that he had these painted because the villagers had no particular religious sensibilities and so required some reminder of spiritual values when they came into the meeting room of the project office.

At our next meeting Dev continued this discussion and noted that the eastern area of Palpa has a unique religion which is neither Hindu nor Buddhist, but an indigenous religion. This was, however, being eroded through the use of Brahmin priests during festivals. They exploited the people, he said, by demanding gifts for doing these services. He connected this observation to a recent letter in a local newspaper that complained that government officials came to villages and expected lavish hospitality, but when the villagers went to town to see the officials, they denied all knowledge of them. He said that religion was at the root of all these problems. The caste system might be related in the ancient Vedic scriptures, but Dev asked if there was any "scientific" proof that this social system was inviolable. There was none, he added, answering his own rhetorical question.

My conversations with Dev illustrate that the discourse of development in Nepal is by no means without its contradictions when translated into the words and actions of those whose task it is to put development into practice (Harper and Tarnowski 2003; Heaton-Shrestha 2004). Dev's description of some of the problems of development in Nepal reflects the fact that no single perspective can encompass the variety of possible situations encountered by one actor in the course of his or her life's work and the reactions that they might have to those situations. Religion, which serves in one social context (Dev's relationship to the Magar villagers of the project area) to represent the possibility of at least a spiritual redemption from a "crude" [kaccā] life becomes in another context (Dev's identity as a Magar man in relation to the high caste, Parbatiya elite of the town) a frustrating limit to possibilities for action. Nested dichotomies of ethnicity, residence, religion and morality intersect to produce a profound feeling of personal ambivalence towards his work due to the contradictory interpellations through which one person can be identified (Morley 1992: 63).

This ambivalence was by no means limited to Dev or even to Nepalis working in the development sector. Foreign nationals working for several organizations in Tansen often expressed similar sentiments. The complexity of the social situation in which they work was recognized by these people, but so too was the fact that in order for their work to be effective and become meaningful within the transnational context of INGO administration, such complexities had to be reduced to a commoditized form, that is one that could be exchanged. As a Western anthropologist, I was by no means exempt from these contradictions. Mention of my trade of English teaching for information points to the fact that my own experience of modernity in Tansen involved the conceptualization of my presence in the town and, therefore, identification in terms of development (helping Nepalis become more like Westerners) through the commodification of culture (selling or bartering my own language). Many of the research techniques and modes of presentation that I used in my research (quantitative survey, interviews with experts, etc.) were familiar to development workers and their clients, our mutual subjects, the people of Tansen and Palpa.

I have become increasingly aware of how this had an effect upon the 'facts' I collected during my research and their subsequent analysis. Equally, I have through this self-reflection become more sensitive to how the act of representation carried out by the local cable television organization that I had gone to study, was also involved in acts of objectification and the construction of images of 'culture' that were implicated in the complex articulation of power in Tansen.

Power in relation to individuals such as Dev Rana, organisations like the local television station and anthropologists working at home or abroad are articulated within a series of nested dichotomies that are hierarchically structured according to one order of priority in some instances, but altered or even inverted in others. My interest in the contradictions inherent in the experience of modernity and development in Tansen as represented in the work of RCTV is predicated upon the fact that as a Western researcher in Tansen these contradictions played a key part in my own experience of that community and the representation of that experience in this work. This experience of the contradictions inherent in modernity is typical of bourgeois subjectivity within the modern world system (Morley and Robins 1995) and in the following chapters I will show how the development of local media, especially television, in Tansen exemplifies the experience of inherent contradictions that are part of Nepal's particular formation of modernity.

Notes

1. De Folo continues: "No one who awakes early in Tansen will forget the billows of white foam rolling over the deep hollows of the valley below the city. The man who watches the counterpoint of mist and sunlight and rolling whiteness will always remember that something 'different' takes place in Tansen" (de Folo 1994: 12). One hotel owner has taken advantage of these geographic and climatic conditions to name his property *The White Lake* in reference to the view of the clouds in the valley below which can be seen

from his rooms. I return to consider these 'romantic' constructions of Tansen and the wider Palpa region in chapter 5.

2. In the 1990s the Upper House (*Rastriya Sabha*) of the Parliament was comprised of a majority of members elected by a vote on the floor of the Lower House and a minority of members who were appointed by the King (Borre et al.: 1994).

3. The Parbatiya Hill Castes include *Bahun* (*Brahmin*), *Chetri* (*Kshatriya*) and 'untouchable' Occupational Castes such as *Damai* (Tailors), *Kami* (Ironsmiths), *Sarki* (Leather Workers) and *Sunar* (Gold and Silversmiths). Comparative ethnographic information about the different ethnic and social groups of Nepal can be found in Bista (1967) and Salter and Gurung (1996).

4. The pejorative connotation of the term *Bhotia* should be recognized, along with the fact that this is a term used by others and in the literature in general of these high Himalayan groups, rather than an indigenous term of self-reference (Salter and Gurung 1996: 11).

5. These tensions have been particularly evident since the overthrow of King Gyanendra in 2006 and the entry of the Maoist movement into the interim government of Nepal. A variety of political groups claiming to represent the interests of Tarai communities have begun to employ violent methods to bring their grievances to national attention.

6. However, as chapter 4 explains, the Ranas themselves were enthusiastic in their adoption of British modes of dress and the consumption of imported luxury goods. The extent to which isolation was actually maintained in practice is also examined in chapter 4.

7. Prior to 1947 the British Raj in India, which had been on friendly terms with the Rana regime since Jung Bahadur Rana sent Nepali troops to help put down the Indian Mutiny in 1857, supported the Ranas. Not surprisingly, the first Congress-led government of independent India did not view the status quo of the Rana regime in the same light and not only gave King Tribhuvan asylum in India, but also tacitly supported the armed opposition to the Ranas (Joshi and Rose 1966).

8. The four parties which have dominated parliament in Nepal are the Nepali Congress (broadly centrist); the moderate, left-wing Communist Party of Nepal (United Marxist-Leninist); the Rastriya Prajatantra Party (a right-wing party of ex-Panchayat members who actively support the power of the Palace); and the Nepal Sabhavana Party (which campaigns on behalf of Tarai communities and receives only limited support even in this region). There were and continue to be numerous other small political parties that have failed to win representation in national or even local assemblies.

When I visited Nepal in for the first time in 1994 the country's first democratically elected government of the 1990s, led by the Nepal Congress's G.P. Koirala (brother of B.P. Koirala, Nepal's first democratically elected Prime Minister) was beginning to suffer its death throes. A year later when I returned to begin fieldwork, the second government under Prime Minister G.M. Adhikari of the Communist Party of Nepal (United Marxist-Leninist) was facing a no-confidence motion in parliament. The government under which I lived for most of my time in Nepal, a coalition of the Congress, Rastriya Prajatantra Party and the Nepal Sabhavana Party, led by S.B. Deuba (Nepal Congress) survived until March 1997. Whelpton (2005) provides a summary of political events between 1997 and 2004, including the murder of King Birendra and his immediate family by Crown Prince Dipendra in 2001. More recent events include the seizure of absolute power by King Gyanendra in 2005, the Second *Jana Andolan* (People's Movement) in 2006, creation of an interim government including the major mainstream political parties and the Maoists, and the decision to transform Nepal into a republic that should be ratified during a meeting of an elected Constitutional Assembly in 2008.

9. An explicit question on ethnicity was only included from 1991 in the national census of Nepal, so it is difficult to give accurate figures on the changing ethnic composition of Tansen. According to the 1981 census, however, only 2% of the urban population gave Magar as their mother tongue (HMG, Nepal 1984), whilst the 1991 census listed the Magar population as just over 15% of the total (Shrestha, V.P. 1994). By 1994 Tansen's population had risen to 16,169 people and much of this rise can be accounted for by immigration from areas within Palpa district. According to my own survey carried out in the last two months of 1995, half of all immigrants came from within Palpa. Interestingly, the figures for residency for Newar and Magar respondents to this survey show almost perfect symmetry: whilst 80.5% of Newars questioned had been resident in Tansen since birth and 19.5% were immigrants, 81% of Magars were immigrants and only 19% resident since birth. This difference was also reflected in the average length of residence for each group: this being 15.6 years for Newar immigrants, whilst Magar immigrants have been resident for 5.6 years on average (further detail on these figures can be found in chapter 5).

10. Nevertheless, the houses or land for building are often owned by Newar families.

11. We should note, however, that this is a relatively recent phenomenon for Tansen. Prior to the fall of the Rana regime in 1951 the population of the town was only about six thousand people (Landon 1993), although this would have been very large compared to the other towns in the hills outside the Kathmandu Valley. Despite more than doubling in size since then, people still frequently refer to Tansen as a 'village' (gāu) in everyday speech. Even a young man in his mid-twenties nostalgically remembered a time in the recent past when "we didn't need television to tell us the local news, but instead we learnt through word of mouth what was going on in the town."

Chapter 2
Conceptualizing Media Outside the Mainstream: Tansen's Television

> It matters for the quality of public life that its central institutions—the media—involve an asymmetry between a relatively small group of producers and participants, and a vast mass of non-producers . . . It matters, similarly, that this asymmetry is naturalized and challenges to it de-legitimized.
>
> Nick Couldry (2000: 193)

Introduction

Several terms, such as 'small', 'alternative' and 'non-mainstream' were used, more or less synonymously in the opening chapter to identify and describe Ratna Cable Television and Communication for Development Palpa's work in Tansen. These are only a sample of the great profusion of terms that have been proposed as appropriate for these types of media activities and organizations. Such terms include, in no particular order: minority, community, local, radical, activist, indigenous, free, oppositional, social, grassroots, participatory, independent, popular, self-governing, emancipatory and citizen. This list is not exhaustive of all the possibilities, and, amongst the profusion of terms, there is clearly much scope for confusion.

Should this concern us? For Clemencia Rodriguez the range of proposed terms actually reflects the diverse forms that media can take in the many contexts within which they are deployed. She states that,

> The lack of a rigid definition for apprehending the texture of citizens' media should point to a new direction in our attempts—as media scholars, activists, or policy makers—to understand movements towards democratic communication. Instead of assuming that the problem lies in not finding a unifying formula to define all the different forms that citizens' media take we must question our need for this type of definition. The problem should not be traced back to the object that rejects tight definitions, but to the subject who tries to impose them, that is to the subject who prefers rigid definitions as a condition to comprehend social phenomena. On this basis, our attempts to define citizens' media should

27

focus on the citizens, and their creative intentionality in altering the mediascape rather than centering on the external and objective forms that citizens' media can take (Rodriguez 2001: 165).

Echoing this concern with the potential for definitions to constrain rather than enable understanding and the discussion of research methodology in chapter 1, Tony Dowmunt notes that,

> Any useful definition of alternative media, or of what constitutes resistance to the [mainstream media] empires, is bound to be complex, and will need to be informed by detailed investigation of what exactly is being resisted, by whom, in what contexts. Maybe we have to move away from generalized assertions, towards analyzing alternative media more 'ethnographically', in particular contexts, mirroring the way that audience research now concentrates on "the investigation of television consumption in its 'natural' setting, as contextualized activity" (1998: 245, quoting David Morley).

However, even if no single definition can encompass the reality of media practices encountered around the world, the wide range of definitions does serve as a useful resource for helping us to identify features that may be characteristic of these media.

The first thing to note is that definitions are often 'negative', identifying these media by what they are not, rather than in terms of any of their 'positive' features. 'Non-mainstream' is obviously the clearest example of this type of definition in the above lists, although the prefix 'non-' can obviously be applied to any number of terms to convey the idea that we are dealing here with media that are different from those that we might more commonly encounter. The problem is that what we 'commonly encounter' may vary quite considerably from place to place. Commercial broadcasting might be non-mainstream in a place where media are rigorously controlled by the state, but mainstream in a place where a liberal, market-based political economy reigns supreme. Such a definition also suffers from confusion about how the mainstream should be defined. Publicly funded television in the United States might be regarded as non-mainstream media in contrast to the dominant position of the commercial networks, but it may also conform quite closely to the professional standards, content, aesthetics and rules of access that are encountered in other media organizations.

What this negative definition does give us, however, is the sense that we are dealing here with a mediascape that is uneven and contoured like an undulating physical landscape. There are commanding heights from which powerful media flow in torrential quantities, just as there are places that are virtually deserted or inaccessible. These are the places, the so-called "fissures in the mediascape" (Rodriguez 2001) within which the media that we are concerned with here are often found to exist. This is also the reason why such media are often discussed in negatives way using the more pejorative sense of this term. Non-mainstream media may be regarded as insignificant or irrelevant in the face of the supposedly overwhelming scale and importance of mainstream media, whatever the circumstances under which the latter are produced. Marginalized in both quantitative and qualitative terms, why should we pay attention to non-mainstream media?

Some of the other definitions, which provide a more positive identification, answer this question of why people bother to produce media in such seemingly barren circumstances or pay any attention to them, either as audience members or researchers. These media have often been too readily dismissed as an irrelevance in the face of the obvious dominance of the media that are under the control of the states or large-scale commercial enterprises (Downing and Husband 2005: 68–9). As Molnar and Meadows (2001) indicate, this marginalization is not based purely in the economic realities of media production:

> A range of ideas and assumptions about our world compete for acceptance through cultural institutions, like the media. Alternative views tend to be systematically marginalized or ignored. That there are alternatives is also difficult for some to accept because of the patient and systematic reinforcement or preferred ideas. But alternatives do exist (Molnar and Meadows 2001: 196).

Couldry (2000) reinforces this point through his analysis of media power, which builds on Bourdieu's work, by examining the ways that the constantly reaffirmed assertion of the legitimacy and primacy of so-called mainstream media are a crucial component of their 'symbolic power'. As he states,

> The power of media institutions is both a cultural and an economic phenomenon. To claim that either has analytic priority is as absurd as a sociologist of religion arguing that studying the economics and organizational aspects of religious institutions is somehow 'prior' to studying the cultures of belief which help sustain them. The media have their own 'culture of belief', and we need to study it. Doing so means thinking seriously about space and the media's impacts on the territories which they play a central role in mapping (Couldry 2000: 194).

Nevertheless, the fact that media institutions and those who rely on them to assert their own political power can, as Couldry recounts, react aggressively in defense when this power is challenged indicates that it may be precisely at these times and places of challenge that we should look to find the greatest insights into the operation of media power.

This study contributes to the agenda for the analysis of media power that is mapped out by Couldry by examining some of the work of Ratna Cable Television in Nepal. As such, it takes us beyond the territories within which so much theorization of media power takes place, that is literally Western, industrialized, modern nation-states (cf. Curran and Park 2000), by offering a detailed study of media making in context. It thus offers material for comparative analyses through the study of how media simultaneously contribute to the construction of a sense of locality and are themselves constructed within the constraints of a locality.

The remainder of this chapter is divided between an introduction to the study of alternative media and then a description of Ratna Cable Television in its first years of operation. The aim in this chapter is not to identify any essential definition of what alternative media are that can then be applied to somehow explain RCTV. It will become apparent that such a definition cannot be achieved and would be of little help in understanding an organization that even in its brief history up to the point at which this study was conducted demonstrated great complexities and contradictions. The task of unraveling these truly begins in the chapters that follow.

Defining Alternative Media

As the above introduction has indicated, one step beyond the negative approach to definition is the commonly-encountered term 'alternative media'. This is only one remove from the negative definition, because it immediately begs the question of 'alternative to what?', which is usually answered in terms of the familiar generalization of 'the mainstream', whatever that might be in the context under examination. As Atton (2002: 9) says, "custom and practice" have led the term 'alternative' to be widely adopted as an accepted way to identify the types of media we are considering here, but "to deploy 'alternative' as an analytical term . . . might afford us little more specificity than saying 'non-mainstream'" (ibid.: 10). Having said this, he prefers this term to other commonly encountered terms, such as 'oppositional', 'activist' or 'radical' because it allows us to encompass media that do not, in their content at least, have to be defined by any particular political stance or take overt political action as their raison d'être.

Many of the other terms listed above indicate the central point made by Atton in his analysis of alternative media, which is that we must pay as much attention, if not more, to their modes of production, as we do to the content of these media. He proposes "a model of the alternative media that is as much concerned with how it is organized within its sociocultural context as with its subject matter" (2002: 10). Definitions based on scale, either in terms of the media organization itself ('small'), of the location ('community'), or of place ('local' or 'grassroots') speak to social aspects of the model. Equally, definitions that focus on the types of people involved, both as producers and audiences, such as 'citizens', 'indigenous' or 'minority' point to the special relationship that the media producers might have with their audience or the specific cultural goals that they may pursue. Social relations within the group of media producers themselves are evoked through terms such as 'participatory' and self-governing', whilst the relations between the group and other agents, institutions or social forces are indicated in words like 'free' or 'independent'. Finally, the goals to which media are directed may be indicated through a term such as 'emancipatory' or 'popular'.

Taking any one definition alone leads to the sorts of confusion experienced by the proverbial blind men describing the elephant; each leaves us with only a partial and misleading understanding of what it is we are encountering. The first step, then, is to employ a model that encompasses each of these areas of concern. Atton (2002: 27) suggests that such a model can be constructed from a typology which encompasses the above definitions and directs our analysis towards: content; form; reprographic innovations and adaptations; distribution; social relations, roles and responsibilities; and communication processes. He points out that the first three of these elements of the typology relate to media products and the last three are concerned with processes. By presenting a typology that balances out the relative contributions of product (content or form) and process (production and consumption), he underlines the important point that it is important to take what we might call the social products into account when analyzing 'alternative' media and evaluating their impacts.

As mentioned above, negative evaluations of alternative media often take their ephemeral existence or evident lack of influence upon mainstream media content as indicative of a lack of worth. However, this is to ignore the profound impact that they have on the lives of those involved in these media activities or in the often neglected localities where they work. The production of media *content* might be the ostensive purpose of alternative media, but the *social relationships* that are also created in the course of this work are no mere side-effect. Relationships are obviously created internally, so to speak, amongst the people involved in the act of creating alternative media. The formation of a group in this way, united through a shared commitment to the goals and processes of media creation, is often of great consequence for those involved. This may at first appear to be of little note for others, but it would be a mistake to thus dismiss such work as parochial. Apart from acting to energize others through their example, alternative media groups also frequently form networks, which Ginsburg (1991) claims is one of the most important political outcomes of the indigenous media activity. The idea that this process of network formation is the basis of social capital formation (Putnam 2000) in the context of the work of RCTV in Tansen is further discussed in chapter 6.

I will discuss Ginsburg's and Eric Michael's work on indigenous media in Australia in further detail in order to reinforce the importance of this point regarding the social potential of alternative media. Faye Ginsburg's influential article "Indigenous media: Faustian Contract or Global Village?" (1991: 94) offers the following outline of her thesis:

> I am proposing that when other forms are no longer effective, indigenous media offers a possible means—social, cultural, and political—for reproducing and transforming cultural identity among people who have experienced massive political, geographic and economic disruption. The capabilities of media to transcend boundaries of time, space, and even language are being used effectively to *mediate*, literally, historically produced social ruptures and to help construct identities that link past and present in ways appropriate to contemporary conditions [emphasis added].

The key term here is 'mediate' and its importance to Ginsburg's approach to the analysis of indigenous media should be noted, because her essentially positive reading of these is derived from her use of the concept. 'Mediation' in Ginsburg's analyses performs much the same role as 'articulation' does within Stuart Hall's cultural theory (see Morley and Chen 1996); it serves as a general term to describe the way in which the cultural representations made by a person or people *speak of* their identity in a way that enables them to both *speak to* and be recognized by others. Silverstone's (1999) discussion of the rhetorical and poetic characteristics of mediation also helps to explicate the way in which media practices are generated by and generative of notions of subjectivity. Mediation is, as he notes, structuration, because it "is only completed in the mind or the life of the reader or viewer" (ibid.; 46). Similarly, according to Turner (1995a: 105), "the praxis of image production by indigenous and other peripheralized social groups typically has the character of mediation, in a double sense: connecting the present reality of the group to its own past and future, and articulating its external relationship to the dominant national or world (i.e. Western) culture and society in which it is embedded."

The control of media by minority groups provides them with an opportunity for "a more positive model of exchange" (Ginsburg 1991: 106). Indigenous media may produce an autonomous location within the global and national *mediascape* (Appadurai 1990) from which those who have previously been disadvantaged within the global or national political economy of media can operate either independently of or in a more equal relationship with other media organizations. Indigenous media not only mediate spatially arranged social relationships but also relations in time. According to Ginsburg (1991: 106) "many in this generation [of Australian Indigenous Peoples] want to engage in image-making that offers a face and a narrative that reflects on the present, connects them to a history, and directs them toward a future as well."

Ginsburg argues that, because of this process of mediation, indigenous media "are of critical theoretical and empirical significance for current debates in several fields regarding the politics and poetics of representation, the development of media in Third and Fourth World settings, and the expansion of ethnographic film theory and the canon associated with it" (Ginsburg 1991: 93).[1] This potential can only be realized through the development of a theoretical position that encompasses both positive and negative political outcomes of indigenous and other alternative types of media use. In other words, we must countenance the possibility that these acts of alternative mediation can inhibit as well as foster social relations between the producers of media and between producers and their audiences. Ginsburg offers two contrasting case studies of Aboriginal media in Australia that demonstrate the different ways in which indigenous media groups may be articulated within the structures of the nation-state.

The first organization represents a 'top-down' approach. *Imparja*, meaning 'tracks' or 'footprints', was set up in 1985 and operates within the framework of the state-licensed, independent, satellite television network. Since it began broadcasting in 1988, the privately owned company which is controlled by an autonomous body, the *Central Australian Aboriginal Media Association* made up of both Aboriginal and European Australian members, has been producing programs of interest to an Aboriginal audience in a variety of languages. But these amount to little more than two to three hours out of seventy hours of programming a week because the station relies on advertising revenue for the vast majority of its funding. This means that the station must appeal to a large audience of mass consumers and in the context of Australia this means a white, 'European' audience. It also means that the schedules rely on a great deal of material bought from outside production companies and this further reduces the 'Aboriginal' character of the station. Even more important than this is the accompanying insistence on the part of both audience and advertisers that Imparja's programming is of suitably high, professional standard. This demand brings with it an attendant requirement for a skilled workforce and discounts the possibility of the use of low cost material produced on amateur format video and film by other Aboriginal filmmakers. Only ten percent of staff is from the Aboriginal population. This illustrates what Stuart Hall describes as the ideological effect produced by the "professional code" within the media, so that despite being officially neutral towards or even allied to radical and minority interests within society, they find themselves operating "within the 'hegemony' of the dominant code" (Hall et al. 1999: 59). "The case of Imparja makes clear," says Ginsburg (1993: 570), "that even well-intentioned attempts to increase the visibility, accomplishments, and concerns of Aboriginal people are often fraught with complexities that white policy makers would rather ignore. Multicultural rhetoric of inclusion can gloss over the fact that the scale and 'rules' of mass media can easily overwhelm local Aboriginal concerns."[2]

The efficacy of the 'top-down' approach may be questionable, but the opposite, 'bottom-up' or grass-roots approach may also face related problems even as it seeks to avoid the pitfalls highlighted above. The *Warlpiri Media Association*, the second example, which has been most extensively analyzed by the late Eric Michaels (1994), is a small-scale organization that grew up in the early 1980s around the activities of a group of video makers in central Australia. Originally producing tapes of local cultural events for dissemination in schools and amongst local social groups, in 1985, the Warlpiri Media Association built its own low-power transmitter. Decades of neglect by the state meant, somewhat ironically, that, in Ginsburg's words, "a bureaucratic vacuum" (1993: 565–6) surrounded some groups, which placed them beyond the remit of existing legal regulation of the Australian media. The small scale of production also means that local concerns can be concentrated on in ways that are beyond the capabilities of an organization like Imparja, but also creates its own vulnerabilities. Relying, as they do, on the skills of a few talented individuals the organization can easily collapse if these personnel should leave. The dynamism and energy that animates such grass-roots organizations is also notoriously difficult to duplicate through bureaucratic means in other contexts whether they be instituted by the state or parastatal organizations (e.g. international non-governmental organizations).

To summarize, we may quote Debra Spitulnik who notes that the study of indigenous media is important because of its "sustained attention to the fact that mass media are at once cultural products and social processes, as well as extremely potent arenas of political struggle" (1993: 303). We should be aware, however, of the possibility of a complacent, not to say romantic, view of these organizations. Ginsburg (1993: 574) herself points out that the "image of a 'primitive' but seemingly empowered 'Other' appeals to western, Rousseauistic fantasies" and Spitulnik (1993: 305) discusses how the indigenous label may itself hide a huge variety in the manner in which such minority groups are articulated with the dominant culture. Indeed, it is important to ask what sort of position the group seeks to establish within the nation-state. We could interpret a situation like that of the Warlpiri Media Association as a clear example of resistance to the state and white-owned institutions' overwhelming control of the Australian media. But as Eric Michaels points out in the original studies upon which Ginsburg based her analyses, the situation is not quite as straight forward as this.

Eric Michaels originally studied and worked with the Warlpiri Aborigines in their production and consumption of television programs in central Australia. His original research project set out to understand the different ways in which print media and electronic media were being used by this community as part of a wider interest in literacy practices (see Ruby 2000: 221–238 for a general overview of Michaels' work). According to Michaels (1994: 81):

> We are used to selling literacy as a pro-social, pro-development medium. We are used to denigrating video and television as antisocial and repressive...[W]e have come to regard the Western world's media development sequence as somehow natural: from orality to literacy, print, film, and now electronics. But Aboriginal and other 'developing' peoples do not conform to this sequence, and produce some very different media histories.

Whilst Warlpiri culture is not literary in any conventional Western sense, Michaels, building on the pioneering work of Nancy Munn (1973), notes that the Warlpiri people have developed a complex system of graphic representation, chiefly manifested in the form of sand drawings that are used as part of traditional story telling. He argues that attempts by researchers to 'prove' that Warlpiri graphic art is a form of proto-writing have been disappointing and goes on to claim that the underlying premise of this sort of research, that the Warlpiri use their graphic art to somehow 'stand-in-for' writing is inappropriate. Such analyses fail to take into account the extent to which the social relations that are articulated by written media in 'literate' societies are distinctly different to social relations in 'non-literate' societies. In particular the absence of an author conceptualized as the individual who wrote something or otherwise made a cultural artifact is absent in the Aboriginal setting. According to Michaels (1994: 108–9):

> To understand Warlpiri video and its challenge to imported TV, one must appreciate this sense of *Jukurrpa* [The Law, Dreaming] as a model of social reproduction—the management of information transmission across generations—and identify the ways in which novelty must be counterinterpolated to the system . . . Warlpiri artists demonstrate their own invisibility in order to assert the work's authority and continuity with tradition. They do not draw attention to themselves or to their creativity.

This reading of Aboriginal cultural production is followed to its logical conclusion in an earlier section in Michael's book entitled "'Traditional' Aboriginal Television" (1994: 30–32), which poses the question "what might television look like if it had been invented by Warlpiri Aborigines?"[3] Here Michaels discusses the absence of change, or rather the *appearance* of unchanging and eternal Dreaming Law in Aboriginal society through which the problem of history is abolished (ibid.: 32). Each act in the present is a transformation of an original act in mythic time so that when the 'present' is compared to the 'past' there is no discrepancy. Spatial metaphors are also used via the spread of the kinship network so that all ritual specialists participate in the 'Truth' without ever maintaining the whole of the 'Truth'. "Information is dispersed in time and space through a network that eventually encompasses the continent, and perhaps the world, in which each adult individual has particular, but constrained, speaking and knowing rights. Significantly, this system is not hierarchical, something extraordinarily difficult for people from class societies to appreciate, whether that society is British colonial administration or a film crew" (ibid.: 32).

This does mean, of course, that any comparison of indigenous media would have to be very sensitive to these institutional and contextual factors, especially given Michaels' processual understanding of culture, which he shares with Faye Ginsburg and Terence Turner. In fact, as he suggests with regard to analyses of the content of Aboriginal media, indigenous media soon begins to fragment even as it is recognized it as an object of analysis:

> Here I want to emphasize *the continuity of modes of cultural production across media*, something that might be too easily overlooked by an ethnocentric focus on content. My researches identify how Jupurrurla and other Warlpiri video makers have learned ways of using the medium that conform to the basic premises of their tradition in its essential oral form. They demonstrate that this is possible, but also that their efforts are yet vulnerable, easily jeopardized by the invasion of alien and professional media producers (ibid.: 121).

Michaels argues that the 'professionalization' of Aboriginal media under the guise of the encouragement of its 'development' simply leads to it being forced to conform to a Western information economy, whereas the value of Aboriginal media is precisely in the capacity it has to transform our own media practices once we grasp that members of this extremely complex, information rich (if economically poor) culture are using media in innovative and truly counter-cultural ways:

> If we take 'community' rather than 'Aboriginality' to be the subject, and make 'local' the qualifier, only then do we avoid the traps of racism and paternalism in our rhetoric and practice . . . Warlpiri Media Association programs only become 'Aboriginal Content' when they are exported from Yuendumu, and perhaps only when they are expropriated from Aboriginal Australia. In the context of their transmission at Yuendumu they are simply local media. I am proposing that such content only becomes 'Aboriginal' when it becomes 'their' media. 'Our' own media never really qualifies (Michaels 1994: 43–5).

This point regarding the appropriation of media is important because it emphasizes that we are not simply talking about acts of taking possession of things and their conventional uses. We are also talking about the way in which things, especially seemingly powerful things such as media, come to be regarded as appropriate for people, potentially any people, to use as a vehicle for self-expression, self-representation and empowerment. This is about cultural transformation, but transformations that happen through the exertion of some degree of control by all of the actors involved and not just some. It is this appropriation of power that Rodriguez refers to in an anecdote about the response of a South American woman to the video of her home that she had recorded earlier: "'I never realized my kitchen could be so beautiful!' The solidified perception of her kitchen was now shaken by the new perspective allowed her by the video camera" (2001: 2). The veteran radio broadcaster and oral historian, Studs Terkel (2008) also writes,

> My moment of ultimate astonishment happened about 30 years ago. It was at a public housing project. A young mother. I don't remember whether she was white or black. The place was mixed. She was pretty, skinny, with bad teeth.
> It was the first time she had encountered a tape recorder. Her little kids, about four of them, demanded a replay. They insisted on hearing mama's voice. I pressed the button. They howled with delight. She put her hands to her mouth and gasped. 'I never knew I felt that way.'

It is this capacity to elicit a revelation of identity, as well as to represent that which is already known, that forms the basis of much alternative media work. It is what underlies Rodriguez's insistence that we should speak of citizens media, rather than alternative media, because it is through this type of media work that people come to recognize and come to share their selves as active political agents.

> Referring to 'citizens' media' implies first that a collectivity is enacting its citizenship by actively intervening and transforming the established mediascape; second, that these media are contesting social codes, legitimized identities, and institutionalized relations; and third, that these communication practices are empowering the community involved, to the point where these transformations and changes are possible (Rodriguez 2001: 20).

The work carried out by Terence Turner with the Kayapo people of the Brazilian Amazon exemplifies this point about the transformative value of alternative or indigenous media production. In the early 1960s, when Turner first went to live and work amongst the Gorotire Kayapo, "the Gorotire had no alternative but to depend on two rival institutional representatives of the Western world system [the Missionaries and the government agency, the *Servico pela Protecao aos Indios* (SPI)] in which they were embedded for the satisfaction of their medical and commodity needs" (1991: 288). These agencies monopolized all forms of transport to and communication with the urban centers from which these state and religious institutions were administered. After a description of a women's naming ceremony performed on their first day in the village and the architecture and material culture of the new village by the SPI station in which the Gorotire Kayapo had been settled, Turner goes on to note that,

> The changes [village architecture and plan, and clothing] had no intrinsic meaning for the Kayapo, but had been imposed because of meanings they held for the dominant outsiders, the whites. They simply seemed an alien overlay beneath which the authentic Kayapo culture still persisted, manifesting itself in collective ritual events like the ceremony we had witnessed that first night in Gorotire, and in enduring social institutions like the men's house and the stubbornly matri-uxorilocal extended-family households that bordered the village 'street'. The native social and cultural forms appeared to have persisted in spite of their encompassment by the situation of inter-ethnic contact, rather than because of any stable or harmonious accommodation with it (ibid.: 291).

Turner describes the depression he felt at this time due to his conceptualization of the situation in Gorotire as one of cultural 'rescue'—"from this point of view, anthropology, like Kayapo culture itself, defined itself in abstraction from the 'situation of contact,' as the antithesis of 'change' and the enemy of 'history'" (ibid.: 292).

Turner refers here to the cosmological beliefs of the Kayapo, which described a universe of concentric circles of life and nature at the centre of which stood the Kayapo. This central position was also conflated with the notion of humanity and so the Kayapo saw their being and its cultural manifestation in ritual as immanent in this cosmology. "The cosmological terms in which this traditional Kayapo view of the social world were cast left no room for a consciousness of the structure of this integral process of social production as itself a social product. It was, rather, seen as the natural structure of the cosmos" (ibid.: 295). The contact situation has altered this worldview.

> The Kayapo have come to see themselves as one 'Indian' people among others, with a 'culture' of the same order as their own. The political corollary of this new level of cultural self-awareness is that the Kayapo have begun to see the preservation or loss of their cultural identity as a matter for conscious concern and concerted political action. From seeing themselves as the prototype of humanity, in other words, the Kayapo now see themselves as an ethnic group, sharing their ethnicity on a more or less equal footing with other indigenous peoples in their common confrontation with the national society (ibid.: 296).

Instead of seeing their concentric cosmology as having a core position occupied by the Kayapo and surrounded by areas of 'natural' non-human life, the Kayapo cosmology acknowledges the encompassment of the central Kayapo and Indian areas by the Brazilian state. The social polarities have been reversed. Indians react to the surrounding natural zone in a transformative way, whereas the Brazilians have a destructive relationship. This is a thesis that retains the fundamental acknowledgement that profound and often destructive cultural transformation is taking place amongst the people and communities of the Fourth World, but it is a transformation that now encompasses the contradiction and struggle be-

tween the Indians and the Brazilian state. "In place of the ahistorical and acul-
tural vision of Kayapo society offered by the traditional world view, it defines
the very survival of their society and culture as contingent on their successful
resistance to the destruction of their natural environment by the dominant
whites" (ibid.: 299). Turner sees his own initial 'objective' fieldwork stance as
part of the alienation felt at the time by the Kayapo. The notion of 'culture' (indeed the Portuguese word 'cultura' itself) has been appropriated by the Kayapo
and "the essential idea underlying these expressions is that 'culture' is the means
by which a society maintains its morale and capacity for action, including both
political action vis-à-vis the national society and the reproduction of its own
pattern of life" (ibid.: 304).

The Gorotire have been able, in the years since Turner's first fieldwork, to
take over all positions of power and administration in the area. "In short, the
Gorotire have not so much overthrown as made their own the architecture of
dependency which comprised these functions, when monopolized by representatives of the national society. They have converted it into the foundation of internal communal autonomy and local control over the principal nodes of articulation with the encompassing national and world system" (ibid.: 302).

Kayapo groups have used video recording technologies since 1985, but until 1990, when the Kayapo Video Project was established at the instigation of
Terence Turner, this use was purely at the "home movie" level (Turner 1992: 7).
Since 1990, however, access to editing facilities and technical assistance has
enabled the Kayapo to produce representations of their culture and, perhaps
more importantly, to record political events such as the meetings of local leaders
or the foundation of new communities. In these cases, the use of video has actually transformed the events themselves by turning what would have previously
been *subjective* events subject to possible contestation into *objectively* established public facts.

> The notion of an objectively determined social Reality [sic.] permanently fixed
> by public documents, which many non-literate societies first acquired through
> the medium of writing, has come to the Kayapo and some other contemporary
> non-literate peoples through the medium of video. To this extent, it seems fair
> to say that video has contributed to the transformation of Kayapo social con-
> sciousness, both in the sense of promoting a more objectified notion of social
> reality and of heightening their sense of their own agency by providing them
> with a means of active control over the process of objectification itself: the
> video camera (Turner 1992: 11).

As noted above, the use of video technology did not initiate the process of cultural objectification by the Kayapo, but, given their non-literate situation, it has
provided a useful tool through which collective agency based upon ethnic identity can be deployed within the framework of the encompassing national society
and Western world system (ibid.: 12; see also Oakdale 2004).

The Kayapo situation is obviously of greater complexity than any simple
model of resistance to state domination can allow for and Turner (1992: 5) notes
that "the relatively small world of indigenous media...nevertheless contains

important differences: hence the need for more empirical studies." It is important to note that the Kayapo use of video

> has not merely preserved traditional customs but in fact transformed their understanding of those customs as customs and their culture as culture. Turner also found that video equipment, expertise, and products often fed into existing factional divisions. Particular Kayapo leaders used the equipment in their own interests, sometimes as a tool to subdue their enemies, sometimes as evidence of personal power (Aufderheide 1993: 588–9).

Patricia Aufderheide goes on to note that:

> The Kayapo are not alone in their experience of video as yet another measure of internal power, but outsiders know very little about this aspect of grassroots video use. Until we do, generalizations about the empowering qualities of media production will remain at the rhetorical level (ibid.).

This case study of alternative media—grassroots video in Aufderheide's parlance—attempts to answer her criticism of such generalizations through its sustained attention to exactly those aspects of social organization and cultural reproduction that have often been overlooked in previous studies of such media.

The analysis of these media organizations in the work of Ginsburg, Turner and Michaels acknowledges that cultural artifacts and forms have been transplanted or diffused from their Western places of origin and are effecting a transformation of the societies and cultures in which their use has been adopted. The point of origin of their analysis is, however, historicized because it is emphasized that this transformation is taking place under the profound impact of Western imperialism and colonialism. Thus, their analyses are never situated in the context of the transformation of a romanticized, pristine culture. Rather, they are analyses of how cultural transformations induced by the frequently violent apparatuses of the post-colonial nation-state may be ameliorated through the use of mass communication technology and media.

Again, 'articulation' must be highlighted as the key term in Turner's analysis because, as Stuart Hall has pointed out, it is a word that has a useful double meaning and both these meanings can be utilized within social and cultural analyses. Not only are people enmeshed within (that is, articulated in the sense of connection with) social, economic, political and cultural structures, but we also enter into dialogue with and attempt to influence the formation of those structures through what we make of the cultural resources that are available to us (that is, how we articulate in the sense of speaking of the position in which we find ourselves). And to be articulate does not simply mean to speak, but it means to speak eloquently often despite the restrictions that our circumstances place upon us. Types of communication using forms other than speech can be judged as aesthetically effective and, therefore, analogous to eloquent speech (see especially Gell 1998 and 1999; Morphy 1992; Deger 2006; and Wilmore 2008).[4] As Hall and Grossberg (1996: 142) put it, the theory of articulation asks how an ideology discovers its subject rather than how the subject thinks the necessary and inevitable thoughts which belong to it; it enables us to think how an ideology empowers people, enabling them to make some sense or intelligibility of their historical situation, without reducing those forms of intelligibility to their socio-economic or class location or social position.

Turner acknowledges the influence of Hall's work in one of his most strongly argued essays in support of the Kayapo use of media, specifically video (Turner 1992). Here he explains that "indigenous self-documentation tends to focus not on the retrieval of an idealized vision of the pre-contact culture but on 'processes of identity construction' in the cultural present" (ibid.: 6). Media technology provides the means through which the Kayapo can articulate (that is communicate) their knowledge of the social, political and economic structures and institutions with which they are articulated in the modern world system. By focusing on indigenous media we are able to recognize very clearly that the 'nodes of articulation' described by Turner are not simply abstract positions within a theoretical socio-cultural landscape, but always exist in a concrete form. Modern, electronic media form an increasingly important, although not the only, means through which these various articulations are established, reproduced, or altered.

The means through which these articulations occur are neither mysterious nor avoidable in most instances. Even the most shoestring alternative media organizations require some source of income in order to produce and broadcast programs. Advertisers are reluctant to buy airtime, professional broadcasters will not buy programs and government or non-government development agencies are suspicious if the programs made by alternative producers do not match a required level of clarity. Such "broadcast standards" (Reeves 1993) are, of course, set by these funding agencies themselves and require equipment and facilities that are expensive beyond the capabilities of most alternative or indigenous producers to finance. It is, of course, nearly impossible to escape from this vicious circle. It is also the case that claiming alternative media are not of broadcast standard also hides a multitude of political and ethnic prejudices behind an aura of technological and 'objective' reasoning (Hall et al. 1999). This argument is similar to those made by Eco (1995) and Mishra (1999) regarding so-called new media, because it posits that an alternative may in fact only reproduce the familiar and mainstream, though with one crucial caveat. Whereas Eco is at pains to demonstrate that other, counter-informational ways of writing and reading exist through which a multiplicity of messages can be articulated in a particular medium (in the case of Eco's study, in comic books), this possibility is denied by critics for whom media are always overdetermined by their original formal characteristics.

Counter-cultural activity by alternative media organizations could be subject to disciplinary control if they were always in competition with major commercial and/or national media and thus inextricably enmeshed in the structures of power in which these 'mainstream' media are implicated. However, this is not always the case for two reasons. The first is a simple concomitant of the above point about the disparity between the financial, and hence the technological, resources of 'professional' media organizations (both publicly and privately owned) and alternative media organizations. The vastly different economies of scale involved in the purchase and operation of 'broadcast standard' and 'amateur' communication technology means that we are in effect considering two entirely different spheres of media production. This factor is reflected in the difficulty that national governments have often had in controlling the activities of alternative media organizations.

Secondly, if these factors have often divided alternative media organizations and their products from the media mainstream, it is also the case that their producers are often keen to differentiate their output from that of the mainstream. It hardly needs to be said that a key motivation for alternative producers is the recognition that mainstream media reflects ideologies and goals that are at the very least irrelevant to their own cultural traditions and political aspirations, if not actually hostile to these aspirations.

These two factors—the desire to produce different media and the economically entrenched technical disparity, when taken together result in media that are recognizably different to the mainstream. This is not meant to imply that all alternative producers are relentless innovators. Indeed, as Nancy Sullivan (1993) points out, some of the power of indigenous media actually comes from the producers' appropriation of Western, mainstream media forms. Sullivan claims that when Western media are turned, as it were, back upon themselves, so that instead of transmitting 'Our' representations of the 'Other' we see the 'Their' own self-representations, the effect can be startling and disrupt the unchallenged reproduction of Western hegemony. Gross (1998) makes a similar point with regard to the way in which production *of* media *by* and *for* lesbian and gay audiences in the USA and Europe has led to the creation of positive minority identities that offer an alternative to the, at best, stereotypical media representations of lesbian and gay lives within media made for mainstream consumption or, at worst, the total absence of representation, let alone positive representation.

Criticism of the Indigenous Media Concept

As we noted above, analyses of alternative and indigenous media have often been overlooked by media researchers, on the grounds that these media are too small to be of consequence. Nevertheless, some analyses have actually generated a quite hostile reception and in this section we examine the bases of some of these reactions. Faye Ginsburg's work in particular has been provocative because she claims that cultural reproduction and survival is enhanced through the use of the very cultural forms that other cultural commentators, both Euro-American and Indigenous, have identified as offering the greatest threat to their survival; that is modern mass media, especially television. For some, such as James Weiner (1997), the notion of a so-called "televisual" indigenous culture is at best an oxymoron and at worst an offensive apologia for the growing dominance of mass media over Indigenous Australian and other Fourth World peoples' lives. For Weiner the question posed by Ginsburg in the title of her 1991 paper "Indigenous Media: Faustian Contract or Global Village?" offers no proper choice because the corrupting gift offered by Mephistopheles *is* the global village. Both perspectives have some merit and first I shall look at why Weiner's argument needs to be carefully considered. I will argue, however, that Ginsburg offers the most cogent analysis of these contemporary, cultural confusions.

We must bear in mind that Ginsburg has restricted the socio-cultural contexts in which indigenous media use occurs to Fourth World contexts, as noted above. These can be regarded as obvious instances in which one cultural community, the Indigenous, is in danger of being swamped by the society and culture that encompasses them, that of the Colonizer. This is clearly a situation that poses a much greater challenge to a culture than even the most pessimistic of commentators could claim regarding the effects of imported Euro-American commodities and media upon the consuming peoples' culture. Real colonization has had far more devastating effects than mere Coca-colonization! This is the minor argument contained within Ginsburg's study: indigenous media help the reproduction of Aboriginal culture and society in situations where the very survival of that culture, let alone its reproduction in a recognizably 'traditional' form, is at stake. It is in this analytical context that the notion of 'resistance' is typically encountered. We may note here the familiar visual trope of the 'savage' who has put down his spear and taken up the camcorder (cf. Turner on the Kayapo).

It can, however, be argued that modern media are intrinsically harmful to the successful reproduction of traditional ways of life because they are themselves a product of Western, industrialized cultures and as such the conjuncture of the two in the form of media use would be profoundly contradictory. James Faris (1993: 12) claims that there is "more West in Western products than has carefully been discussed in the anthropological literature on the subject." He expands upon this viewpoint in another article:

> There is, as noted, obviously nothing wrong with Kayapo, or any other people, videotaping whatever they may like. But as I have tried to stress, the means of realizing both the power of the technology and its influence are not available to the Kayapo, nor are the motivations of cultural presentation for non-Kayapo consumption. I find their use of video, as described by Turner, rather forlorn. It is almost as if, now, they are equal partners with news photographers and photojournalists. The Kayapo and others of the Third World do not join the global village as equal participants, as just more folks with their video cameras. They enter it already situated by the West, which gives them little room to be anything more than what the West will allow . . . The problem is not the cine camera or camcorder (this is not a Luddite objection and I have already noted the limitations imposed by the device). It is that we of power are the subjects, the viewers, the wanters, the covetous (Faris 1992: 176–177).

James Weiner (1997: 198) makes a similar statement:

I argue that these [Western] foundations [of representation, visualism, and sub-jectivity] are integral to the filmic media themselves—as we must agree they are if we are to accept that they are cultural products through and through—and that they could be opposed to and even subversive of non-Western modes of knowledge and its acquisition, revelation, and articulation.

These are important points to consider, especially as both Faris and Weiner make it clear that they are not simply arguing for a crude form of technological determinism, but instead claim that because mass media technologies have been developed in the West as the means of articulating a specifically Western set of socio-economic relationships, the indigenous users of these media will simply become enmeshed within this circuit of mediated relationships. If we accept such assumptions, Weiner's claim that the Aboriginal cultures that are repro-duced may be no more than "ersatz" cultures is likely to be true. A cultural form may be reproduced, but it is emptied of all meaning because it no longer retains its "ritual 'use-value'" (Weiner 1997: 199, note 2).

Weiner uses this term in relation to Benjamin's (1992) seminal critique of the changed status and role of art in society in the era of mechanical reproduc-tion. Benjamin contrasts the aura of the work of art that is manually produced, which arises from its unique place in the present time and place conjured up through a ritual act (or, in a secular context, a ritual-like act), with the mechani-cal (re-)production, and hence ubiquity, of the photographic arts. In Weiner's view, mechanically reproduced cultural forms lack any "epiphanic" quality, "the making visible of a manifestation of divine power or, in general, the unseen, the invisible, the unrespresentable . . . [which] are what social life and ritual are about *in these settings*" (Weiner 1997: 199; emphasis added). Thus, they are merely pathetic reminders (in the sense of arousing our sympathy and sadness) of what was once a vibrant and living reality. Gaenszle (1997: 369) refers to this as the "'folklorization' of tradition, i.e. its reduction to a mainly aesthetic enter-prise." He continues: "though it may still affect the 'Lebenswelt', culture loses its pervasive, unquestioned founding qualities. It is often reduced to nothing more than an occasional reminder of one's 'true' identity."

Work on indigenous media could be vulnerable to this criticism and would be of little interest if it did not develop beyond the scope of a simplistic cultural survival thesis. But it does, and theories of indigenous media rely on an anthro-pological definition of culture that, as Eco (1995: 162) observes, is

> for obvious reasons among the most difficult to accept. On the one hand, it forces us to question our ethnocentricity and the confidence that *our* way of liv-ing and thinking is the only valid one. On the other hand . . . every time a cul-ture refers to a different model as a 'cultural phenomenon' the threatened cul-ture uses the expressions in senses 1) [culture as refined aesthetic taste] and 2) [culture as a superior attitude of mind], in the belief that the *other* is being held up as the only positive model.

Weiner tends to make this error in his criticism of so-called televisualist anthro-pology because he directs his ire at the weak, 'rescue anthropology' version of indigenous media studies and thus confuses the anthropological description of cultures in which mass media undoubtedly play a role with the description of the aesthetic function of representation in his 'own' cultural setting (i.e. in the ethnographic setting in which he worked). Undoubtedly, in settings where a living tradition of ritual unaltered by any outside force is in existence the introduction of mass mediated forms of cultural representation would have the effect he describes, but this is clearly not the case in the situations described by Ginsburg, Turner and Michaels. As Deger (2006) notes, Weiner's critique of the indigenous media concept fails to situate either his argument or the lives of the creators of indigenous media in an historical perspective and simply assumes the universal applicability and validity of the Heideggerian philosophy upon which he bases his argument.

David MacDougall has noted that "as indigenous groups take greater control of the visual media they may well alter traditional representations of themselves" (1997: 285). The effect that this has had upon anthropology, especially anthropological filmmaking, is what Ginsburg (1995) refers to as a "parallax effect", using the way that astronomers measure the distance to stars based upon the perceived change in their location in the sky when observed from different positions as a metaphor for the ability indigenous media have to change anthropologists' perceptions of the people they study. She describes how an object, in this case the cinematic representation of indigenous culture, "appears to look different from the observational perspective of ethnographic film" (Ginsburg 1995: 65) than from the perspective of an indigenous filmmaker. Film-makers and producers of other media who are positioned in radically different cultural and socio-economic locations in the global landscape experience their own variation on the parallax effect: the objects that they train their gaze upon may appear very different to each of these observers. Rather than undermining anthropological or other external representations of indigenous groups, Ginsburg argues that indigenous media provides an opportunity to analyze and understand how such differences in interpretation arise and her argument can easily be expanded to apply to alternative media more generally.[5] Her approach has clear affinities to that of Sol Worth and John Adair's work on the Navajo Film Project (Worth and Adair 1972), which had the express aim of examining whether

> motion picture film, conceived, photographed, and sequentially arranged by a people such as the Navajo would reveal something of their cognition and values that may be inhibited, not observable, or not analyzable when investigation is totally dependent on verbal exchange . . . [And whether] the images, subjects, and themes selected and the organizing methods used by the Navajo filmmakers would reveal much about their mythic and value systems (Worth and Adair quoted in Worth 1981: 6)

Ginsburg also says that "indigenous producers...clearly recognize their media works as a form of social action when they become authors of representations about themselves" (1995: 70). Ginsburg is not making an appeal here to a notion of a privileged *authentic* media on the grounds that 'natives' have made their own representations, as Weiner (1997) claims. Instead, she is recognizing that the production of alternative visions of culture and society through various media serves to challenge the "static and reified understanding of culture" which lies at the heart of much Western discourse about indigenous societies and is "part of a desire on the part of Aboriginal people to 'talk back' on their own terms to those who might have presumed to speak for them" (Ginsburg 1995: 68).

However, MacDougall (1997: 285) says in reference to the analysis of indigenous media and alternative uses of media in general that "in neither of these cases does visual anthropology pose a fundamental epistemological challenge to what has been called 'the anthropological project'." He continues: "they merely make anthropology more sensitive to the politics and possibilities of visual representation. The more substantive contribution to anthropological thought comes not simply from broadening its purview but from its entering into communicative systems different from the 'anthropology of words'" (ibid.: 285). But Turner and Ginsburg are correct that studies of indigenous media *may* provide a challenge to conventional anthropological epistemology because they challenge us to think more clearly about what 'culture' actually is.

Whilst previous research was carried out within broadly functionalist traditions of anthropology, within which the question of the internal stability of cultural forms and hence the uniform character of media representations of that culture by members of that culture was considered to be unproblematic (Chalfen 1992), Ginsburg and others associated with research into indigenous media, Terence Turner and Eric Michaels in particular, have been forced to reconsider the anthropological approach to culture itself. Ginsburg (1995: 68) calls for the abandonment of a "static and reified understanding of culture" in favor of "a praxis-oriented" notion of culture (ibid.: 73). Turner (1995a: 105, emphasis in original) argues that the making of indigenous media "is a *praxis* in Marx's sense: the praxis of creating culture" in so much as "groups who begin to objectify their own identities through media such as video thereby transform their identities in essential ways, but even more importantly, they shift the focus of attention from what it is they represent (the text, if you will) to the *process of producing* the representation" (ibid.: 104–5, emphasis in orig.).

Culture has often been used in somewhat metonymic ways to stand for a people. But, if the artifacts that people use are obviously 'alien' (as imported electronic communication technology may appear to some to be in a Kayapo or Warlpiri setting), and if the use of those artifacts is passionately advocated by those people, anthropologists must think carefully about the fundamental presuppositions of their project. This is by no means a wholly new criticism of cultural anthropology. Some of the issues raised by indigenous media studies do, however, echo those raised by MacDougall (1997: 286) when he claims "that categories of anthropological knowledge will have to be seriously rethought, both in relation to science and to the representational systems of film, video and photography."

Most important is the fact that the tautologous definition of culture as both the object of anthropological study and the analytical category through which this study is carried out has to be reconsidered. Taking an alternative, 'processual' definition of culture as our analytical starting point means that, in the words of Shohat and Stam, anthropological analysis is "not merely a question of communicating across borders but of discerning the forces which generate the borders in the first place" (quoted in Ginsburg 1995: 64). Anthropologists cannot regard culture, be it the culture of 'tradition' or of 'modernity', simply as a static and unchanging thing, but must acknowledge that they must study the ways in which the artifacts and components of a culture come into being, are reproduced and possibly transformed over time.

Raymond Williams (1994) has called this the "emergent" property of culture. "New meanings and values, new practices, new relationships and kinds of relationship are continually being created" (ibid.: 606), whilst at the same time we often observe that some elements of any given culture are stable with various forms and clusters of forms persisting from one time to the next. This persistence of cultural forms may be measured in moments or generations, but it is certain that no matter how long a particular cultural form might have existed, its continued existence, that is its dominance as the "species specific" (Williams 1994: 606) mark of a culture, cannot be guaranteed. A major task for any cultural analysis then becomes the study of emergence and the reasons why some cultural forms come into existence but may subsequently either whither or thrive. As Rodriguez says,

> Citizens' media are similar to living organisms that evolve and develop uniquely in permanent interaction with their complex environments/contexts: at some point they strengthen their struggle against one target, but later they can abandon that target and take on a new one, which in turn, can be abandoned to focus on a third one. It is in this play of articulated historical conflicts and struggles where the richness of citizens' media resides, in terms of their potential as forces of resistance (2001: 158).

This is also the point at which we leave the overview of theories of alternative media to describe the particular history of Ratna Cable Television and Communication for Development in Tansen. As will become apparent in this description, RCTV/CDP's history in the years leading to their creation and in the first 5 years of their existence illustrate many of the features of content and processes of production that were identified in the foregoing discussion. It also indicates the necessity for the type of detailed contextual analysis that I have argued for in chapter 1 and the early part of this chapter. This context is provided in chapters 3 through 7. Chapter 8 will consider the significance of the example of RCTV/CDP for our understanding of alternative media in all their various guises.

Introducing Ratna Cable Television (RCTV)

Ratna Cable Television was a private, family-owned business, which at the time of my fieldwork was the sole supplier of cable television in Tansen.[6] The company provided access to the Star TV satellite television network, which is owned by Rupert Murdoch's News Corporation, produced a weekly program on local news and events, and also ran a lucrative electronic-goods repair shop in the town's bazaar. The late Buddha Ratna Shakya was also the founder chairman of Communication for Development Palpa [CDP] (*Bikāskolagi Samachār*), a non-governmental organization that was established to co-ordinate the various relationships that RCTV had with government at local and national level and other NGOs and international non-governmental organizations. Buddha Ratna ran both his commercial business and CDP with his son, Mahesh, who shared the family home that also served as the production studios for RCTV.

The Shakyas originally lived in Taksar Tol, where they followed the family business of manufacturing *kuruwa* and other metal ware until the early 1980s.[7] The first member of the family to leave this trade and to enter into the electrical repair business was Buddha Ratna's older brother who had done a correspondence course in radio repair run by an Indian company. Subsequently Buddha Ratna went to Poona in India to study radio repair and Mahesh learnt the trade from his father.

Buddha Ratna had always been involved in the cultural life of Tansen, for example composing *bhajan* (hymns) for various festivals in Tansen, most notably Gai Jatra, a festival commemorating the recently deceased in early Autumn, and Buddha Jayanti, the Spring festival which celebrates the life of Gautam Siddhartha, the historical Buddha (see chapter 7). During the early 1970s, an organization called the *Deurali Pariwar* (Deurali Family) was founded to perform the songs and dance for Gai and Bhagwati Jatra and Mahesh Shakya was instrumental in this. The name was chosen because of the significance to village life of the *deurali*, a cairn at the meeting point of roads.[8] A *deurali* would be a place where people would stop to rest and where, inevitably, someone would strike up a song or play a musical instrument to keep everybody entertained. All of the members of the Deurali Pariwar were young, unmarried men who would get together on a regular basis to meet, compose songs and perform dances. Educational institutions were one of the main forums in which they performed. They began by performing folk songs or those written by other artists, but they rapidly progressed on to composing their own songs and performing original dances. Interestingly, all the members of the group adopted 'Deurali' as their stage name and Mahesh still used this name in all his cultural activities, including the production of the local television program. The Deurali Pariwar eventually broke-up after about seven years in 1977 when the men began to get married and enter jobs that took them beyond Tansen.

The Shakyas were developing their electrical repair business and expanding into television technologies in the early 1980s. In 1980 a Nepali engineer, who was not from Palpa and had experience working in Russia, came to Tansen as part of the team working for the District Telecommunication Office installing the town's first telephone lines. He had a video recorder and discovered that it was possible to connect his deck to the television sets in the neighbors' houses and show Hindi movies on a number of televisions simultaneously. The engineer taught Mahesh and his father how to do this and subsequently they started the cable installation side of their company, changing its name to Ratna Cable

Television, initially with the idea of showing Hindi movies during times when there was nothing on Doordarshan, the only channel that you could get in Tansen at this time.

The Shakya's house had been the first in Tansen to get pictures from Doordarshan in India. Prior to that, some people in Tansen had televisions, but they were used exclusively with video decks because there had been no Doordarshan transmitters that could be picked-up in West Nepal. There was no Doordarshan transmitter in Gorakhpur so one would have to attempt to pick up the signal from Lucknow, just over two hundred and thirty kilometers to the south-west. The Shakyas overcame this problem by constructing an enormous aerial to receive terrestrial television pictures. When they did successfully manage to pick up the Doordarshan signal on a regular basis they would often have many people come to their house to watch television. They attempted to pick up Nepal Television when the station first started broadcasting in 1985 via a transmitter in Kathmandu, but were less successful because atmospheric conditions considerably affected reception. Sometimes they would broadcast the NTV signal through the infant cable network if the reception was of good enough quality. In addition, in the late 1980s and early 1990s, Mahesh Shakya had frequently gone to the town of Butwal, thirty nine kilometers to the south, to install aerials because at that time there was a shortage of skilled technicians there who knew how to do this.

The Shakya's satellite equipment was bought in early 1992. It cost eighty thousand rupees in total and comprised a Japanese transponder and an Indian made reception dish. It was bought with the intention of broadcasting via cable, never as equipment purely for private use, and they had always wanted to profit from the dish via the installation of a town-wide cable network. They decided to invest in expensive Japanese equipment because cheaper equipment was not so widely available at that time, and the quality of the Indian equipment was, they said, so poor.[9] (However, Indian made satellite equipment was apparently only a tenth of the price that the Shakyas paid.)

About one month after the installation of the dish, they linked it into the cable network.[10] The cable network was based on a series of linkages that could be connected to a household's television set from a central cable connected to the Shakya's satellite receiver. Normally a maximum of three households received a signal from the end of a sub-link to this trunk line. These three connections were easy to establish once the initial sub-link was installed; so easy in fact that 'amateurs' were able to tap into the cable network and receive a signal, albeit of an inferior quality. The Shakya's referred to these in English as "leak lines."

The Shakyas had, as mentioned above, also intended to broadcast films through a video deck onto the cable system, an idea then popular amongst cable operators who had started to become established in Butwal and Pokhara. However, they were very keen that they should not just broadcast Hindi movies. The next important development in the development of RCTV, therefore, was the videotaping of the town's Bhagwati Jatra, which was then shown through the cable system. The video camera used was borrowed from an old musician friend of Buddha Ratna who lived in Bhairahawa where his business was based. This program was so popular that the Shakyas decided to begin a regular local program consisting of local news, public information features and documentaries. They were able to make their first broadcast in the August 1992 (24th Shrawan 2049 VS) and did so with the help of several people from outside of the RCTV business.[11] An important first volunteer was an ex-Deurali Pariwar member, who was at that time the principal of a local private boarding school.

The cable system spread rapidly through the town with about 300 having been connected by RCTV by 1995, but many more picking up the signals by simply attaching a cable directly to the line of a neighbor. According to one estimate there were as many as ten thousand viewers of cable television, including the local program every week in the Tansen Municipality area (Deurali 1995).[12] However, these viewers were largely limited to the central 'bazaar' areas of town because the lower housing density and steep streets in the outlying areas made installation of a cable line impractical.

The relative wealth of the residents of the central bazaar area compared to the rest of the Municipality was also a significant factor in the pattern of cable distribution. The cost of cable installation was initially three thousand rupees payable either in one installment or in fifty rupees per month.[13] This was unsuccessful in terms of ensuring that sufficient revenue was raised to make the business profitable. The installation fee was therefore changed to compulsory installation fee of five hundred rupees and then fifty rupees per month thereafter. Under this new arrangement, apart from the money, the customer also had to supply the cable to RCTV. Despite this, the cost of a cable link was still considerably less than the forty five thousand rupees that a new Japanese satellite dish cost at this time or even the six thousand rupees cost of an Indian-made dish. Ordinary terrestrial television aerials could sometimes get the satellite signal if they were close enough to a dish. An Indian made black and white television set cost about six thousand to ten thousand rupees and a color set three times that amount. There was a nominal license fee for ownership of a television levied at local government level, but nobody paid it and the municipality did not pursue this matter. It was hoped by Municipality officials that this situation would change due to the re-organization of local government finances and taxation following the introduction of new legislation by the coalition government of Sher Bahadur Deuba in 1996 (Adhikari, G. and Rajkarnikar, D.G., 1994; *Kathmandu Post* 19th October 1995)

The Shakyas controlled the two channels received by viewers of the Star TV network on the cable system. Zee TV, a Hindi language light entertainment channel, was broadcast almost continuously on one channel and the other channel alternated between BBC World Service TV in the morning and Star Plus (British and American light entertainment programs), Prime Sports (all English language, except for optional Hindi cricket commentary available on a separate frequency), or El TV (a Hindi language channel showing old movies and film music) during the day and evening. Owners of a private satellite dish could receive at least nine channels on the same satellite transponder used by RCTV and the lack of choice available via the RCTV was the main reason cited by customers who wished to buy their own, private dish. The Shakyas claimed that the age of their satellite equipment was one reason why they could not provide more than two channels at a time, but the inadequacy of the available cable was another reason. All television viewers in Tansen could in theory also receive two terrestrial television channels, Nepal Television (the only national station) and Doordarshan (the Indian national broadcaster). These terrestrial channels had only recently become widely available in Tansen with the construction of a transmitter by NTV on Srinagar Hill and by Doordarshan in Gorakhpur. However, the reception quality of both remained poor. It was ironic that for most people in the bazaar the NTV transmitter was poorly positioned so that signals tended to pass directly over their residences.

The 'local program' (*sthāniya karykram*) began at one pm every Saturday, this being the weekly holiday in Nepal, and normally lasted one to two hours. Viewers of the cable channels lost their picture and received static for a few seconds whilst Mahesh or his father disconnected the satellite downlink from the cable network and replaced it with a connection to their own video recorder. They could then broadcast their programs to the cable viewers. At one pm the streets of the bazaar were a little emptier than they were before and the introductory music of the program could be heard coming from many houses (see Wilmore 2008 for further consideration of this).

The following schedule of RCTV's local program for 21st October 1995, gives an example of a typical Saturday broadcast:

1. Views of Tansen to the accompaniment of modern style music.
2. Introduction to the program by a male announcer.
3. Local news read by female announcer. This featured a march through Tansen by local school children to mark United Nations' World Peace Day; fashion awards at the college campus; events and speeches held at the town's police headquarters to mark Nepal's National Police Day.
4. Public information announcement concerning garbage problems in Tansen sponsored by the Municipality administration.
5. Advertisements for local businesses giving festive greetings from the owners to commemorate the occasion of *Tihar* (*Diwali*).
6. *Chitragit* (Pop Videos): Four Nepali music videos recorded from NTV broadcasts. Ballads and love songs shown being sung in the studio and inter-cut with scenes of the singers walking through rural landscapes.
7. Local advertisements and Tihar greetings again.
8. Professionally produced advertisement for a Nepali brewery.
9. *Uttar Ramayana*: Hindi language serial based on the Ramayana epic.
10. Repeat of the brewery advertisement.
11. Close of program by male announcer.
12. Scenes of Tansen as at the beginning.

The schedule for the weekly local program had not changed significantly since broadcasts began three years previously. However, for reasons that will be discussed in detail below, the length of the program was generally only one hour a week during the time of my fieldwork (September 1995 to September 1996) and the proportion of material originating from sources other than RCTV, such as the *Uttar Ramayana* serial, had increased.

The actual broadcasting of the weekly program was, as the above suggests, a relatively simple matter of reconnecting a couple of plugs and playing a video-cassette. What this indicates is that all the RCTV output was pre-recorded onto VHS-format videocassette. The technology available to RCTV did not allow for any live broadcasting. Mahesh acted as the production manager and edited all programs made by RCTV as well as producing the finished, broadcast version of the week's program. Originally, this was done simply by recording tape-to-tape using two standard video decks. This was extremely time consuming and severely restricted the types of presentation format of the programs. From September 1994, however, Mahesh used a JVC s368 editing desk donated to CDP by the Asia Foundation, an INGO funded by the US government, and this greatly facilitated his work. Even so, recording original footage and editing the program was extremely laborious and at a rough estimate, it took between seven to ten hours to produce ten minutes of broadcast material.

One-off programs, documentaries for example, and the regular weekly news show were produced in the same manner, which involved several stages:

1. Recording of 'raw' video footage in the field
2. Script writing
3. Recording of backing vocals and continuity material in the studio either on video or audio cassette
4. Editing of the program.

A team of volunteers carried out all the above processes, except the final stage, which was the sole responsibility of Mahesh because he was most proficient in the use of the editing desk. There were between three and four regular volunteers at any one time. They included: a male local high school teacher, who was the main camera man and news editor; a female textile factory manager; a male lecturer in business studies from the local college; a female high school student; and a young man who ran a tourist art shop and provided all the graphics for the programs. Many other people had been involved in working for RCTV as volunteers in the past and some continued to on an irregular basis. The above people are mentioned to briefly indicate the sorts of people who are involved. All were volunteers and no one was paid by RCTV, although an employee at the repair shop had on occasions helped out as a camera operator. All those who worked in the production of the local program did so as private individuals and did not need to be a member of CDP or an employee of RCTV.

Many other people from Tansen were involved in programs in the first year or so of RCTV's existence, either as interviewees on discussion programs, musicians and dancers, or guests and presenters on programs addressing specific issues such as health education. By 1995 this sort of contact was more infrequent, as RCTV had come to rely on material that they had not produced themselves. Nevertheless, it was still the case that many of the town's citizens will have seen an RCTV camera operator at work covering a news story somewhere in the Municipality on a fairly regular basis. The high school teacher who read the news was sent on a journalism training course for a few weeks by the now defunct local newspaper, *Satya*, and Mahesh had some video editing lessons provided by the Asia Foundation and NTV, but these were the only members of the organization to have received training in skills directly relevant to work on the RCTV programs.

The rapidly growing ambition of the Shakyas and their supporters can be seen from their early experimentation with the limited equipment that they had available to them.[14] In October 1992 (1st Kartik 2049 VS) they broadcast their eleventh program, which included the first outside broadcast program. This was made at Lipin Devi, a nearby village, and focused on the village temple's *mela* (fair). They had to make this program using a conventional videocassette recorder and a very long cable attached to the electricity supply of one of the villager's houses! The thirteenth program, which was also broadcast in October (15th Kartik 2049 VS), included a documentary made by another organization for the first time. This was made by Helvetas (a Swiss INGO that had been active in Palpa for many years) and was about the opening of the new road between two nearby settlements (Aryabhanjyang and Rampur). The first locally-made advertisement, for a tailor's shop in the bazaar, was also screened during this broadcast.[15]

The fifteenth program broadcast in November 1992 (29th Kartik 2049 VS) featured the first health program broadcast, involving a doctor from the United Mission to Nepal's Tansen Hospital, and a children's program presented by a teenage schoolgirl. This girl's older brother, Rajeshwor, made his first broadcast in the sixteenth program (November 1992; 6th Mangsir 2049 VS) as an announcer. The first women's feature was presented in November 1992 (13th Mangsir 2049 VS) during the seventeenth program, but this program was probably most note worthy for the introduction of the first weekly news report. Two weeks later in December 1992 (27th Mangsir 2049 VS) the local teacher who was to become the program's regular news editor made his first broadcast.

By now RCTV was coming to the attention of various people and groups outside of Palpa. The twenty first program (December 1992; 11th Paush 2049 VS) featured an interview with Prithvi Raj Ligal, who was Vice-Chairman of the National Planning Commission during the time of my fieldwork. Then, on 31st December 1992, the first magazine article featuring RCTV was published by the Kathmandu based weekly *Janmanch*. It was written by Asesh Malla, who was a well-known drama writer and member of the board of Nepal Television. Malla also came to the town in the following year and was interviewed by RCTV for their twenty sixth program on February 1993 (17th Margh 2049 VS). At first RCTV re-used videocassettes, so much of the early material is no longer available. However, prompted by Malla, who urged them not to destroy such a valuable record of the town, they now began to save a copy of all material broadcast. Because of this article in *Janmanch*, RCTV came to the immediate attention of NTV and the Ministry of Communication. It should be noted that both the above men had connections to Tansen, with Prithvi Raj Ligal being born and brought up in the town and Asesh Malla's father-in-law living in Tansen.

The fact that there was some confusion regarding the precise status of *Ratna Cable Television* and *Communication for Development Palpa* should be highlighted here. Ratna Cable Television was a private business owned by the Shakya family, and Communication for Development Palpa was a non-governmental organization. The pretence that CDP as such produced anything was maintained to prevent any difficulties with the central and local government, because it was the case that initially everything RCTV did with regard to broadcasting was illegal or at least took place outside of the framework of the laws that then regulated broadcasting in Nepal. The local program was broadcast through the RCTV cable network, but officially all the programs were made by CDP. The reasons why this distinction was maintained is discussed in greater detail below and in chapter 6, which analyses the politics of the local program.

It is sufficient to say at this point that all people living in Tansen referred to the organization as RCTV or simply "local television" or "the local program" (often using the English phrase instead of the Nepali, *sthāniya karykram*). As was mentioned in chapter 1, this initially created a problem when I started fieldwork because I would sometimes ask people if they watched 'local television', meaning did they watch RCTV/CDP broadcasts, and receive a positive reply only to discover that they thought I was talking about Nepal TV. 'Local' in this sense meant Nepali as opposed to Indian television (Doordarshan). I cleared up this confusion by always specifying that it was Tansen's local television (*Tansenko staniya telebijan karykram*) that I was talking about.

At the time of its inception and up to the early months of 1993, RCTV was not so much an illegal organization as one that had no precedent, there being no provision for the registration of a private or community communication organization in Nepali law. Following the publicity surrounding RCTV in the last month of 1992, the then Chief District Officer (CDO) and vice-CDO received many orders to close down RCTV from the central government in Kathmandu, but it has been claimed by the Shakyas and their supporters that the CDO saw the potential development benefits of the organization and so always stalled or simply ignored the order.

Page and Crawley (2001) assert that by the time cable television started in Nepal the national government had recognized the potential of the medium from observation of the Indian experience and put a regulatory framework in place, although the situation in Tansen shows that this was not the case in the early part of the 1990s. Nevertheless, regulations introduced in 1992 enabled the launch in Kathmandu of a large-scale commercial cable network owned by an entrepreneur named Jamim Shah in 1998 without any of the problems experienced by similar organizations in India (see Page and Crawley 2001: 89–93 for a description of the rivalry between small-scale individual cable operators and larger commercial networks in India). Their description of the situation may be correct with regard to the majority of small-scale cable operators in the towns of Nepal, who were simply ignored by the national government prior to the introduction of the National Broadcasting Act in 1992. However, this Act, which consolidated the government's control of the state broadcasters Radio Nepal and Nepal Television, whilst allowing private cable *distributors* to operate, prohibited the production of original programming for broadcast through private cable networks. RCTV began operating shortly before this Act came into force, and by ignoring this restriction forced both national and local level government agencies to seek a compromise with the organization.

It is at this point that the figure of Vinaya Kumar Kasajoo became especially important in the development of RCTV. Kasajoo was the editor of the now defunct local newspaper *Satya* (Truth) and was then editor of a weekly, rural newspaper called *Deurali*, which received support from several international non-governmental organizations, most notably the *Asia Foundation* (USA) and *Mellemfolkeligt Samvirke* (Danish Association for International Cooperation). He had great knowledge of media practice, both in Nepal and internationally, and had been involved in political activism, but not explicitly party political activity, for many years (see Kasajoo's website, www.kasajoo.com, for further details of his work and writing). It was Kasajoo who advised RCTV to become a non-governmental organization, eventually christened *Communication for Development Palpa*, so that they could clarify the legal status of the organization and get access to donations from INGOs. Therefore, RCTV became the name of the organization that dealt with the installation of cable links, the supply of Star TV programs, and which broadcast the local programs that were officially made by CDP.

A meeting was held to draw up a constitution for CDP and the Municipality then officially registered the organization as an NGO. The authorities accepted CDP with little complaint, their only restriction being that they could not use the word 'television' in their title as there was fear that this would set a precedent for other organizations that might want to broadcast. The local and national government would not have to formulate any specific policy regarding the administration of broadcasting organizations, relying instead on the bureaucratic and legal framework provided for charities and NGOs.

Prior to the launch of CDP, the group had no constitution or officially documented policies, and was made up of an informal committee that normally had between five and seven members. These included Buddha Ratna Shakya, Mahesh Shakya and a couple of other family members, along with a teacher from a private boarding school and an old friend of Buddha Ratna who was a businessman living in Bhairahawa.[16] It was this friend who provided the camera that they had used to make their first programs. The start of RCTV was also the catalyst for the reformation of the *Deurali Pariwar*, this time made up only of those who still lived in Tansen. They concentrated their efforts on producing and organizing the content of cultural programs broadcast by RCTV/CDP.

The creation of CDP also brought people to the group (here referring to the television production group in general rather than just the *Deurali Pariwar*) who previously would not have come to help purely private RCTV, because it was now perceived to be a *social* organization rather than a *business* organization. Vinaya Kasajoo said that CDP was "a kind of umbrella organization under which people came forward to help a nice and respected family as friends."[17] Kasajoo gave an example of this. During the Rana administration there were many singers and musicians at the *darbār* (palace and centre of government). Amongst these was a classical singer and again, through music a friendship began with Buddha Ratna Shakya. From the Rana period until the late 1980s this singer had worked at the District Administration Office at the Durbar and his most recent job before retirement was as the head of the Telecommunication

Office; therefore, Buddha Ratna did a lot of work for the Telecommunication Office. When RCTV started producing the local program one of the first people to help was the singer's son, who was a teacher at the local college campus and also the chairman of the Tansen branch of the Japanese sponsored Reyukai Cultural Organization. The singer's son was, however, involved with RCTV before the formation of Communication for Development Palpa and this would seem to indicate that people's perception of the Shakyas as a "respected family" and their previous connections of friendship and work probably had more to do with the example Kasajoo offered than the legitimation offered by the 'official' status of CDP. The general significance of these sorts of informal business and working relationships to the development industry in Tansen is considered in more detail in chapter 6.

The period from the twenty-sixth broadcast in February 1993 (17th Margh 2049 VS), which featured the interview with Asesh Malla referred to above and the first original drama program made by the group (a two minute long comedy routine on the subject of public hygiene), up to October 1995 (Kartik 2052 VS) was a time of rapid evolution and optimism for RCTV. In June/July 1993 (Asad 2050 VS) the group participated in a trade fair in Tansen organized by the local Chamber of Commerce and Industry by experimenting with FM radio broadcasting. Following a newspaper article on this experiment two Radio Nepal engineers came from Kathmandu to see the RCTV set-up. The central government in Kathmandu also confirmed the registration of CDP in this month.

Following the sixty-seventh program in November 1993 (28th Kartik 2050 VS) there was a halt in broadcasts because their only camera was not working. Through contacts that Vinaya Kasajoo had made as a journalist, RCTV was able to improve their equipment. In 1993 an INGO contributing to national media development, Worldview Nepal, gave them a camera and a monitor. Mahesh Shakya and Vinaya Kasajoo also went to Kathmandu to buy a new camera having been promised ten thousand rupees from a Nepali human rights organization, International Institute for Human Rights, Environment and Development (INHURED), on the provision that they make some programs of concern to the NGO. Only one camera of good enough quality was available and this cost sixty thousand rupees. Another ten thousand rupees came from RCTV and the remaining forty thousand rupees was loaned to them by Kasajoo.

The quality of the programs produced by RCTV greatly improved following the addition of this equipment. This was primarily because with a battery-powered camera they could record material without the restriction of having to be linked to a conventional video recorder and mains electricity supply. The first fruits of this freedom were seen in the seventy-ninth program (February 1994; 14th Phalgun 2050 VS), when a documentary on Magar culture was broadcast, using footage from villages in the areas surrounding the town. A feature on the important temple at Bhairabsthan, approximately ten kilometers west of Tansen, was the next documentary to be broadcast.

The other major donation of equipment from an INGO was an editing desk from an American INGO, the Asia Foundation. The then director of the Asia Foundation had been closely involved in the setting up of the Deurali rural newspaper, coming to Tansen twice to discuss this with Vinaya Kasajoo. She returned to Tansen for the inauguration of Deurali and on this occasion met with RCTV for the first time. They discussed their needs with her and in 1995 they acquired videotape-editing equipment. The hundred and seventh program (September 1994; 25th Bhadra 2051 VS) was the first to be completed using the editing desk donated by the Asia Foundation.

In the intervening months, the Congress government had lost a vote of no confidence in the first parliament elected after the 1990 spring revolution. The subsequent general election (November 1994) led to the formation of a minority Communist Party of Nepal (United Marxist Leninist) government. The Minister of Communication from this administration, Pradeep Nepal, came to visit RCTV, along with NTV General Manager, Thapanath Sukla, in January/February 1995 (Margh 2051 VS). The Minister promised that an NTV transmitter would be constructed on Srinagar Hill above the town to provide a regular television signal in Palpa for the first time since the broadcaster's inception ten years previously. To prove their intentions an NTV team came to begin test signal work on Srinagar.

In February/March 1995 (Phalgun 2051 VS) a NTV news program, *Samachar Samichya*, broadcast a feature about RCTV and two months later in April/May 1995 (Baisakh 2052 VS) Thapanath Sukla, the NTV General Manager, visited again. Following discussions with Sukla, Mahesh went to Kathmandu for a few days training at NTV and had discussions with NTV management about the use of the new antenna, then under construction. The advantages of using the NTV transmitter were obvious because all the television sets in Tansen and surrounding areas, not just those on the RCTV cable network, would be able to pick up the broadcasts. RCTV had just secured their first regular advertising contract with a national company, a brewery, and Mahesh hoped that access to the transmitter would significantly boost the revenue to the organization from advertising.

However, the time of the Dasain festival in October 1995 (2052 VS) proved to be the zenith of RCTV's fortunes in these early years of its existence. The NTV transmitter came on line at this point and perhaps inevitably this detracted from the RCTV program because there was alternative Nepali language broadcasting available for the first time in Tansen. RCTV also had to reorganize their broadcast on Saturday to fit in with the NTV schedule; somewhat ironically, this meant completing the local television broadcast before the beginning of the popular Hindi movie broadcast on Saturday afternoon. Mahesh also took the decision to reduce the length of the weekly broadcast to just one hour on a regular basis from this date because he said that he could no longer cope with the long hours required to produce the program.

The collapse of the Communist (UML) government just before Dasain was of more serious consequence for RCTV. Mahesh had hoped that access to the NTV transmitter and the subsequent boost to revenue would enable him to give up his job in the repair shop and concentrate full time on producing RCTV programs. He had also hoped to encourage further investment from INGOs, which would enable him to gain access to recording equipment of a professional standard, which would mean that he could produce material for sale to other broadcasters, including NTV. The very high cost of this equipment made these look like unrealizable aspirations and such hopes were decisively dashed by the incoming Congress-led coalition government of Sher Bahadur Deuba which immediately withdrew the previous government's promise to consider granting access to the NTV transmitter. RCTV's future was uncertain throughout the time that I was conducting my fieldwork in Tansen (October 1995 to September 1996), but was still broadcasting the local program on a weekly basis and waiting for a message from the Minister of Communication, Kishwor Nepal of the Congress Party, when I left.

Since the time of my fieldwork in Nepal, Communication for Development Palpa and Vinaya Kasajoo's organization Rural Development Palpa (RDP) have continued to produce various media. The local television program continued to be broadcast, although in the much-reduced format that was used in 1996. The Shakyas continued to negotiate for the award of an official television broadcasting license with the various administrations that have controlled the central government of Nepal in the past ten years. However, in 1999 competition from a rival cable operator based in the Kathmandu Valley led to difficulties for RCTV. Accusations from the rival operator of involvement with Maoist rebels led to the Ministry of Information and Communication fining RCTV and suspending their license to broadcast (Edwards n.d.). Mahesh was also threatened with imprisonment due to this incident and, as Edward's states, this was avoided "thanks to Ratna's local protectors . . . , but their position remains precarious." A change of name to Shrinagar Cable followed this incident.

In 1999 Radio Madan Pokhara, an off-shoot of Rural Development Palpa run in conjunction with Radio Sagarmatha (a development oriented FM radio station based in Kathmandu founded by the Nepal Forum for Environmental Journalists [NEFEJ]), began regular broadcasts. This trend towards diversification in media production has continued through the launch by CDP in June 2001 of a website (www.tansenpalpa.net) devoted to the development aims of the NGO.[18] These aims were further entrenched in 2003 when CDP launched a community multimedia center with support from UNESCO (see Pringle et al. 2004; Martin et al. 2007). Although the founder of RCTV and CDP, Buddha Ratna Shakya, sadly died in 2006, the organization has continued to thrive and transform as the circumstances of Nepal's and Tansen's own political, economic and media landscapes have changed.

Conclusion

This chapter has examined the ways in which media have been conceptualized outside the mainstreams of theory and practice. In the first section we examined debates about the definition and worth of non-mainstream media organizations, especially as they have been utilized by indigenous peoples in order to understand their particular and varying characteristics. The task of conceptualizing media in this case has generally been undertaken by theorists or critics of such media, who may or may not be directly involved in the work of media production itself. This section showed that there cannot be any single or essential definition of media, but the combination of the insights derived from these attempts provides the components of a viable analytical model (Atton 2002). As Couldry states in relation to his own work, modeling of this sort is "an abstract way of bringing out the complexities in a process of naturalization which would otherwise be an undifferentiated object...The value of the model depends on how well it helps us articulate what people actually do, think and say in their dealings with the media process" (2000: 179). By drawing our attention to the fact that media production involves the articulation of complex social relationships in order to make and distribute successfully the concrete products or texts, this model helps us to appreciate that the formation of such relationships may prove to be most important outcome of alternative media production.

The second part of the chapter provided a description of one example of the 'actual doing' of media, Ratna Cable Television and Communication for Development Palpa. It will already be obvious from this description that RCTV/CDP provides ample evidence for the different aspects of the model outlined above, as well as combining features of several of the types of non-mainstream media that were identified in this discussion. The creation of RCTV/CDP was motivated by the need to provide media serving the needs of the immediate locality and community. Some elements of ethnicity or indigeneity in the media can be discerned, albeit weakly, in terms of their emphasis on Nepali language broadcasting, as opposed to Indian and Hindi language media. The small-scale, volunteer-based and often precarious existence of the organization is also characteristic, although it has managed to survive several serious threats to its existence. At the same time, however, the need to identify sources of funding and other resources has led to links with NGOs and INGOs that extend the relationships involved in the organization's work beyond its immediate locality. The combination of commercial activities with community-focused development activities also indicates that we cannot draw any strict distinctions between the two in this case. Whether the content of RCTV/CDP programs could be described as radical or oppositional in any straightforward sense is questionable, even if the creation of the local program broadcast through the cable system was in itself a radical act, as the repeated attempts by central government to close the operation down attest. Finally, the creation of the RCTV/CDP local program, coming as it did shortly after the events of the first Jana Andolan may be seen as an example of emergence of new political subjects that Rodriguez (2001) claims is indicative of citizens media. By employing new production technologies (video), new forms of distribution (cable), new types of content (local news), new forms of social organization (volunteers) and new forms of institutional arrangements (non-governmental organizations), RCTV/CDP was able to enact the freedoms of information and expression that were enshrined in the 1990 constitution of Nepal (see Onta 2006). Even so, the period before RCTV's creation, and especially the formation of the Deurali Pariwar, indicates that this was not an unprecedented act of cultural innovation, even if the technologies used were new. Chapter 4, which looks in more detail at the history of Tansen as a whole, provides further evidence of the milieu of cultural innovation out of which RCTV emerged.

All the elements of the model can be discerned in this description, but it is equally clear that they are present in a complex admixture and seldom in any of the purity of form that would be required to make RCTV/CDP a paradigm case of any single variety of non-mainstream media. Not only is this an example of a hybridization of several different types of non-mainstream media, but it also indicates that the distinctions between non-mainstream and mainstream are not always maintained in practice. Most obviously here, the distinction between commercial and non-commercial, or even anti-commercial, are blurred, despite the split between RCTV (the business) and CDP (the NGO). Other examples of compromise between possibly contradictory motivations and goals in the work of the organization will become apparent once the more detailed examination of the following chapters is completed. Such compromises are highlighted in this study not to be critical of RCTV/CDP and their work, for surely any organization can be seen to require such pragmatics if it is to survive. Rather, the goal here is to examine, beyond the mere fact of the existence of such compromises, how and why they came about, and how they were or were not resolved given the context within which the organization worked. RCTV/CDP has clearly changed even in the short span considered by this study, and the application of any model to the analysis of these types of media must be grounded in history and processes of change.

This concern with history is crucial for analysis, because just as mainstream media organizations must work continuously to maintain their legitimacy as sites of discourse and action (Couldry 2000), so too must non-mainstream or alternative media work to maintain their legitimacy in the eyes of those whom they claim to serve or represent. Indeed, they may need to work even harder because their existence is often questioned politically and precarious economically. The important question to ask, then, is how such work of legitimation occurs in the face of the survival pressures that non-mainstream media must endure. As the examples described by Rodriguez (2001) show, many non-mainstream media (citizens' media in her parlance) do not survive beyond a brief efflorescence of enthusiasm at their inception. Most importantly, this question, despite its incorporation of pragmatic concerns into analysis, moves us away from seeing the survival of non-mainstream media simply in terms of the materiality of resource issues or the availability of skilled and enthusiastic labor. These media cannot survive if they are not seen to be legitimate expressions of identity and action by those who work for them and by the audiences or people they seek to serve.

Therefore, before continuing with our study of RCTV/CDP, we must look in more detail at the general crisis of legitimacy in national media in Nepal that formed the immediate prelude to events in Tansen. As we shall see in the following chapter, this crisis in national media was only one part of the wider crisis that engulfed the Panchayat regime at the end of the 1980s.

Notes

1. The Fourth World is defined by Graburn (1976: 1) as "the collective name for all aboriginal or native peoples whose lands fall within the national boundaries and techno-bureaucratic administrations of the countries of the First, Second, and Third Worlds. As such, they are peoples without countries of their own, peoples who are usually in the minority and without the power to direct the course of their collective lives."

2. Molnar and Meadows (2001: 58) note, however, that Imparja's Indigenous staff rose from these very low levels to about 40% of total staff numbers by end of the 1990s.

3. This is based on the conclusions drawn from his original (1986) unpublished project report *The Aboriginal Invention of Television: Central Australia 1982–86* commissioned by the Canberra Institute for Aboriginal Studies.

4. According to Howard Morphy (1992: 203), "it is aesthetic effects in combination with cognitive understandings that give concrete form to abstract conception, and enable people to use that conception for particular purposes."

5. Ginsburg's use of the parallax metaphor is heuristically useful in that it helps to explain the potential value of indigenous and anthropological representations of society and culture as an aid to cross-cultural communication and understanding. However, it is, not surprisingly, an imperfect metaphor. The parallax effect in astronomy is useful because the positions from which observations of distant stars are made are known with a high degree of certainty, thus making the unknown factor, distance to the star, known with equal certainty once the elementary geometric calculation is made. Ginsburg's metaphor starts to break down once we begin to ask whether any comparable certainty over the identification of cultural and socio-economic location is possible. The parallax effect is at best a useful way of re-imagining familiar debates about the representation of culture in mediated contexts.

6. The description of RCTV/CDP that follows is written in the past tense to emphasize that we are dealing with the situation as it was up to the late 1990s. This media organization has continued to change since this time and has also suffered the sad death of its founder, Buddha Ratna Shakya. Writing in the past tense emphasizes that we are speaking of things as they were, not as they are today, and helps to avoid the creation of an a-temporal 'ethnographic present' in this work.

7. A *kuruwa* is a brass water pot used during many sorts of religious ceremony and commonly given as a gift to newly weds or honored guests

8. The name has also been appropriated by, amongst other people, a cigarette manufacturer and a rock group! The former played upon the image of smiling villagers, both male and female, enjoying their product around a roadside cairn in their advertising.

9. Many of my Nepali informants frequently expressed their belief in the superiority of Japanese-made goods over their Indian equivalents. It appeared to be a familiar trope in conversation, although evidence was only ever anecdotal.

10. The development of the RCTV cable network in Tansen in the early-1990s is very similar to the first networks in India, which have been described as 'mom and pop operations'. "Individual entrepreneurs were using makeshift technology; there was neither infrastructure nor the most rudimentary common technical standards. There was no license, legal framework or institutional protection. Cable operators served purely local needs and they had to provide their own protection" (Page and Crawley 2001: 89–90). The ways in which RCTV sought protection and defended their operations in the face of the lack of any legal or institutional framework for cable television broadcasting in Nepal forms a significant part of the narrative presented below and in chapter 6.

11. Vikram Samvat (VS), occasionally transliterated as Bikram Sambat (BS), is the calendar used in Nepal for all official purposes. It uses the lunar months for scheduling

rituals and festivals, and these are named in the dates that follow. The Nepali New Year begins in mid-April.

12. Page and Crawley (2001: 89) note that it was only after the provision of cable networks became more widespread in India in the late-1980s and early 1990s that satellite television was transformed "from a private facility for wealthy homes to a mass entertainment and communication phenomenon." This observation certainly holds true for Tansen and Nepal in general.

13. The average (median) income per month in Tansen according to a survey carried out for my research in November and December 1995 was NRs 4,000 (US$73) to NRs 5,000 (US$91) (see chapter 5 for further information about incomes and standards of living).

14. RCTV's decision to make their own programming a regular feature of their cable output stands in marked contrast to the situation elsewhere in South Asia where, according to Page and Crawley (2001: 310), "there has been very little generation of local programming", despite the existence of cable operations that are very similar in form to RCTV. This suggests that the factors that lead to or prevent the creation of original programming through cable television and video are not simply technological or even economic, but must be sought in the specific social and cultural characteristics of the community in which the cable operators are based. Page and Crawley's description (ibid: 311–3) of cable operators' original video programming and organization in Chennai (India) and Mishra's (1999) study of Delhi cable operators do, however, bear comparison with RCTV's work and could provide interesting material for a more detailed comparative study.

15. This business was connected to the television organization because it was owned by the family of the durbar singer's son's sister-in-law (his older brother's wife).

16. The business man was a *tabla* (classical Indian and Nepali drum) player, which was how Buddha Ratna had come to meet him.

17. Interviewed 9th April 1996

18. Further information about local media in Tansen can be found at this website.

Chapter 3
Communication for Development: Nepal's Media Revolution

So often in the 'nation-building' policies of the new states one sees both a genuine, popular nationalist enthusiasm and a systematic, even Machiavellian, instilling of nationalist ideology through the mass media, the educational system, administrative regulations, and so forth.

Benedict Anderson (1991: 113–4)

South Asia has no shortage of nationalities, ethnic groups and communities who might benefit from new media technologies, nor of development needs which the media might help to meet. But early expectations of the benefits of mass media technologies in these fields now look exaggerated and there is greater appreciation of the complexity of social influences, of which the media are only a part.

David Page and William Crawley (2001: 29)

Introduction

It is important to understand the main features of Nepal's national mediascape in order to place the activities of the media producers and consumers of Tansen into their wider context. Crucial to this is the idea of development (*bikās* in Nepali) that can be seen to overdetermine much of the media activity of Nepal in recent times. This process of development and attitudes to it will be described in this chapter in relation to the national context and the implications for this at the local level of the town demonstrated in later chapters.

One of the great canards of early research into electronic media, which not surprisingly has been popularized by the media industry itself, is that they act as

63

a focus for national unity (Smith 1995). Electronic media within this research paradigm are assumed to have an instrumental role in the creation of a mass audience based upon the unification of a national population around a common mediated culture and "have been deployed by central governments as an integrative force" (Page and Crawley 2001: 26). However, Benedict Anderson (1991: 22) has argued that although "beneath the decline of sacred communities, languages and lineages, a fundamental change was taking place in modes of apprehending the world, which, more than anything else, made it possible to 'think' the nation", the ways in which this change has been experienced in various places is complicated by the particular characteristics of the "local colonial state" (ibid.: xiii). In particular, the role played by media in the creation of states in the colonial and post-colonial eras has not followed any simple pattern determined solely by the characteristics of the communication technologies through which national identities have been made manifest. This chapter follows the research agenda mapped out by Anderson by examining how ideas of national identity in Nepal have been articulated through the state's development of media and communication technologies and how this development discouraged the articulation of minority cultures and languages (Page and Crawley 2001: 26). The ultimate failure of this attempted articulation and the corresponding de-legitimation of the state's program of development is a central theme of this narrative.

Media and Communication Prior to 1950: The Absence of the 'Masses'

> And it was in the month of March of 1950 when the privileged nobility of Rana days possessing a receiver set (to possess a radio was a privilege then) heard privately the revolutionary 'Awaj' (voice) of the newly set-up radio (people who were afraid to mention the name of that Radio then used to term that broadcast as 'Awaj' or voice only.) Like a lightning flash, the 'Awaj' or the voice of that revolutionary radio gradually resounded throughout the nook and corner [sic.] of the Kingdom (Khatri 1976: 33).

In 1976 at the height of the Panchayat era the Department of Communication of His Majesty's Government of Nepal published the short book from which the above quotation is taken. As such, it is a document of value to an historian of mass communication and media in Nepal for what it tells us about the rhetoric of the Panchayat state in this sector of national development, quite apart from what it tells us about these events. It is perhaps no surprise that the breathless, almost messianic tone of this quotation is continued throughout Khatri's book, a paean of praise to the wisdom of the policy of guided development and partyless 'democracy' at the core of the Panchayat system. And just as Khatri's words contain the solecism of the lightning flash "gradually" resounding throughout the Kingdom, the Panchayat system contained at its core the contradiction that it tried to modernize the country through the mediation of a centralized state controlled by an absolute monarch.

Khatri is, of course, guilty of hyperbole; we have no way of knowing today who made up the audience for the first broadcasts of the Nepali Congress sponsored *Nepal Prajatantra Radio* (Nepal Democracy Radio) or even how many people listened. But we can be sure that, due to the low power of the equipment available to the rebel broadcasters, it probably had a very limited geographic coverage from its base in Biratnagar in the eastern Tarai and this would have greatly limited its potential audience.

Nevertheless, the symbolic impact of this event goes beyond any immediate instrumental role that it might have played in the events of 1950, such as acting as an effective means of communicating the aims and demands of the revolutionary forces to the population at large. For the first time in living memory the supposedly total control of the Rana family over technologically sophisticated means of communication was being challenged from within Nepalese territory, in the same way that their monopoly over the means of violence was being simultaneously challenged by armed uprisings in the Tarai and Palpa (see chapter 4). As Joshi and Rose (1966: 490) observe, the leaders of the 1950 revolution "soon discovered that the governmental machinery that had seemed omnipotent from the outside was, when viewed from the inside and in its reality, quite weak and fragile." That this reality remained hidden for so long is perhaps a testament to the effectiveness of the Rana's policy of limiting the population's access to information about the regime through any form of free and independent media.

We should be careful, however, not to regard the will of the political elite as the sole cause of the almost total absence of any form of mass media or mass communication system in early modern Nepal. For there to be a mass media there has to be a prior concept of a 'mass', that is an audience—in this case a national audience—with which to communicate. It remains highly debatable whether the concept of the *nation*-state is applicable to Nepal during the time prior to and during the rule of the Ranas.

Before 1950 the relationship of the individual inhabitants of Nepal, most of whom were peasant farmers, to the state was mediated through a set of exchange relationships with local representatives of the state in their role as landowners. According to M.C. Regmi (1984), these relationships were invariably not directly between the primary producer (the farmer) and the representative of the state (the landowner), because most landowners were absentee landlords who rented their state-appointed landholdings to comparatively wealthy, local landowner/farmers, who also took over many of the administrative and legal functions of the state in their locality. According to Regmi (ibid: 29), "the modern conception of the state exercising full jurisdiction over all communities and regions in their territories did not apply to the kingdom during this period." The essential point is that prior to the middle of the Twentieth Century the function of communication technology and media in Nepal was *qualitatively* quite different to their role in the post-revolutionary state.

This point is seldom brought out adequately in studies of mass media in the Nepalese context, which have tended to emphasize purely *quantitative* aspects of change in the provision of media and communication technology between the pre- and post-revolutionary eras.[1] To reiterate, it makes little sense in the context of pre-1950s Nepal to speak either of mass communication or mass media, because there simply was no 'mass' with which to communicate. There were, of course, many millions of people living within the territory of the state, but whether they either felt themselves to be citizens of a single nation-state or were treated as such by the state must at least be open to question. It is also the case that even if, as Habermas (1992) points out, the size and social scope of the public sphere in Eighteenth and Nineteenth Century Europe was restricted there was still sufficient freedom for the concept of agency operating within autonomous civic institutions to develop. The development of a public sphere in this Habermasian sense was, however, impossible within the context of the Rana state (Burghart 1996).

Prior to 1950, the only indirect means of personal intercommunication in Nepal was the postal system carried on foot along the trails of the Himalaya, organized according to a long established system of rights and obligations to receive and carry mail. Mail was "carried by runners who were paid by making a permanent land allocation to them. This practice created families of hereditary runners" (Bajracharya and Shrestha 1981: 156–7). The illiteracy of the vast majority of the population at this time and the fact that a postal service is primarily only useful for intercommunication between specific individuals meant that the postal service could only function as a means of communication between government and administrators at central and local levels. As Ludwig Stiller (1976: 119) notes, referring specifically to the period between the end of the Anglo-Nepali war in 1816 and the rise of the Ranas in the middle of that century:

> Under the decentralized form of government that was characteristic of Nepal during these early formation years, individual districts had strong bonds linking them to the centre but few bonds linking them to each other. Apart from national projects such as the *hulak* [postal] system, the munitions industry and the army, there had been little change in the local social structures that had once found political expression in the mini-states of a divided Nepal. These social structures continued largely as closed societies.

He goes on to relate that,

> establishing the *hulak* system along the main east-west trails under the pressure of military expansion seems to have exhausted the central administration's energies and imagination. No further steps were taken for years to establish more than the most tenuous linkages between the different districts of a region to supplement the strong linkages between the centre and individual districts. In particular, the advantages that could have been derived from developing regional trade linkages were totally ignored. The districts remained isolated units, and, being isolated units, they were unable to contribute to an expanding economy (ibid: 134).

We will shortly investigate what social and cultural factors might have militated against this trend towards regional and sub-regional fragmentation when we come to look at the process of nation building in Nepal. What is already evident here is that certainly in the pre-Rana period and for much of the century between the rise and fall of the Rana regime, the rulers of the Nepalese state had neither the resources nor the political will to use what communication technologies were available to them to do anything other than ensure the maintenance of their centralized control over the different parts of the kingdom.[2] As Seddon (1979: 28) notes, "under these circumstances the state apparatus was quite incapable of laying down the technical and social infrastructure essential to national integration and development." To use Anderson's (1991) terminology, the idea of "simultaneity" upon which the imagined community of the nation was founded could not be fully realized within the context of this infrastructure.

However it is the case that despite the turbulent events of Nepalese modern history, the political entity that is the Nepali state continued to exist. Having been unified under the house of Gorkha the state remained intact and largely independent, despite the trauma of defeat by the East India Company and the annexation by the British of huge portions of the lands that made up the country, including parts of the most valuable territory in the Tarai. What if anything ensured this survival?

The answer lies, though it might seem paradoxical, in the very weaknesses described above because the Nepalese state was an almost paradigmatic example of a "soft state" (Myrdal 1977: 150) within which "national governments require extraordinarily little of their citizens" and where "even those obligations that do exist are inadequately enforced." The political traumas of this time had little effect upon the individual citizens of the state; life, though incredibly hard physically and psychologically, would for these people go on much as it had before (Stiller 1976). But at the same time such lives were not totally devoid of any collective sentiment. For Stiller (1976) it was the common religious heritage of the Himalayan peoples that united them both in contradistinction to the successive Muslim and British regimes that dominated the plains of India, and in common bonds of allegiance to the Hindu monarchy and its representatives. These bonds were manifested at almost every turn within the ritual life of the population (Quigley 1993).

In 1854, the Rana regime promulgated a new legal code, the *Muluki Ain* (literally 'the law of the land'), which for the first time created a systematic set of principles through which each of the different groups that made up the population of Nepal could be classified and their legal relationship to the state described (Höfer 1979). We can speculate that one of the reasons for the interest of the Rana regime, specifically its founder Jang Bahadur Rana, in the systematic codification of the Nepalese legal system was the need to create a system of social order that relied on foundations other than that of the monarch's authority alone, given that, for all their regal trappings, the Ranas were not the ultimate source of ritual authority within the kingdom. The codification and promulgation of a new written legal system also shows some degree of interest in the modernization of the state on the part of the Rana regime (Pfaff-Czarnecka

1997: 427; see also Whelpton 1983 for a discussion of how Jang Bahadur Rana was partly inspired to carry out these reforms by his visit to Europe in 1850). What is significant, of course, is that the basis for this codification was the Hindu religion and the caste system, as they were conceptualized by high caste members of the ruling Gorkhali (and broader Parbatiya) elite.

At its most brutal this meant that even those groups that had never practiced the Hindu religion or had a system of social organization based upon caste principles were required to conform to these principles in their relations with the state through the legal system.[3] In this way, a factor that had *tended* to create some degree of sociocultural unity within the Himalayan region and by implication within the area controlled by the Nepalese state, that is 'Hinduization', was elevated to a position of official state policy to which the inhabitants of that state had to either actively conform (through a process of 'Sanskritization' if they had not previously been Hindu in any conventional sense) or acquiesce at times of contact and exchange with the state (if they were unable or unwilling to renounce their traditional religious and cultural identity) (Quigley 1987) .[4] Even ethnic groups who already had a system of social organization based on caste principles, such as the Newar, were affected by the promulgation of the Muluki Ain, because in each case it was the 1854 code or one of its subsequent revisions that had preeminence in the eyes of the state. Throughout the time of the Rana regime, this official policy of Hinduization would serve to mediate relations between the state and its citizens and became, almost by default, the basis of a *national* caste hierarchy (Liechty 1994: 511). From the 1950s onwards, and most vigorously during the time of Panchayat rule, it would become a key element in the discourse of Nepalese nationalism.[5]

An important caveat must be added here before proceeding. Those who have examined this question of the role of the legal code's role in the formation of the Nepalese nation-state in the Nineteenth and early Twentieth Centuries have tended to assume that the situation described in the documents published by the state correspond to the practices of the people on the ground. As will already be apparent from the above description of the organization and functioning of the state at this time, this is at best a questionable assumption. It is beyond the scope of this study to investigate this issue in relation to the role of the legal code in the social history of Nepal in detail. We must at least acknowledge, however, the warning of Pratyoush Onta (1994: 9) that

> historical accounts . . . based on normative and political texts and codes designed by ruling classes, tend to be limited in what they can say about the social structure of past societies as experienced by people occupying various social strata. It is also unclear to what extent these formulae of rulers can be said to have initiated change. To say . . . that the 1854 code divided the people into four general classes is easy. To study its internal logic, as done by Andreas Höfer (1979) and other, is not that difficult either. But without knowing how much of that code was actually implemented, we cannot adequately assess its role in bringing about a change in social structure.

Whilst the precise focus of the question raised by Onta, the 1854 Muluki Ain, cannot be examined in detail, his general call for a properly *social* history certainly is at the heart of this study which seeks to analyse the notion of mass media and mass communications roles within Nepalese society in relation to an example of alternative media.

Before continuing discussion of the search for a national identity and the role of media and communication in this search in greater detail, it is necessary to look at some of the developments in Nepalese print media under the Rana regime. As I have already indicated above, due to the paucity of developments in this field under the Ranas, this will inevitably be a brief discussion.

Jang Bahadur Rana brought the first printing press in Nepal into the country after his trip to Europe in 1850. In 1862, the Manoranjan Press was set up specifically to produce copies of official government publications, such as the legal code or books on military practices, and private access to this press or the establishment of any press in private hands was strictly controlled. However, such was not the case in India where several groups of Nepalese expatriates started to publish newspapers and books in the last decades of the Nineteenth Century.

The Rana response to the persistent trickle of these publications into Nepal from India was mixed. For example, an official national newspaper, the *Gorkhapatra*, was founded during the reforming Prime Ministership of Dev Shamser, which began on 5th March 1901.[6] Dev Shamser also founded several vernacular schools and, according to Stiller (1993), he even placed suggestion boxes at strategic locations around Kathmandu "to solicit opinions from the people."[7] The alternative response from the Ranas came swiftly following Dev Shamser's reforms. On 26th June 1901, a coup d'état led by Chandra Shamser removed Dev Shamser from office. Chandra's 29-year premiership and that of Bhim Shamser that followed marked a return to the strict, although seldom entirely successful, control over any potential outlet for anti-Rana sentiment within Nepal. The *Gorkhapatra* survived, but for many years it existed merely to publish government pronouncements and fiction, and had very little real news content. As it was under government control and editorially emasculated, this is perhaps not surprising. The development of electronic media under the Ranas was limited almost in its entirety to the private telephone lines, cinema and gramophones imported into Nepal, along with myriad other luxury items, to be the playthings of the bored aristocratic class (see Appendix A in Liechty 1994 and Liechty 1997, for a discussion of the predilection of the Rana aristocracy for imported goods; also chapter 4).

The essential phrase in the above paragraph is, of course, "within Nepal", because, the Rana regime felt "secure inside Nepal but felt helpless to control agitators in India" (Stiller 1993: 167). Whilst political conditions inside Nepal were not conducive to the publication of newspapers, the Nepali diasporas in India had the freedom to produce newspapers and magazines that were critical of the regime, the first of these being *Gorkha Bharat Jeevan* published in Varanasi in 1886 (Shakya 1997). Hutt (1997: 117) observes that "up until the twilight years of the Rana regime in Nepal much of the modernization and development of Nepali literature took place in India, where educational facilities were more generally available and Rana censorship largely ineffective." However, when we talk about Nepal in this context we are really returning to an earlier geographical meaning, that limits its place of reference to the confines of the Kathmandu Valley. Beyond the Valley, as the discussion of Tansen's history in chapter 4 will show, the reality of Rana control was somewhat different, even before the "shattering" revelation of the regime's weakness after the 1950 revolution (Joshi and Rose 1966: 490).

'Communication for Development': Media During the First Democratic and Panchayat Eras (1950–1990)

The presentation of raw statistics alone can be deceptive, as Alan Macfarlane (1993) points out, if we wish to estimate how much of an effect nearly five decades of 'development' has had in Nepal. Whereas in 1950 there were virtually no roads, no communication infrastructure bar the postal service and a single telephone exchange in Kathmandu, a literacy rate of only 2%, and only one daily newspaper published in the entire country, by 1990 there were over a thousand kilometers of metalled roads, almost four hundred and fifty newspapers registered with the government (*Communications in Nepal* 1988; figures for financial year 1986/87), national radio and television networks, and a national literacy rate of almost 40%.[8] All this seems to indicate that Nepal has progressed greatly over the decades since 1950. By way of contrast, however, Macfarlane (1993: 109) states with simple severity that "the figures giving total numbers of schools, hospitals, health workers, miles of road constructed, are meaningless without taking into account the quality of what is being developed." It is important, therefore, to look in some detail at both the quantity and quality of the media available to the people of Nepal, and to do so in a broadly historical perspective. In doing so we will see how the slogan adopted by the National Communication Plan of 1971, "Communication for Development", came to be given substance and created the context within which Tansen's local media came into being.

There was from the time of the very first post-Rana government an expression of a need for a dramatic change in the provision of media and mass communication in Nepal. As was stated earlier in this chapter, the very existence of the revolution that had been carried out by the activists of Nepal's political parties was predicated upon the growing awareness of those activists that legitimacy for their political aims had to be sought in an appeal to the needs of the majority of the population rather than those of the small elite who had benefited up to then from the resources of the country. These resources did, of course, include that majority of primary producers who farmed the land to create that wealth.[9] This is not the place to examine whether the wealth of the nation is any more equitably distributed today than it was before (it most certainly is not—the disparity between the lives of those who live in the 'thatched huts' and those in the 'stuccoed palaces' to use Regmi's (1978) contrast still exists).

Rather, given the legacy of Nepal's history described above and the given facts of extreme differences in the ways of life of Nepal's populace (including here differences of culture and language, socio-economic organization and income), we examine on what basis a true system of mass media and communication could be said to have developed.

We must first understand that, whilst the leaders of the 1950 revolution might have appealed to the national interest in justifying their actions, unlike the events of 1990, theirs was not a movement based on widespread popular unrest. Primarily the crisis of 1950 was one of legitimacy for the ruling elite brought about by the rejection of their government by the notional head of state, King Tribhuvan. The political parties and groups who sought to capitalize on this crisis did so after the event and did not contribute directly to the precipitation of that crisis in the first place. Indeed, it is notable that the settlement reached between the Rana government, the monarchy and the Nepalese political parties only involved the later group after an extended period of secret negotiations between the existing Rana government in Nepal and the Indian government acting on behalf of the monarchy's interests.[10] Political activity in Nepal after the settlement of 1951 was characterized, therefore, by an extreme suspicion on the part of the political parties regarding the motives of the Indian Government, the old Rana elite, who had retreated into the wings but not wholly left the political stage, and the King, who now held the balance of power. As John Whelpton (1997: 46–47) observes of the monarchy at this time,

Once the Ranas were dislodged . . . the monarchy was in a strong position to portray itself as the embodiment of national identity, particularly after the accession of Mahendra, who was less beholden to India than his father had been. In addition to the religious awe surrounding Hindu kingship and to his prestige as the direct descendent of the founder of the nation, the occupant of the throne was helped by the royal family's century of political emasculation: it was the Ranas, not the Shah kings, who bore the responsibility for collaboration with British colonialism. The monarchy was in fact able both to claim credit for ending Rana autocracy and also count on the loyalty of individual members of the Rana family who retained high positions in national life, in particular the army: a century of inter-marriage between Ranas and Shahs meant that, in a sense, 1950–51 simply saw an exchange of junior and senior roles between two wings of the same family.

Perhaps it is not surprising given the politics of this time that the politicians who emerged out of the revolutionary movement, many of whom had not actually been resident in the centre of political life, Kathmandu, for some time having lived in exile in India, spent much of the decade after 1950 trying to consolidate their personal power-base within the political landscape. Between 1951 and the general election of 1959 there were numerous changes of government, all of which were appointed by the king in his role as head of state, but on the basis of *ad hoc* assessments of the support that individual members of a particular government could garner from within the political class and on the streets of the capital city (Joshi and Rose 1966).

This extreme fluidity in the political system is reflected in the mass media of this time. The availability of print media had increased dramatically and by 1960 there were over thirty seven different newspapers and periodicals available in Kathmandu (Aditya 1996). But their distribution was almost exclusively limited to the central Kathmandu Valley area or the larger towns of the Tarai, and circulation numbers were very small. Partly this was due to constraints imposed by the available printing technology, transportation problems throughout the country, and a tiny readership base due to low levels of literacy. But it also reflects the political role that these publications played at this time. Most owner-editors were either political actors themselves or used their publications to lobby on behalf of a particular party or faction. As Joshi and Rose (1966) explain, these newspapers functioned not to inform the general population of political events in the capital, never mind elsewhere in the country, but instead acted as an adjunct to the rumor mill and networks of gossip through which political life took place.

Given that the interests of Nepal's politicians were expressed through these means and not forgetting that the resources of the state were wholly inadequate to the task of modernizing the country's communication infrastructure or the fact that few administrations stayed in power long enough to put any policy decisions into effect, it is not surprising that apart from one or two projects (including a telephone line to Palpa) very little was done in the 1950s to promote the development of mass media and communication in Nepal. "During the First Five Year Plan (1956–61)", say Khatri (1976: 33), "little attention was paid to the development of mass-media including Radio Nepal. Although there was a reference on [sic.] the importance of information in the concluding paragraph of the plan there was not a single specified project related to radio or any other mass media."

The event which probably had the greatest impact on the political elite's awareness of issues concerning Nepal's lack of communication infrastructure was the general election of 1959, the first such plebiscite held in the country's history. The election had to be extended over a month long period due to the problems of terrain and the lack of communication infrastructure (Hoftun and Raeper 1992: 8), and because of these difficulties the election process gave the major political parties that contested seats on a nation-wide basis, direct experience of organizing a truly national political system for the first time. This election also demonstrated that social and cultural diversity within Nepal was matched by an equal diversity of political opinion. Although the Nepali Congress Party achieved a solid majority within parliament, they did so with only 37% of the popular vote (Borre et al. 1994: 9).

Barely a year after the election of Nepal's first democratic government in 1959, King Mahendra used the emergency powers granted to him under a constitution that he had played a major role in formulating. He exploited the violence of some of the political opponents of the Nepal Congress government as an excuse for staging what was in effect a constitutionally sanctioned coup d'état, under the pretext that the government could not maintain social order.

The leaders of the Nepal Congress, including Prime Minister B.P. Koirala were arrested and for two years the king ruled under the authority of emergency law.

Despite bringing the democratic experiments of the previous decade to an end, the subsequent actions of Mahendra and his inner circle of advisors in the palace show that they understood from the experience of those years that the complexities of the nation-building process in post-1950s Nepal were daunting. Whilst the use of force could suppress opposition to the monarchy's rule for a limited time, it could not be a long-term political solution, as the downfall of the Rana regime had shown. The three decades that followed Mahendra's coup were a time during which the monarchy and the state sought to construct an ideology that would sustain a viable national coalition of interests. As such it consisted of elements that would often appear in theory, if not in practice, to be contradictory. This ideology had three main components—the benevolent dictatorship of the King underwritten by the state's promotion of a policy of Hinduization, modernization and development of the country as the guiding principle of government policy, and the adoption of a political system based on partyless *Panchayat* 'democracy'. The popularization of this ideology would involve massive investment in the communication infrastructure of the country, itself a key index by which the attainment of development could be measured, and the concomitant exercise of strict control over the media to prevent open dissent towards this state ideology.

Control of the media took the form of both direct censorship and more indirect methods. In January 1960 all party newspapers were closed down following the preceding ban on political parties. In total the Kathmandu Magistrates Office cancelled the official registration of sixty-five different publications (*Communications in Nepal* 1988). Indirect control of the press came about through the promulgation of the 1963 Press and Publication Registration Act, which imposed strict demands upon the publishers of any periodical. These included rules on the number of copies of a publication that had to be produced in any given year, the minimum number of pages that they should contain, minimum page sizes and minimum print run. Subsequent revision of these rules in 1966 meant that an automatic ban on publication could be imposed if any of these requirements were not fulfilled. This revision of the law also imposed minimum levels of collateral that the publishers had to provide as a guarantee. These were equivalent to ten thousand rupees for daily publications, fifteen thousand rupees for weekly and twenty thousand rupees for other types of publication, which were prohibitively expensive sums for the time. New rules issued in 1985 and amended in the following year, apart from revising the above requirements, set up a committee consisting of government appointees selected from amongst the ranks of the government and the Nepal Journalists Association to deal with the distribution of state resources to approved publications. This measure, combined with the overwhelming dominance of the government's contribution to the advertising revenue that most publications relied upon, meant that even the supposedly private press in Nepal, never mind the newspapers published by the state-owned Gorkhapatra Corporation, were dominated by the Panchayat government.

The clear aim of these financial and production requirements was to place a prohibitive burden upon those who wished to enter the market and control the editorial content of news publications without resorting to the measure of outright censorship, which would have been unpopular (at least in public) with many of the foreign governments who were providing increasing amounts of financial and material aid to Nepal at this time. However, the effect was in practice somewhat different. As a report of Worldview Nepal (*Communications in Nepal* 1988: 14) states, "despite formulation and promulgation of different 'Acts' and 'Rules' they were hardly executed.[11] On the contrary, promulgation of different rules and regulation off and on [sic.] created mistrust among publishers and they feared them and fought for survival."

This is not to say that newspaper publishers and editors did not face persecution and prosecution under the Panchayat regime. Vinaya Kasajoo, the publisher/editor of Tansen's local newspaper, *Satya* (literally meaning 'truth'), which is no longer published, described to me the problems that he had faced in first getting permission to publish any newspaper at all and then the subsequent terms of imprisonment that he had faced when the authorities accused him of contravening the state's press regulations. But the important lesson is that *Satya*, like many other (mainly weekly) newspapers did stay in publication throughout the years of the Panchayat regime, even if many of them were unable to stay in regular existence. The numbers also rose dramatically following the 1980 referendum on the Panchayat system during which the restrictions on party political activity were temporarily lifted.[12]

Another means through which state control over newspapers, specifically their content, was maintained was through the monopoly over the gathering and distribution of news within Nepal held by the state owned *Rastriya Samachar Samiti* (National News Agency) or RSS. Originally two privately owned and controlled news agencies, *Nepal Samvad Samiti* (established in December 1959) and *Sagarmatha Samvad Samiti* (established in May 1960 by three daily newspapers), had provided news reports to the Nepalese press. In February 1961, however, the government merged the two organizations and in the following year established the RSS under majority state ownership. Apart from the work of foreign owned news agencies, no other Nepal news organization was permitted to gather and distribute news to the Nepalese press.

The Panchayat regime looked towards the electronic media, primarily radio, over which it had a total monopoly within Nepal as the primary means of communication with the population. Ostensibly, this was due to the country's harsh terrain and low literacy rates, which meant that printed media would be able to reach only a small proportion of the total population. In reality, all governments in South Asia have tended to regard electronic media in a different way to the printed media (Page and Crawley 2001: 35). Whereas the latter have been largely left to the private sector and controlled through indirect forms of restrictions (see above), the electronic media have come under direct state control and been used "as a tool of national policy" (ibid.). As the author of an official government publication stated, "Radio Nepal [the sole radio broadcaster during the Panchayat era] has to play a very important and significant role in arousing development consciousness among the masses, to secure their active co-operation and participation in the national reconstruction work" (Khatri 1976: 38).

Even so, the actual geographical extent of Radio Nepal's coverage was limited for several reasons. Most obviously, it took some years for adequate technology to be available within Nepal. Donations of expertise and materials by various foreign governments meant that by the early 1980 short wave radio transmissions could be heard in most areas, but Radio Nepal's Medium Wave channel, which had been started in 1985, was only available in the Central and Western Development Regions. Up to 1985 Radio Nepal had relied solely on public funding, but the Medium Wave service was a direct result of the decision made to open up Radio Nepal to commercial sources of funding in the 1980–1985 National Development Plan.

A second, potentially more serious problem is found at the opposite end of the communication process. Radio receivers are, of course, relatively expensive consumer items in a country where even in 1991 the average yearly income was only US$180 per capita (HMG 1994). If this is so today, then it was even more the case during the Panchayat era. The number of people who actually owned a radio receiver varied massively between different parts of the country. According to figures gathered as part of the decennial national census, in 1981 the total number of radios in the country was 255,526 (17 per 1000 people). This ranged from a high of 30,000 (71 per 1000 people) in Kathmandu to only 76 (1.7 per 1000 people) in Mugu, a mountainous district in the Mid-Western Development Region. Palpa's total at this time was 4,127 radios (19.2 per 1000 population).[13] The actual size of the audience is more difficult to estimate as in each case a single radio set would be listened to by many more people than just the owner of the receiver. Statistics from studies carried out in 1989 and 1991 suggest that approximately 34% of rural household and 51% of urban households own radio sets, which means that each set would serve approximately seventeen people in rural areas and eleven in urban areas given average household sizes (Aditya 1996: 48).[14]

Even if we could conclusively answer this question of total audience size, it would tell us little about how people were responding to the radio programming that they heard (Ang 1996). One vital point with regard to this is that from almost the start of the Panchayat era the language policy of Radio Nepal was changed so that all spoken language broadcasts were only made in Nepali or, in the case of a few daily news bulletins, in English.[15] Prior to this, broadcasts had also been made in Hindi and Newari. As Grandin (1989) and M. Shrestha (1994) explain, this restricted language policy was one of the main grievances voiced by non-native Nepali speakers when they criticized radio broadcasting in Nepal. The language policy of Radio Nepal proved to be particularly problematic in relation to the Tarai where the majority of the population spoke languages such as Bhojpuri and Maithili that were served by the output of All India Radio (Page and Crawley 2001: 61).

A related issue is the fact that even when the Radio Nepal service split into a commercially funded, broadly entertainment-based Medium Wave channel and a publicly funded Short Wave channel (broadcasting its traditional mix of public service programs), the sociocultural and demographic diversity of the audience meant that for many people in Nepal the content of radio programming seemed to be an irrelevance. To move briefly towards the present day, my study of listening habits amongst Tansen's population showed that women by-and-large claimed that they only listened to popular music programs, if they listened at all, whereas men claimed that news programs were their favorite. Grandin (1989) reported similar listening patterns in his study of music and media consumption in a neighborhood of Kirtipur, a town in the Kathmandu Valley. Likewise, rural audiences reported that they found programming targeted at urban listeners irrelevant to their lives and vice versa for urban audiences (Serle et al. 1993). Whilst it is obvious that commercials advertising consumer items may seem irrelevant to listeners in a village kilometers from the nearest bazaar, Grandin also relates how listeners in Kirtipur also complained of radio advertisements that seemed to imply everyone could afford what they offered, when clearly this was not the case.[16]

Even as the Panchayat government began to recognize the potential role of media and communication technology in the promotion of its ideological goals, specifically as they related to building a united and 'developed' nation, the practical realization of these aims began to unravel due to the different reactions of Nepal's socioculturally diverse population to this ideology. The leaders of the Panchayat state wished to arouse "development consciousness among the masses" (Khatri 1976: 38). As such, the Panchayat followed the direction of all South Asian governments of this time in that "their policy towards the media has largely been based on a functionalist approach, in which the media are seen as a causal influence for continuity, integration and normality in society" (Page and Crawley 2001: 32).

But could a mass public be brought into existence in the precise national form that the Panchayat rulers of Nepal desired? Functionalism in the context of national policy towards media does not just consist of abstract social theory, but requires the practical and material manifestation of a political ideology. In the case of Nepal, each of the three elements of Panchayat ideology, *Hinduization*, *Nepalization* and *Development*, attempted to resolve this question by providing a set of key symbols around which a national consensus could be built. Each of these elements, however, contained contradictions that led to the amelioration of these efforts at the very least, or, at worst, led to the opposite result by opening or widening social, economic and cultural fissures within the population of Nepal. We will now briefly address each element in turn.

Hinduization

The earlier Nineteenth Century absorption of Nepal's multiplicity of ethnic and religious groups within a legal framework based upon the principles of Hindu caste hierarchy has been discussed above. Despite the official rejection of these principles by the constitutions that have organised the institutions of the state since 1963, the Panchayat state continued to treat the king as a semi-divine figure within the context of the World's only Hindu monarchy.[17] Successive national census results have still been offered in support of the claim that Nepal's population was predominantly Hindu in its religious affiliation, which has been made by the ethnic groups within Nepal that have dominated all governments, primarily high caste Parbatiyas (Bahuns and Chetris).[18] It was a central premise of Panchayat ideology that the population of Nepal, despite its underlying diversity, should be united through their common identity as subjects of a monarch whose rule was divinely sanctioned by deities to whom they related in their own daily worship.

Nevertheless, critics of the methodology of census collection in Nepal and the presentation of the subsequent data have argued that results which identify the majority of Nepal's population as Hindu have only been obtained by means that bordered at times on deception (Pfaff-Czarnecka 1997). The question of religious syncretism in Nepal is, of course, a famous one and this was exploited within the census by asking leading questions, such as whether a person worshipped a particular Hindu god and using an affirmative reply as evidence that that person was Hindu. As Damian Walter has observed (pers. comm. 1996), it is invariably the case in Nepal that the religious practices of any group are never entirely alien to another group. In this respect, the division of the Nepalese population into entirely separate religious groups is as much an artefact of the census itself than a reflection of any intrinsic reality existing prior to and underlying the census results.[19] This should not be taken to imply that religious differences do not exist, but, as David Gellner (1988) has persuasively argued, these differences tend to lie within practice rather than doctrine. Chief amongst these is the fact that different ethnic or kin groups will rely on priests from different religions to perform their rituals. But even here there can be no definitive rules. Many of the priests of ostensibly Hindu temples in Tansen are, as is the case in 'Newar' settlements elsewhere in Nepal, from Buddhist Newar families.

In addition, syncretism should not be mistaken for harmony, as has often been the case with casual foreign observers and sometimes even academic students of Nepalese society. As Hoftun and Raeper (1992) observe, the Panchayat regime was happy to utilise this image of an harmonious religious community to convince outside observers, not the least being foreign governments and other donors of development aid, that all was well in the kingdom of Nepal. As they say,

> This potent picture had been created and maintained for many years by tourists, anthropologists and foreign scholars. These westerners wanted to believe in Nepal as a society of peace-loving people living in one of the most stable societies in the world. It was true that poverty was part of this picture—but it was a gentle, persevering poverty—not a condition which would lead to violence and upheaval. Further more, poverty and hardship were often linked in westerners' minds with religion and inner (and coveted) spiritual peace derived from Hinduism and Buddhism (ibid: 75).[20]

However, as with totalitarian regimes in general, it is unlikely that these propaganda-like images of stoic tranquility were recognized in the daily experience of the majority of Nepal's population, although at present this can only be an assumption, as the subaltern history of Nepal remains largely unexplored territory at this time.

Nepalization

Whilst the census has created a false picture of the dominance of Hinduism in Nepal by over representing the number of respondents who claim this as their sole religion, the opposite technique has reduced the figures for speakers of languages other than Nepali, and in particular the number of Hindi speakers. The census of Nepal treated certain variants of Hindi, which the census of India regarded merely as dialects of Hindi, as completely separate languages. This included Bhojpuri and Maithali and in this way the number of Hindi speakers as a percentage of the national total was reduced, if only on paper. The reasons for this language policy were twofold. Firstly, it gave some legitimacy to the claim made by Bahun and Chetri castes, which comprised native Nepali speakers, that their dominance of government was only representative of the numerical dominance of the Nepalese population as a whole.

The second reason can be found in the regional politics of Nepal. As Fredrick Gaige's (1975) seminal work on this subject demonstrates, the situation of the Tarai and its inhabitants within the nation-state has always been a subject of concern for the government of Nepal. At its most brutal, this has led to outright conflict between the polities of the hill and mountain region and the polities of the plains, although the last manifestation of this was almost two hundred years previously during the Anglo-Nepali war. During the Rana era, these anxieties led to the use of the Tarai as a jungle barrier to prevent incursions into Nepalese territory from the plains. Following the eradication of endemic malaria in the Tarai in the 1950s after an USA sponsored program of insecticide spraying, the Tarai became the area within Nepal with the fastest growing population. It also became an area of massive importance to the economy of Nepal as its agricultural land far outstripped the hill region in terms of productivity and it was the area within which, apart from the Kathmandu Valley, the most rapid urbanization and industrial growth was located. Its position as a border region between the Nepalese hills and the Indian plains is obviously crucial in this regard, but this is also the reason for continued anxieties and unrest, of which the issue of language in the national census is only one manifestation.

Immigration into the Tarai region occurs not only from the direction of the hills but also from India, and it is the questioning of the loyalty of these peoples to the Nepalese state by successive governments that decades before the rise of *janajati* (ethnic) politics in the hill region, led to the formation of political parties based on demands for greater autonomy in the Tarai. Most prominent amongst these since the mid-1980s has been the *Sadbhavana* (Goodwill) *Party*, although more militant organizations that have not shied away from using violence have been at the forefront of more recent protest movements. Despite this party's claims for the special status of the Tarai within the Nepalese state, it remains the case that because the institutions of the state have been structured by the society and culture of the hills, and these institutions have jurisdiction and authority throughout the territory of Nepal, whatever the individual sentiments of the Tarai dweller they have had to carry out their political opposition to the state through those self-same institutions. The linguistic and ethnic diversity of the Tarai population also makes it difficult for parties to mobilize the Tarai as a cohesive political force (Whelpton 1994). This problem is borne out by voting figures. In 1959 the Tarai Congress, the forerunner of the Sadbhavana Party failed to win a single seat. When elections were held in 1991 the Sadbhavana Party won only six seats (2.93% of the total) and polled only 4.1% of the total popular vote, rising to 10% in the seventy six seats it contested.

Gaige uses the term 'Nepalization' to describe this phenomenon of the spread of the Nepali-speaking hill culture into areas that have only come under the control of the Nepalese state comparatively recently. Areas with their own linguistic, cultural and religious traditions have been forced, if not to abandon, to at least subordinate these traditions to the 'official' practices of the nation in their interactions with the state (most noticeably in education). But, he is also careful not to present this as simply an abstract process or a *fait accompli*; rather, it is the result of clear and conscious policies made in the fields of politics, administration and, above all, in education by the Panchayat regime. So, for example, Gaige (1975) was able to show that the ethnic and cultural background of a majority of those working in local government and administration in the Tarai when his study was carried out was in the hills rather than in the Tarai itself. Invariably they were recruited from the triumvirate of castes, Bahun, Chetri and Newar, who dominate the state throughout Nepal (ibid: 166, table 19).

Similarly, applicants for citizenship were required not only to have been resident in Nepal for a considerable length of time, but they were also required to provide proof that they were literate in Nepali as well as able to speak the language. These highly restrictive laws only came into force in the 1960s and effectively disbarred the vast majority of immigrants to the Tarai from legal recognition or involvement in the political process. Panchayat political constituencies included a level of organization, the *anchal* (zone), between that of the district and the national level. Each zone to which Tarai districts belonged also contained hill districts and, according to Gaige, the relative imbalance between the politically active populations of these areas meant that it was invariably the case that Tarai districts were represented by hill dwellers at this zonal level. Numerous other examples of how institutions of the state were, and indeed still are, dominated by 'Hill people' and 'Hill interests' can be offered, but the general point has been made.[21]

The single greatest factor in the process of Nepalization and the construction of Nepalese nationalism is, as S. Shah (1993) states, education. In Nepal, as in all developing countries, education also formed one of the key components of the development efforts of the state. So, whilst increasing the literacy rate was seen as one of the most important factors in the modernization of Nepal, this literacy would emphatically be Nepali literacy. Various amendments to the educational policy pursued in Nepal have been made since

1950, most notably with the so-called New Educational System that was put into operation between 1971 and 1976 with the supposed aim of reducing the elitist character of the educational system (Vir 1988). However, the fundamental character of the Nepalese educational system has remained the same up to the present day. Students proceed through a series of year grades subdivided between primary and secondary institutions. The culmination of this progress comes in the final two years of secondary education when students may be submitted for an examination, the School Leaving Certificate (SLC), which allows for the student to matriculate if passed. The vast majority of students, however, never reach this level and most leave before taking their SLC.[22]

The official language of instruction throughout Nepal is Nepali, the language of the Parbatiya ethnic groups who have dominated the political life of Nepal since the Gorkha conquests of the Eighteenth and Nineteenth Centuries (see Hutt 1988). In both the earliest years of primary education and the upper years of secondary education, however, this is sometimes not the case. In the first instance, recent reforms have allowed for the teaching of very young students in their mother tongue. In the latter case, knowledge of English becomes increasingly important, because it is one of the compulsory components of the SLC.[23] Since the post-1990 liberalization of policy on the control of schools, this has led to a rapid proliferation of private 'boarding schools' offering a completely English medium curriculum (with the exception, of course, of Nepali language classes). Not surprisingly, this is primarily an urban phenomenon as it is only in the towns that parents with a sufficient income and teachers with the requisite skills are available to make such schools viable.

Development

The general point made above about the growth of distinctions within the educational system should now be addressed, because this links us directly to the next major topic of relevance to the construction of Nepali nationalism, which is the ideology of development, *bikās* in Nepali. For, as Stacy Pigg (1992) has shown, this ideology, which is meant to unite the nation through the common goal of the struggle to modernize society and economy, by its very logic also divides the country (both materially and symbolically) into areas of lesser and greater development (*bikasit* and *abikasit* respectively). Not surprisingly, the key axis around which these developmental distinctions arise within Nepal is that of rural and urban society, the country and the city. Meanwhile Nepal itself is characterized as *abikasit* in relation to countries, including its giant neighbor India, that are relatively more *bikasit*, that is developed.[24]

Pigg explains in her influential 1992 article that although 'development' is embodied in objects (she cites new breeds of livestock, water pipes, electricity, videos, schools, commercial fertilizer, roads, airplanes, health posts and medicines as examples of what 'development' typically connotes in common usage) and as such is quantifiable with areas being classified as of greater or lesser development depending on how many of these things they have, the essence of development is in the relationships that then pertain between these areas and the people that inhabit them. Whilst urban areas are places of 'much development' (*dherai bikās*), rural areas and villages tend to be, at best, places of 'little development' (*thorai bikās*), or even 'no development' (*bikās chaina*). She claims that

> this inverse relation between rural areas and degrees of *bikās* gives rise to two ways of representing national society and locating oneself in it. One uses the terms of *bikās* as coordinates to demarcate social territories and pinpoint social positions; the other turns *bikās* and village into the compass points according to which socially located people orient themselves (1992: 499).

Pigg uses Benedict Anderson's notion of the 'imagined community' to argue that in the absence of a colonial presence in Nepal, *bikās* has become the ideology through which a sense of national community has been created despite the problematic "relation between the political entity that forms a basis for a national, Nepalese identity and other social identities" (ibid: 496). But in turn she shows how the prosecution of those same ideological goals has contributed to the creation of new material and symbolic fissures within the population that it seeks to unite.

Communication and movement across these fissures in the socio-economic landscape is also structured according to the logic of bikasi ideology and the patterns of consumption upon which it is predicated. According to its logic, the term 'villager' (*gāūle mānche*) has pejorative connotations that are reinforced through numerous channels of everyday discourse. Pigg provides examples culled from school textbooks and literature distributed by INGOs, including pictures that compare and contrast children supposedly of the present shown in rags carrying heavy loads in *dokos* (the traditional wicker basket seen throughout Nepal) slung across their foreheads, with children of the future in clean clothes and who are playing happily or reading school books. "In fact", says Pigg, "Nepalis are likely to read these pictures as renderings of present-day class difference. Childhood defined as work is the childhood of the village laborer; childhood defined as diligent study and carefree play is the childhood of the landowning or professional, largely urban, elite. What this picture conveys is that everyone's tomorrow will (or should) look like some people's present" (ibid: 500–501).[25]

Social relations, at least as they pertain to class, are mediated through development/*bikāsi* culture and rest upon the ability of agents to influence the flow of resources, encompassing multiple forms of capital (economic, educational, political and cultural), between positions within that landscape. So, for example, the chairman of an NGO based in its office in an urban centre might be assessed by his colleagues and peers in terms of her or his ability to attract funding from foreign donor agencies, whilst a politician representing a village development committee (formerly village panchayat) might be similarly assessed according to whether he or she could attract I/NGOs to work within the local area and provide elements of development infrastructure. We can speak of these agents as powerful in so much as they are positioned at boundary points within the developmental landscape across which resources flow, but as the above discussion makes apparent, there clearly is a hierarchical relationship between those living on the different sides of each boundary. [26]

Blaikie, et al. (1980) describes this situation in terms of a series of embedded, core-periphery relationships. So, whilst Nepal is as a periphery of India, the Kathmandu Valley and its cities is a core area of Nepal and Palpa district is a peripheral area. Within Palpa, of course, the villages of the rural hinterland are peripheral to the core area of Tansen town. Using a metaphor coined by Pierre Bourdieu (1998), we may speak of the differential 'exchange-rates' that exist when making transactions between these core and periphery areas; an agent situated in an upper part of the hierarchy can make an intervention in a lower echelon, but it is extremely difficult for the reverse to happen. It is also the case that the structure of Nepalese bureaucracy, which gives substance to this analytical distinction between areas, makes it almost impossible for agents situated in a lower echelon to cross over more than one boundary at any one time.

Conclusion: The Failure of Panchayat Ideology

The failure of the Panchayat administrations to build effective systems of communication and media in Nepal between 1960 and 1990 cannot be wholly attributed to the inadequacy of the resources available to meet the required needs of such a system. Whilst it must be admitted that the geography and poverty of Nepal have presented huge obstacles to the introduction of modern forms of mass communication, the problems faced within the communication sphere are not just 'quantitative' in character. Given the situation created by the political and cultural policies followed by the Panchayat state, these problems could never be overcome simply by increasing the amount of resources devoted to the mass communication system. This system was introduced with the over-riding, if not sole, aim of giving support to the Panchayat state through the promotion of the linked ideologies of Hinduization, Nepalization and Development described above. Broadcasting in Nepal, in common with the rest of South Asia,

> was an instrument of cultural autarchy, a means to literacy and an educational resource. Using a technical infrastructure built with public resources, it was a vehicle for setting out the preferred ideology of the state as articulated by the government, a means of building a national identity and promoting national culture (Page and Crawley 2001: 263).

This goal proved to be unattainable in Nepal for several interconnected reasons. First, although classic, essentialist theories of political-economy based upon the experience of European history, have tended to make the assumption that entities centered on linguistic and geographical factors exist and are simply called into being by the nation through instrumentalist means, such as media and communication technologies, these assumptions were never tenable in the context of Nepal.[27] Indeed, as was argued above, the factors which have been assumed to work most forcefully to bring about unity, such as education and media, often have contradictory effects and new forms of identity based upon rediscovered or reinvented ethnic, gender and/or religious difference have come into being.

The preceding sections of this chapter have dealt with the implications of this point in detail. It is this general failure of communications policy prior to the revolution of 1990 that forms the backdrop both to the development of local media in Tansen and its analysis in this study.

A second point derived from the general lessons learnt from studies of media audiences in many different societies also leads us to question whether grand aims such as nation building can be realized in practice. Far from eliciting a common response from the reading, viewing or listening publics, audience members have repeatedly been shown to react quite differently to identical messages depending upon variation in their social characteristics or position vis-à-vis the originator of the message.[28] Whilst this is hardly surprising, it has also been shown that media, both in terms of their technological form and content (hardware and software), can provide material and symbolic resources through which these same characteristics and positions can be actively supported or resisted.

This chapter described the introduction of and uses sought for media by successive political regimes in Nepal and described how transformations in the use of these media can be related to changes in the 'nation-building' aspirations of these regimes. This history has been characterized by the essential contradiction identified by Anderson in the quotation at the start of this chapter. Individual regimes have sought to foster national unity with a view to preserving their power and legitimacy in the eyes of both the citizens of Nepal and internationally, but these efforts have also threatened to bring other, competing identities and loyalties to the fore. For the sake of this summary, we may broadly divide this history into three periods: Pre-Panchayat, Panchayat and post-Panchayat.

During both the first and second periods, communication within Nepal was monopolized by the state with a view to protecting the domination of the ruling regime. In the first period, however, the state attempted to isolate the populace from influences that might challenge the traditional systems of authority and control upon which the regime relied. It was impossible to maintain such restrictions, even before the use of electronic media became common, given the close proximity of 'free' Nepali media in India, which contributed to the collapse of this regime.

The Panchayat regime, recognizing that this was the case, reversed the policy of a closed media, if not the policy of a controlled media, and used new systems of communication to encourage mass support for the regime under an aggressive nationalist ideology which promoted 'Nepali' culture, Hinduism and 'Development' (bikās) as the shared ideals of all citizens. The spread of new forms of media, especially electronic media like radio and television, was promoted by the regime as a key indicator of the achievement of these development goals and, therefore, of the legitimacy of the regime.

Joshi and Rose (1966), writing in an era before the concepts of 'development' and 'modernization' had come to be widely criticized, considered that only one out of their three requirements for nation-building had been achieved in Nepal. Neither "rationalization of the political process in conformity with the circumstances, needs, and history of the country", nor "rationalization of the problem-solving administrative machinery" had been achieved in the fifteen years following the 1950 revolution (ibid.: 515–516). They believed that only the last of their criteria, the creation of "a sense of national unity and solidarity", had been achieved during this period and even then, they qualified this statement with the observation that "this sense of Nepali nationalism is still largely confined to the people of central Nepal" (ibid: 517). Nevertheless, they continued,

> there are indications that it [Nepali nationalism] is spreading to the remoter hill areas to the east and west of Kathmandu and even to the Tarai under the avowedly nationalistic goals of the present [Panchayat] regime. The development of transportation and communication facilities, the continuing expansion of educational facilities, and the dominant political role of the Crown may help to unify the country in the psychological as well as the political sense.

This statement serves as a useful example of 'classic' assumptions regarding the largely functional and supposedly politically unproblematic role of mass media and communication in the process of identity formation, especially as it relates to questions of national identity (Page and Crawley 2001: 32).

Over thirty years later, this assumption has been shown to be only one amongst a whole gamut of possible outcomes of the production and consumption of mass media in the context of the nation-state. Other possibilities can be shown to exist.[29] Kievelitz (1996) argues that variable and apparently contradictory situations can arise from the process of nation building; the use of mass media is a key component of this process.

One possibility is that the lives of the nations citizens may be affected by the spread of what Ulf Hannerz (1992) has referred to as "the global ecumene." Superficially similar to the extreme position of commentators who predict the eventual homogenization of all world culture, the global ecumene describes instead the emergence of a trans-national, predominantly bourgeois, cultural space facilitated by the increasing spread of access to modes of communication and transport that enable the exchange of common cultural forms. As such, the global ecumene is not only a cultural space, but it is also a space structured by national political and economic circumstances, because the cost of access to this space (even in the developed countries of the West, never mind the developing world) restricts the socio-economic composition the ecumene's inhabitants.

The opposite extreme in terms of the *results* of this process of nation building is the recent emergence of what Kievelitz (1996: 5) calls "politically vociferous form[s] of ethnicity [which] only developed as a response to the threat of nationalism which tended to neglect, even tried to eradicate, ethnic difference", referring here to a general process of ethnic identity formation which, he asserts, is "a universal process in time and space." Somewhat ironically, the introduction of modern communication technology and media to Nepal may, as elsewhere, have provided the very means through which this new sense of ethnic identity has been made manifest. Whilst national unity was the idealized aim of successive government's media policies, the results in practice contributed to the growth or re-emergence of fissures within Nepalese society. Paramount amongst these has been the growth of *jati* (that is, ethnic) consciousness and a split between *bikāsi* and *abikāsi* (that is, developed and undeveloped) sections of society. Not surprisingly this latter set of distinctions is primarily made manifest in the contrasting forms of urban and rural society that have arisen in Nepal during the past three decades.

The third phase of this media history, the post-1990 democratic era, might be seen simply as bringing to fruition the trends noted above. Political opposition to the Panchayat regime throughout the 1980s finally forced King Birendra in 1990 to recognize in the constitution and political system political realities that could no longer remain hidden, despite the denials of the official ideology promulgated through the state's media; the different social groups and political interests that existed in Nepal could not be politically subsumed within the framework of the Panchayat system. A unified, Nepalese national identity could be defined in relation to surrounding nations or political entities, most notably India, but within the boundary of the nation itself distinctions arose that, within certain contexts, could not be easily reconciled with this national identity.

It is from such emerging fissures in the ideology that had previously held Nepal together that local media developments in Tansen (specifically cable television) emerged during the post-Panchayat era in Nepal. As we shall see in the following chapters, these fissures were experienced not in abstract sense but in terms of concrete socio-cultural distinctions rooted in the history and experiences of the community. Some of Tansen's citizens used new media technologies and institutions that are typically regarded as products of either powerful state institutions or of global business to give expression to these experiences, and in so doing attempt to exert some influence over the emerging directions that their lives were taking.

Notes

1. This tendency is apparent in work carried out within the boundaries of Nepal's media studies tradition, such as Khatri (1976), Malla (1982), Serle et al. (1993), Sharma (1980) and *Communications in Nepal* (1988). Work by anthropologists, such as Grandin (1989 and 1994) or Liechty (1994, 1998 and 2003), has perhaps not surprisingly, given qualitative variations in media and communication use in Nepal greater prominence.

2. Some sense of the restricted nature of the Rana era postal system is given by the contrast between the number of post offices in the Rana and post-Rana eras. By 1880, forty-three post offices were operating and this had doubled to ninety by 1950. In the three years to 1954 a further thirty-four offices were added to the system, but by 1981 the figure stood at over one thousand two hundred (Bajracharya and Shrestha 1981).

3. For some analysts, most notably and controversially Dor Bahadur Bista (1991), this factor continues to play a crucial detrimental role in the functioning of contemporary Nepalese society.

4. This paper by Declan Quigley is important because he emphasizes very clearly that 'Hinduization' and 'Sanskritization' are quite distinct sociological phenomena, even if the underlying political cause might be the same. The former describes the actions of a particular institution, the state, in promulgating an official ideology, Hinduism and the caste system, through which its constituent systems will be organized. The second describes the actions of particular groups or even individuals to a situation in which their enfranchisement and legitimation by the state depends upon conformity to a set of conventions based upon Hinduism and the caste system.

5. Gledhill (1994) notes that in explicitly colonial situations the objectifying framework of bureaucracy transformed indigenous elite culture, especially in matters such as religious affiliation. "Colonialism draws colonized peoples into the process of 'objectifying' their traditions, and therefore spreads this particular characteristic of Western 'modernity' at an early stage of incorporation" (ibid.: 182). The internal situation in Nepal during the Rana period has clear affinities with the processes of colonialism described by Gledhill. As such we should not underestimate the extent to which the Rana era provides a foundation for the era of 'modernization' that followed the overthrow of the regime in 1950.

6. Initially only a weekly publication, by 1943 Gorkhapatra was bi-weekly, and by 1946 tri-weekly, although it was not until 1961 that it started daily publication.

7. It is unfortunate that, as Stiller (1993: 136) says, "we have today no sample of the suggestions the Prime Minister found in these boxes"!

8. The raw national figure does, however, hide a great disparity within Nepal between both younger and older sections of the population and between men and women. So, for example, in 1991 literacy rates for men and women ranged between 76% [males aged 10–14 years] and 24% [males aged 60–64 years], and 49% [females aged 10–14 years] and 3.1% [females aged 60–64 years] (HMG, Nepal 1995: 378, Table 16).

9. And that wealth should not be under-estimated. According to Stiller (1993), when Prime Minister Chandra Shamser Rana died in 1929 he left a staggering sum equivalent to 41 million pounds Sterling in cash and securities, and large amounts of agricultural land and palaces to his heirs (see also Regmi 1978).

10. King Tribhuvan had, after all, sought refuge in the Indian Embassy in Kathmandu and then in India itself after escaping from confinement in the royal palace.

11. Although the initial effect of the return to dictatorship was a severe drop in the number of newspapers published in Nepal, by 1970 the figure had risen to fifty-two (more than existed prior to establishment of the Panchayat) and eighty-four by 1980 (Aditya 1996: 44, fig. 3).

12. Aditya (1996) gives figures of 459 newspapers in circulation in 1985, a more than five fold increase in five years. According to *Communications in Nepal* (1988: 23–24, Table 2.7) there were 448 government-registered newspapers available throughout Nepal in the fiscal year 1986/87. Of these, fifty-nine were published daily, two twice weekly, three hundred and forty weekly and forty-seven fortnightly. An overwhelming proportion of these were published in the major cities of the Kathmandu Valley and most of these in Kathmandu (223 in Kathmandu, thirty in Patan and seven in Bhaktapur). Of the remainder, 144 were published in Tarai districts and forty-four in hill or mountain districts, including three in Palpa District (two weekly and one fortnightly).

13. Figures from *Communications in Nepal* (1988: 48–52, Table 5.1).

14. The reliability of these figures is, however, called into question by the fact that the two studies referred to here were carried out by independent research consultancies

based in Kathmandu and came up with widely varying estimates for the total number radios in use in Nepal (1.2 to 2.2 million)!

15. Other languages did feature in the musical content of Radio Nepal, but even here attempts were made to limit their extent, either by playing non-lyrical versions of songs from other Nepalese linguistic and cultural groups or singing versions that had Nepali lyrics substituted for the originals (Grandin 1989).

16. Page and Crawley (2001: 28) note; "In the new era of liberalization, the tendency of different governments has been to follow global trends and leave broadcasting increasingly to market forces. One of the questions we examine...is whether this makes sense for states in which as many as 40 per cent of the population is defined as poor."

17. The interim constitution of Nepal promulgated after the 2006 revolt against King Gyanendra's direct rule effectively declares Nepal to be a secular state.

18. The official figure from the 1991 census for Hinduism is 86.5% and Nepali as mother tongue is 50.3% (HMG 1994)

19. Anderson's (1991: 184) observations are illuminating in this regard:

Interlinked with one another, then, the census, the map and the museum illuminate the late colonial state's style of thinking about its domain. The 'warp' of this thinking was a totalizing classificatory grid, which could be applied with endless flexibility to anything under the state's real or contemplated control: peoples, regions, religions, languages, products, monuments, and so forth. The effect of the grid was always to be able to say of anything that it was this, not that; it belonged here not there. It was bounded, determinate, and therefore—in principle—countable. (The comic classificatory and subclassificatory census boxes entitled 'Other' concealed all real-life anomalies by a splendid bureaucratic *trompe l'oeil*). The 'weft' was what one could call serialization: the assumption that the world was made up of replicable plurals. The particular always stood as a provisional representative of a series, and was to be handled in this light. This was why the colonial state imagined a Chinese series before any Chinese, and a nationalist series before the appearance of a nationalist.

20. Hoftun and Raeper (1992: 75) go on to add that, "the main factor of social stability in Nepal was reckoned to be the caste system. The Chetris and Brahmins stood at the forefront of an elaborate and intricate social pattern that kept any possible conflicts at bay. In such a controlled society a political revolution in the traditional sense of the word was simply unthinkable. For this reason also, what happened in 1990 came to many as a shock." They were thinking, perhaps, of comments such as this by Jan Pieper (1975: 69):

It is hard for us inhabitants of an urban environment not rooted in an esoteric world of ideas to understand the importance which the Hindus attach to the supernatural of their cities. The townsfolk live in a strange mixture of veneration and fear, and this made the Hindu urban culture such a suitable foundation for the classical oriental system of total power . . . Urban unrest—so common all through European history—never occurred in India before 1857, and is still an impossibility in the three cities of Nepal.

A contrasting view of "the Hindus attach[ment] to the supernatural of their cities" described by Pieper can be found amongst the illustrations of Hoftun and Raeper's account of the 1990 Jana Andolan: the caption for a plate illustrating their book reads,

"Temple idols used to build barricades around the city centre during the uprising in Patan (end of March 1990)" (eighth plate between pp.116 and 117).

21. To give one more example, this time from my own experience: during the course of my fieldwork, I was invited by a student who I had met in Tansen to travel with him to his family's home in Parasi, the headquarters of Nawalparasi district in the Tarai just to the southeast of Palpa. He explained to me that his family was descended from Bahuns who had originated in the hill district of Gulmi, but during his grandfather's time they had decided to sell their land in the hills and invest it instead in the Tarai. Originally the family had moved to the village of Manari, four kilometers to the east of Parasi, where they still owned land that was farmed by tenant farmers who were Tharu and who dominated the population of this village. Apart from farming the family also ran the local post office and even now, after leaving Manari to move to Parasi, the mother and paternal aunt of my friend were involved in the running of the post office in the town. His father was an officer in the branch of the District Administration that organized agricultural development work throughout the district. In short, this family provided an almost paradigmatic example of how the ownership and control of both land and institutions like the post office or development organizations in the Tarai was in the hands of 'Hill' people rather than indigenous Tarai people.

22. The figures for SLC passes are extremely low as a percentage of the total population who reach secondary level education: 1971 equaled 0.34%; 1981 equaled 1.23%; and 1991 equaled 2.88%. The number of females as a percentage of the total has risen from 32.4% in 1971, to 36.6% in 1981 and 45.5% in 1991.

23. The role of Sanskrit teaching in the Nepalese educational system is also a point of some contention. Attempts to make it a compulsory subject of study have been vigorously rejected by groups for whom Sanskrit is a totally alien language on the grounds that it acts as a *de facto* barrier to their children's educational progress.

24. This ideology of development is inevitably contains within it the conditions that maintain hierarchies of inequality because, as Gewertz and Errington (1991) note, the ultimate end point of development, the living standards of the First World, are unobtainable.

25. People in Tansen would often assert these sorts of rural-urban distinction in terms of different sorts of views, sometimes sentimental and sometimes scornful. So, for example, one male friend upon seeing a trail of mules carrying loads of cement being lead through the streets of the bazaar commented upon the beauty of the girl leading the caravan and attributed this to the simple and uncorrupted life of the villages where, he assumed, they were heading. In contrast to this, another friend who noticed that I was reading a copy of *Deurali*, a newspaper produced and edited in Tansen and aimed at a rural audience, remarked that the Nepali used in its reports was so simple that reading it would make me stupid, implying of course that I would be reduced to the same level of intellect as its rural readership.

26. A vivid illustration of this arose during the early months of my fieldwork when I went with my wife to visit the town of Ridi, on the western border of Palpa district, to see the town's famous *Rishikesh Jatra* [Rishikesh Festival]. Friends in Tansen told us that we could stay at the house of a local politician and telephoned ahead to arrange our accommodation. This politician, a physically imposing man who had served in the Indian army and won several awards for his boxing skills, had represented the town at the district level during the Panchayat era and was now a firm supporter of the *Rastriya Prajatantra Party* (RPP), the rightwing monarchist party. He boasted to us of the development works that he had brought to his 'village', works that included a permanently manned health-post and a microwave telephone. This telephone, the only one in the town, was for public use, but located in a small room on the ground floor of the

politician's house; control over access to it and the collection of payment for its use was also in his hands.

27. Such attempts have been subject to considerable criticism in relation to the history of European nation-states in recent years (see E. Gellner 1988).

28. Page and Crawley (200: 342) note the potentially disabling effects upon South Asian governments' policies of a belief in the "omnipotent power of the mass media to form and educate opinion by conveying information and approved messages."

29. See also the previous discussion of alternative media in chapter 2.

Chapter 4
The Rise and Fall of a Hill Town

What the Gorkha rulers had, that British Indians lacked, was some semblance of sovereignty; here defined as the right to exercise one's will in both external and internal spheres of action. From the Gorkha point of view sovereignty was central to any claim—made either by king or subject—of leading an authentic Hindu life. The Gorkhali entitlement to act did not imply, however, that they could make the world their own, for their powers of agency operated within a larger world already organized for them by the imperial seats of authority at Delhi and London, Lhasa and Peking. Despite their sovereignty, Nepal found itself as a peripheral power constantly seeking some measure of autonomy in terms of the hegemonic discourses of others. The political discourse of Nepal, including its claims of Hindu rule, must always be interpreted, therefore, as a periphery speaking to an alien centre.

Richard Burghart (1996: 261–2)

Introduction

Prior to the annexation of Palpa by the house of Gorkha and the extension of Gorkha's sovereignty into the western Himalayan regions less than 200 years ago, Tansen was the capital of an independent state. This chapter describes how this independence was lost and the subsequent history of Palpa within the state of Nepal in order to explain how the characteristics of Palpa district and more specifically Tansen town, came into being. Such an analysis is essential given that CDP/RCTV claims its key functions and means of legitimation to be the role it plays in expressing the views and identity of the local population in the face of the hegemonic media discourses that speak from the 'alien' centers of Kathmandu (NTV), New Delhi (Doordarshan) and elsewhere (via satellite television). The diachronic, 'historical' perspective offered by this chapter is counter-balanced by the next, which adopts a synchronic, 'sociological' perspective on the town, its population and culture.

As the opening quotation from the ethnohistorical work of Richard Burghart (1996) makes clear, the relationship of a 'peripheral' state such as Nepal to the 'core' states with whom it must deal has been and continues to be a key factor in the historical development of the nation-state. This structure of political economy is mirrored within the borders of Nepal itself, dominated as it is by the distinction between internal 'core' regions of the capital in the Kathmandu Valley and provincial areas like Palpa that are often regarded as 'peripheral'. Just as the hierarchical relationship between states must be taken into account for the wider geopolitics of the South Asian region to be understood, so to must an understanding of the internal social, economic and political complexities of Nepal itself be taken into account.[1] Such an argument clearly serves to emphasize the importance of writing 'local' history, as is the case here, but the implication of this argument is also that the history of Nepal as a whole cannot be written without attention to the role that a multiplicity regions, ethnic groups and polities played in this history. This is particularly so given that the history of this relatively young nation-state is dominated by the processes of its continuing (re-) creation. The history contained in this chapter is local only in terms of its geographical focus, because the implications of this analysis regarding the constitution of the Nepali state are of much wider relevance.

The historical analysis of this chapter also provides the next element of the contextual prism through which the production of alternative forms of local media in Tansen must be understood. It serves to underline the argument contained in the previous chapters that any general understanding of media must take into account the ways in which their uses are adapted to suit local circumstances. The history of Tansen also shows that international cultural, economic and political influences upon the life of this community are not just an occurrence of recent times. Indeed, it can be argued that the existence of Tansen is the result of the interaction of British-India and Nepal in the Nineteenth Century. This chapter, therefore, provides historical depth to the analysis of media development and helps us to avoid naïve accounts that view recent or contemporary times as radically different to what may have come before.

The Conquest and Annexation of Palpa by the Emerging Nepali State (1769–1850)

In June 1804 AD, Palpa became the last independent kingdom within the boundaries of the modern day Nepali state to be absorbed into the realm ruled by the Shah Kings of Gorkha. Since its establishment by the Sen Dynasty in the mid-Fifteenth Century, the Kingdom of Palpa had been a major participant in the competition for political and military domination in the Himalayan region. Now in a matter of weeks, the political entity that was the Kingdom of Palpa disappeared.

The Sen Kings had a shared history and close affinity with the Shah dynasty. Both were reputed to be descended from Rajput warrior kings who had entered the Himalayan region following the Mughal invasions of northern India in the Tenth Century. As Rishikesh Shah explains, the Hindu chieftains from Rajasthan who made their way into the hills to carve out new principalities "sought to trace their ancestry to some Indian Rajput clan or the other, but the links they tried to establish were, at best, tenuous" (R. Shah 1992: 64). The Sen dynasty was no exception to this and variously claimed descent from the kings of Bengal who allegedly fled to the Himalayas after their defeat at the hands of the rising Mughal power in the Indian Plains in AD 1200 and, alternatively, Chittaur Rajputs who fled to Nepal in AD 1304 (Ghimire 1990). Ghimire demonstrates that neither of these claims can be conclusively supported with historical evidence (ibid: 16–17), although he does favor the latter claim in his own account of the Sen Kingdoms of Palpa.[2] Several factors lead Ghimire towards this belief, including documented evidence of marriages between the Palpali Sen and Rajput leaders in India, the common worship of the Hindu deities Kali and Bhagwati, and the use of certain common symbols such as the sun and the moon in royal iconography. Such evidence is, however, circumstantial and alternative possibilities can be considered.

A process of Sanskritization through which the indigenous ruling lineages (Khas in the case of Gorkha and Magar in Palpa's case) took on the military, administrative and ritual trappings of their illustrious neighbors, may be an alternative explanation for similarities between the cultural characteristics of the ruling elite in the Himalayan hill states and the Rajputs in India (Stiller 1995: 48–53; cf. Srinavas 1952). The ruling families in many of the Himalayan kingdoms of the Chaubise Rajya (literally 'Twenty Four Kingdoms'), the loose affiliation of tiny states that existed in the central and western Himalayan region, governed populations that were certainly made up of a majority of Magar, Gurung and other hill peoples. In the case of Palpa, Magar troops formed the vast majority of the army and, because leading soldiers were often rewarded for their services with land grants and land ownership was the basis for a person's standing as a noble, many of the local 'aristocracy' would have been Magar. As Ghimire (1990) notes, intermarriage between members of the nobility would have led to a mixing of lineages.

Stiller's comment on this question is worth quoting: "Without entering into the popular but historically sterile question of which families in Greater Nepal, if any, were spurious, i.e., who claimed Rajput descent without being truly Rajputs, an assessment must be made of the impact of the Rajputs on the history of this period" (1995: 49). Here Stiller acknowledges that whether by actual migration and conquest, by political usurpation of power, or simply by the adoption of an innovative form of rule with an attendant cultural system, the influence of the Rajputs and their turbulent history upon the state of the Himalayas must be acknowledged.

It should be noted that these issues retain their importance even today as the following extract from my field notes indicates. I had met with a young Magar 'social worker' and during our conversation we began to discuss the role of ethnicity in contemporary politics:

> He says that the main social problem in Nepal is linked to the Hindu religion because it is through Hinduism that Bahunism, the institutionalized dominance of the Bahun caste, is made legitimate. He notes that this system is deeply entrenched, Nepal being officially recognized as a Hindu kingdom in the constitution. He sees no difference between the old Panchayat constitution and the post-democracy constitution in this respect.
>
> To illustrate how Bahunism dominates Nepal's 'polluted politics' he cites the dominance of both the Nepal Congress and UML parties by Bahuns. They are both identical in this respect in that they are dominated by 'high level people'. He says that the Bahuns have monopolized power through a policy of 'divide and rule', which has separated brothers along the false lines of left and right even though the parties are identical. He uses the similarity of identical *raksī* (liquor) with only a different color to describe how the parties are the same. They look different, but the taste is the same and you get equally drunk on both of them. The only way that 'low people' can enter this political mainstream is by attempting to raise their caste, but this requires them ultimately to go to Kathmandu and they are then separated from their original community.
>
> He gives an example of how this process of raising of caste can still have great power today even if the rise occurred well over one hundred and fifty years ago. An historian, Vishnu Kumar Palli, wrote a book called *Ithihās Bitrakar Magarharu* ('A History of the Magars') in which he claimed that Bhimsen Thapa, the famous Prime Minister of early Nineteenth Century Nepal, was from a Magar family. Bhimsen Thapa's family then came to Tansen [presumably because this is where Palli lives] to ask the CDO Lalit Bdr. Thapa (who is Magar, one should note) to arrest the author on the grounds that he was slandering their family. The CDO said that if the family could come up with any evidence that what Palli had said was not true then he would immediately arrest him. The family then returned to Kathmandu and apparently after several months sent a letter to the CDO admitting that they could not find any evidence to refute the claims.
>
> He notes that both Chetris and Magars use the surnames Thapa and Rana and that families have inevitably got mixed up during the past centuries. Even so, he says, Magars are still discriminated against in government and are seldom given high office. One of Palpa's MPs is a Magar, but my informant says that he will never speak out in favor of his own community because to do so would debar him permanently from office.

A related point is that, although the 'styles' of rule and the courts of the ruling elite were heavily influenced by orthodox forms of Hinduism derived from a Rajput model, this trend would have cross-cut any 'racial' or ethnic divisions amongst the ruling elite because from the centuries of the Mughal invasions onwards this developed into a common ideology through which monarchical authority was asserted and legitimated in the Himalayan region (Hamilton 1986 [1819]: 101–102; cf. Burghart 1984). Nevertheless, Stiller (1995) doubts whether this ideology led to innovation in the fundamental revenue structures of the hill states. "In many of the hill states the Rajput raja and his immediate followers were apparently not deeply involved in the details of government, and allowed the local structures to carry on much as they had before the emergence of the Rajputs as a ruling class. The raja's main concern seems to have been his position vis-à-vis the other principalities in his neighborhood and the expansion or defense of his personal prerogatives" (ibid: 52).[3]

Our present knowledge of the early history of these Himalayan states is not sufficient to assess the efficiency of their administration relative to those which they had replaced or other contemporary South Asian states. But it is probably the case that the adherence to a shared, religiously-grounded culture did contribute towards the ability to rule during this period. We should not forget that this region is one in which transport and communication is, even today, extremely difficult; three hundred years ago this was an over-riding factor in the life of all Himalayan peoples, both rulers and subjects (Stiller 1995: 1–9 and 1993: 7). Political power was theoretically in the hands of an absolute ruler with his (or, during occasional times of regency, her) centre of power at the court (darbār), but such centralizing tendencies were hard to put into practice.

The system of land control prevalent during this period arose in the context of this extreme environment as an answer to this problem of communication. All land was considered to be the inalienable property of the state, in effect of the king, but in practice, very little land was retained for the direct use of the monarch and the durbar (Regmi 1978). Payment for service to the state in a largely non-monetized economy was usually given in the form of some sort of rights over the tenure and control of land. This could either be in the form of a permanent land grant (birtā) or a yearly warrant for control (jāgir) that could be renewed at the annual assessment (pajani) of the state's servants. As Stiller (1995) states, this system was capable of being used very effectively by the Gorkha king Prithvi Narayan Shah to reward and motivate his troops and supporters because land, at a premium in the Himalayas, was the ultimate reward guaranteeing prosperity and prestige.

At a time of stability and consolidation, however, the system could prove disastrous as more and more land and the income it generated was taken out of the control of the state and put into the hands of 'private' individuals. "The Gorkhali rulers sustained their monopoly over political power by sharing the economic benefits of that power with the aristocracy and the bureaucracy in this manner. Those groups, consequently, appropriated a part of the economic resources that otherwise would have accrued to the state" (Regmi 1984: 213). Ultimately, little income was left for the state to invest in improving the overall economic situation. The birtā/jāgir system was also used to solve the problem of regional administration with the landholder, or his agent, being given many judicial and administrative responsibilities in the area of the land holding. In effect, the state was absolving its responsibility to govern in many areas that were ostensibly under the control of the ruling monarch.

Burghart (1984) warns us to avoid becoming ethnocentric or even historocentric in our judgment of the rulers of the past because it is the case that the ideology of kingship and rule in the pre- and immediate post-unification period was significantly different to that with which we have become familiar through theorization based on European models of political economy. He argues that although the nation-state, "mean[ing] a form of government that is seen to be an expression of the will or character of a culturally unique people and whose political boundaries are delimited with reference to the territorial distribution of the people...is current in present-day Nepal, there is no evidence that it existed in governmental discourse during the period of Nepalese expansion across the southern flank of the Himalayas at the turn of the Nineteenth Century" (Burghart 1984: 101). Instead, Burghart describes a situation in which a distinction is made between the realm (*deśa*) within which the ruler exerts ritual authority and the territorial unit within which the king has proprietorial authority, the organization of which has already been described above. The two need not have necessarily been synonymous. Further hierarchical distinctions are drawn within a realm between the capital (*mūla deś*), which was the center of ritual power located at the site of the ruler's tutelary or patron deity, and the provinces or districts (*prades*), each with their own loci of ritual action. "Provincial ritual enactments of universal import [i.e. those that affected the moral order of the realm] could not be undertaken without the approval of the central authority" (ibid: 106). Having said this, day-to-day governance and revenue collection within each of the districts was carried out by a governor appointed by the king, who took upon himself the functions of the king within the territory under his administration:

> Each lord possessed judicial, fiscal, and ritual duties over territory in the same way that the king possessed these rights and duties over the kingdom. Therefore, the administrative hierarchy of the traditional Hindu polity did not comprise relationships between functionally differentiated parts; instead, it comprised relationships between functionally undifferentiated parts. Each rank within the pyramid of authority was a kingship over an administrative unit that was defined territorially. The territorial jurisdiction of each successively higher rank englobed the territorial jurisdiction of the ranks below. At the highest rank was the king who ruled the largest territorial unit, the kingdom (Burghart 1996: 40–41)

This hierarchical relationship between centre and province could encompass newly conquered territories, a political relationship that would be signified and enacted through the adoption of the vanquished rulers' tutelary deity by the victorious ruler. The Gorkha conquest of Palpa provides a vivid illustration of this process in action as well as of this era's politics.

In the period prior to the unification of Nepal by the house of Gorkha the small states immediately to the west of Gorkha, the *Chaubisi* (Twenty-Four) and *Baisi* (Twenty) Rajas, were organized into a series of military and political alliances. Pre-eminent amongst these was the Palpa Alliance consisting of Palpa, Ghiring, Rising, Gulmi, Argha, Khanchi and Jagarkot. Not only did this alliance consist of states that occupied rich agricultural land, including large sections of the Tarai, and productive mines, but Palpa also had close political ties to the neighboring state of Avādh (Oudh). If it retained its cohesion, this alliance could have blocked Gorkha's advance into the western Himalayas almost indefinitely (Stiller 1995). It was the diplomacy, rather than the military strength, of Gorkha instigated by Bahadur Shah, de facto ruler (if not king) of Gorkha, that led to the destruction of this alliance.[4]

In 1785, the king of Palpa, Mahadutta Sen, formalized a new alliance with Gorkha by marrying his daughter, Bidya Laxmi, to Bahadur Shah. To Hamilton, writing in the early decades of the Nineteenth Century, this appeared to be an act of villainy, perhaps even stupidity. By splitting Palpa away from her allies in the central hills those allies were left without their surest defense, support from the south and possibly from Avādh. The end for these states was not long in coming and by October 1786, they had been conquered. After a decade any value for Palpa that the marriage alliance might have had was ended with Bahadur Shah's disgrace and death instigated by the young and ambitious king Rana Bahadur Shah, who had by then come of age.

By the last years of the Eighteenth Century, Rana Bahadur Shah faced a new threat to the almost unchallenged power of the Gorkhali state in the Himalayan region. The British East India Company had extended its dominion as far as the foothills of the Himalayas and this included de facto control of Avādh. Prithvi Pal Sen had begun to seek help from the Company, including requests for military support, to reinforce his claim to the territory controlled by the Palpali state. This led Rana Bahadur Shah to act decisively to end the threat posed to Gorkha by the continued existence of a state that thrust into the middle of her territory and which could provide a conduit for British intervention in the very heart of the Himalayas.

Hamilton provides us with a concise description of Prithvi Pal Sen's character: "[he] was endowed with great personal vigor, nor was he, I believe, at all scrupulous about personal means; but he seems to have been rash and credulous, which rendered him totally unable to resist the wiles of the people of Gorkha" (1986: 174). It was this fatal character flaw that, according to Hamilton, led him to accept an invitation to travel to Kathmandu in 1804, supposedly to receive the hand of Rana Bahadur Shah's sister in marriage. After arriving in Kathmandu, however, Prithvi Pal Sen was imprisoned, along with his four hundred-strong retinue, and eventually executed. Palpa was occupied only one month later by a force of Gorkhali troops led by Amar Singh Thapa, father of Rana Bahadur's chief minister (*mukhtiyār*) Bhim Sen Thapa.

Prithvi Pal Sen's personal weaknesses probably did contribute to his downfall, but other possibilities are raised by Burghart's interesting work on Nepalese kingship. The Palpali king had already been imprisoned once in Kathmandu following a previous invitation to attend a religious ceremony involving the ritual cleansing of Rana Bahadur's son. Hamilton comments that the official reason for Prithvi Pal Sen's invitation to perform the *ṭikā* ceremony was that "among the hill chiefs he was considered as the most eminent by birth" (Hamilton 1986: 174). As such, the mark of his royal status would guarantee the purity of the child by associating him with the purity of the monarch who was supposedly *primus inter pares* amongst the rulers of the hill realms (*deśharū*), even if by then the de facto political, economic and military domination of Gorkha was obvious to all. Prithvi Pal Sen had been naïve enough to believe in 1803 that this ritual status would protect him and in 1804, he paid for this miscalculation with his life.

As Stiller notes, the annexation of Palpa marked a watershed in Gorkhali foreign policy in the hills because for the first time the Nepalese state came into direct conflict with the British East India Company. "The Nepal government maintained on principle their right to all the lands dependent on a hill kingdom when the kingdom was conquered or taken under Gorkha's supervision. Their claim in 1805 to the Butwal *jamindāri* [lands controlled by the state and rented out to private tenants] of Palpa, however, was summarily rejected in a letter from the governor general to the Nepali *vakīl* [lawyer] in Calcutta" (Stiller 1995: 276). The disagreement between the two powers in this region, which was to lead to full scale war ten years later, was exacerbated by the fact that neither side understood fully the terms through which their dialogue and argument was carried out. The British maintained a sovereign claim upon these Tarai lands on the basis of a treaty signed with the Nepali government in 1801. However, as Burghart (1984) explains, the Nepalese recognized a separation between actual occupation and exploitation of a particular piece of land on the one hand and the monarch's right to claim the land as part of his realm (*deś*) on the other.

The key means through which such claims were signified and upheld within newly conquered territories was "to treat all realms as being equivalent and to respect the tutelary deities of each conquered realm" (Burghart 1984: 105). This was certainly the case in Palpa, but the situation here also suggests that the transfer of power between the Sen and Shah dynasties was not as seamless as this theory might suggest. Immediately after the conquest, in 1806, a temple dedicated to Narayan (Vishnu) was built near Srinagar Hill by Amar Singh Thapa, now installed as the first governor of Palpa, as was the parade ground (*tundik-hel*). Not only was this a temple dedicated to a Vaishnava sect wholly different in its religious character to that of the Tantric deities, such as Bhairab, famously patronized by the Sen kings of Palpa, but it was also constructed in the Newari 'pagoda' style of the Kathmandu Valley's cities as opposed to the *sikhar* (lit. summit, peak) style that characterized most of the temples in Palpa at that time (Ghimire 1990).[5] As such, this temple would have been a highly visible symbol of the arrival of a new authority in the region.

This reminder would have been further manifested every year during the festivals of Narayan and Bhagwati that saw the chariots of the deities taken from their inner sanctums amidst much pomp and ceremony and paraded around the precincts of the town. These festivals still occur today; indeed the Bhagwati Jatra is blessed every year by a descendent of Ujir Singh Thapa, and is attended by the vast majority of the town's residents and many people from the surrounding area (Baniya 2053 VS). It is impossible to gauge the effect that such a spectacle would have had on the people of Palpa almost two hundred years ago, but it would be difficult to surpass as a symbol of political power manifested through the body of the ruler's patron deity.

Mention of the construction of these temples also raises the question of who the inhabitants of Tansen were at this time. Whilst there was already a settlement of some sort on this site, the immediate post-annexation period undoubtedly saw growth. The Sen rulers had a fort on the summit of Srinagar hill above the present day town and the remains of this can still be seen today. Lower down the hill near the present day bazaar we know that the *tundikhel* (parade ground, literally 'archery ground') was created during the Sen Period and this would suggest the presence of barracks, although where they might have been is uncertain. The Ananda Bihar (Buddhist monastery), which overlooks the *tundikhel*, is also thought to have originated during the Sen Period (Ghimire 1990: 123). The personal comments of some present day citizens also suggested that temples erected by the Sen Rulers on the sites of the Amar Narayan and Bhagwati temples may have been demolished to make way for these new buildings, but I have no corroborative evidence for this. Finally, we have the original name of the town itself, *Tansing*, a Magar word meaning 'northern settlement', which clearly indicates prior settlement on this site (Kasajoo 1988:17; cf. Adhikary 1996). The adoption of 'Tansen' as the common form of the town's name was a later change at some point during the past two centuries, predicated, according to Adhikary's research, on the widespread alteration of proper nouns to fit the appearance of *Sanskritic* origin.

Tansen was, however, from the early decades of the Nineteenth Century to comparatively recent times, predominantly a Newar town inhabited by the people who had come to Palpa to help with the construction of the temples already mentioned and, no doubt, the buildings of the governor and military for which there is no surviving evidence. Both Bhimsen Tol, near the Narayan temple, and Taksar Tol near the Bhagwati temple (*taksār* meaning 'mint') were constructed at this time to house this immigrant population and the contemporary vernacular architecture of these areas, along with that of the other original bazaar precincts of Asan Tol and Basantapur reflect their Newar origins, being reminiscent of the houses of the Kathmandu Valley. Nevertheless, both Kasajoo and Ghimire mention that it was only after a disastrous fire destroyed much of the town in 1828 that the inhabitants of the town were allowed to have ownership rights over property in the bazaar and only then did the growth of permanent dwellings begin. Kasajoo refers to the supposed flimsy character of the houses before this time. It is possible that this amendment to the property laws in Tansen reflects a growing confidence in the security and permanence of their rule in Palpa on the part of the Gorkhali authorities, but we should be wary of using this as negative evidence for any opposition to Gorkhali rule in Palpa from 1806 to the late 1820s. There is no evidence for any such opposition.

Apart from working as craftspeople, Newars came to Tansen to work as traders, administrators and servants to the Parbatiya aristocrats who governed the region, such as Amar Singh Thapa and Ujir Singh Thapa. Another intriguing possibility that was raised by several informants amongst the contemporary Newar community was that their ancestors had come to Tansen to avoid socio-cultural obligations, especially with regard to *guthi* (social organizations unique to the Newar population that are used to make funeral arrangements for members and their family) in their ancestral cities of the Kathmandu Valley. Despite this factor, Newar immigrants were quick to re-establish their religious and social customs in Tansen and the Palpa region (Quigley 1986). As one Newar informant explained to me, using perfectly functionalist reasoning, the immigrants found themselves in an alien territory and sought security and strength through the social bonds that such customs helped to create.

The result of this is that by the time the first written accounts of Tansen were published in the early part of this century, the town had developed into a social and architectural copy of the cities of the Kathmandu Valley, albeit on a much smaller scale. Indeed, Tansen is often referred to today as *Kathmanduko bhāi* (Kathmandu's little brother) (Vajracharya 2039 VS). It is important to note, however, that modern Tansen has come into being at a time when the old Newar culture of Malla era Nepal was being challenged by the over lordship of the House of Gorkha. The fabric of the town and the socio-cultural life of the community has, grown up to reflect what we might describe as the co-stewardship of the town, as opposed to the overlaying of Parbatiya political hegemony over the rich substratum of Newari culture that we see in the Kathmandu Valley. The Newars of the Kathmandu Valley have been described by Gellner (1997a: 151), using a term from African sociology, as a "host tribe", because they form a majority in the capital city and region of the state but a minority elsewhere. We can see the situation in Tansen as the inverse of this with the headquarters of the district being Newar dominated, whilst the surrounding areas are largely made up of Magar or Parbatiya communities.

Once again, we should reiterate that this difference has been exacerbated by the difficulty of communication between the different regions of Nepal. In this case, the immigrant population of Tansen was far removed from the ancestral communities of the Kathmandu Valley. The fabric of Newar society and its reproduction is closely connected with the religious and social institutions that are, to a great extent, defined territorially. The organization and practice of many 'local' festivals and cultural practices in contemporary Tansen reflects this history by articulating relationships of caste and ethnicity through which Tansen's Newar community is connected with the ancestral communities of the Kathmandu Valley. Tansen, along with several other long-established, multi-caste towns in the hills, such as Pokhara, Gorkha, Bandipur and Dolakha, maintain close kinship links with the communities of the Kathmandu Valley. "It is not the cities of the Kathmandu Valley which provide anonymity but the small rural bazaar [i.e. those of a smaller size and less internal differentiation than towns like Tansen]. It is not the size of settlement which is the crucial variable in identifying prospective marriage partners but the degree to which public rituals and institutions like *guthi* are (or have been in the recent past) entrenched" (Quigley 1995: 105). The maintenance of *guthi* organizations and public rites in Tansen is, therefore, partly representative of the continued effort of members of the Newar community to maintain a level of orthodox cultural practice that will continue to qualify them as Newars of adequate status in the eyes of their brethren in the Kathmandu Valley cities.

Palpa as a Key Province in the Nineteenth and Early Twentieth Centuries

We should be wary of giving the impression that Tansen was in every way dominated by the Newar population during the period from the annexation of Palpa to the revolution of 1950–51. As with their counterparts in the Kathmandu Valley who were *culturally* dominant within their cities but *politically* emasculated, power in Tansen and Palpa laid firmly in the hands of the Gorkhali elite who were assigned to administrative and military posts in this important province. It should be reiterated that in reality these functions of power in Palpa— administrative, judicial and military—could often only be separated in retrospect because the governor of the district would have control over each (Burghart 1996). This was especially important in the case of Palpa because the town became the headquarters of the Nepali army in the western central region of the country. The standing army stationed in Tansen reached a total of approximately 3400 men at its height in the early decades of the Nineteenth Century, who with their camp followers formed a sizeable part of the urban population.[6] The barracks built in latter half of the Nineteenth Century still dominate the southern end of the central durbar complex, although in the mid-1990s, before the escalation in the Maoist conflict, the army barracks catered to a much smaller garrison of just one company (about 100 men) stationed in a compound adjacent to the *tundikhel*. Several other buildings, such as the Kali temple in the Durbar complex for which the garrison's priest [*purohit*] is the officiate and the arsenal on a remote hill on the outskirts of town known as the Barud Khan, also attest to the military presence in Tansen.[7]

The area around the old barracks in the bazaar is called Silkhan Tol (literally 'armory' or 'arsenal ward') due to the presence of an armory and gunpowder production facilities, the latter operated by Muslim specialists, in this area prior to the construction of the Barud Khan. Today this *tol* is better known as the site of the town's cinema, but it is still possible to collect pieces of slag, the byproduct from smelting metal, along the paths in the vicinity. Parts of Basantapur, Bhagwati Tol, the Sadak and the area which is now taken up by the bus station were known as *khalaṅgā*, meaning a government owned plot of land set aside to house members of the army and militia or their families. After 2030 VS (1973–74), ownership of the *khalaṅgā* land in Tansen was given to those who were then resident there.

The role of the military force stationed in Tansen during the first half of the Nineteenth Century was two-fold: to prevent internal unrest should it arise in this region and to face the potential threat from the forces of the East India Company to the south. As we have no record of any civil disturbances during this time, the garrison's role in countering this external threat in the first half of the Nineteenth Century appears to be of greater importance. During the Anglo-Nepali war of 1814–16, the Palpa garrison led by Ujir Singh Thapa successfully engaged a British force of five thousand men led by Major General John Sullivan Wood. It was this success that led Ujir Singh Thapa to reconstruct Tansen's Bhagwati temple in thanks for this victory (Baniya 2053 VS). Despite victory in

this battle, Nepal lost the war and the Treaty of Sagauli, which brought this conflict to an end, imposed a set of severe terms upon the Gorkhali regime.

Nepal was forced to cede large parts of territory in Garhwal and Kumaon in
the west of the Himalayas, and Sikkim and Darjeeling in the east to the East India Company. But, more importantly, the British also annexed about half of the
territory in the Tarai that had been previously controlled by Nepal. This was a
massive blow to the Nepali exchequer and to the ruling elite because, as is still
the case today, the agricultural and forestlands of the Tarai are the richest of
Nepal's natural assets. The land ceded to the East India Company included the
Tarai territories that had previously been controlled by the Sen Dynasty, in what
is present day Nawal Parasi and Rupendehi districts. These included the important trading town of Butwal, which lies on the very edge of the Mahabharat
range. This brought the border with British controlled territory to within only
twenty kilometers of Tansen and this proximity explains the military importance
of Palpa, and Tansen's garrison in particular, because the town lies on the route
of the main road into the heart of the central Himalayas. Beyond Tansen lay the
important districts of Kaski and Lamjung, the pilgrimage centre of Muktinath,
the semi-autonomous kingdom of Mustang and, ultimately, one of the few reliable passes into Tibet.

However, as was noted above, by the time Percival Landon visited Tansen
in the early years of the Twentieth Century the military role of Tansen had declined very considerably. The explanation for this is simple. Almost as soon as
the Treaty of Sagauli was signed, Hastings, the Governor General of the East
India Company, realized that if Nepal was to remain a viable state the Tarai land
would eventually have to be returned. Hastings offered to pay compensation for
the loss of this land to the members of the Nepali court who held *jagīr* and *birtā*
rights in these annexed areas of the Tarai in the form of an annual payment to
the Nepali exchequer of two hundred thousand rupees, but this was insufficient
to compensate for the psychological impact of this loss on the ruling elite in
Kathmandu and also made no allowance for the potential increase in revenue
that could have been made by the state through the development of forest and
waste land in the Tarai into productive agricultural land and the supply of tim-
ber. Stiller adds that such a payment would "place leading members of the court
of Kathmandu in the pay of the Company's government and subject them to the
Company's pressure in any future dispute or difference over policy" (1995:
312), a position that was clearly untenable. Some land in the Tarai, including the
town of Butwal and surrounding areas, was returned in December 1816 revers-
ing the provisions of the treaty that finally brought hostilities to an end, but the
real turning point in Anglo-Nepali relations came at the time of what the British
have referred to as the Indian Mutiny in 1857.

The Rana family regime led by Jang Bahadur Rana, which had come to
power in 1846 following a bloody coup d'état in Kathmandu, had been assidu-
ously fostering links with the East India Company over the previous decade. In
1857 Jang Bahadur Rana offered military support to the British to put down the
uprising in India and somewhat reluctantly the British accepted, possibly because they saw both the value of having the leader of a Hindu state on their side

and the risk that the commanders of the Nepali forces might not be able to control the troops under their command, who might be considered as sympathetic to their fellow Hindu troops involved in the mutiny (Husain 1970). It was feared that Jang Bahadur himself might be persuaded to turn against the British by one of the rajas of an Indian state, Avādh for example, if it was seen that the military situation was no longer under British control. "Considering all the various risks involved in accepting the Nepalese offer, Lord Canning [then Governor General of the East India Company] was right in accepting Jung [sic.] Bahadur's offer only when he felt the course of the war had turned clearly toward the British side" (ibid: 76). Jang Bahadur personally led a force of eight thousand Nepali troops (later increased to fourteen thousand) to help in the relief of Lucknow, whilst a detachment from the Palpa garrison led by Lieutenant Heera Singh advanced into India to bolster the British defense of Gorakhpur.

As a reward for this aid, the Governor General returned the western Tarai lands between the Kali and Rapti rivers to Nepal. This act led to the establishment of what are today recognized as the modern territorial limits of the Nepali state and the Rana foreign policy of support for the British regime in India that would guarantee those borders throughout the following century. According to Husain, "Jung's objectives were to prove his loyalty to the British, to secure the permanency of the governmental power in the hands of his family and to save his country from future molestation by the powerful British government, and all these goals were ultimately fulfilled" (1970: 79). It is perhaps ironic in the context of this study that one measure of the success of Jang Bahadur in achieving these aims is the subsequent further decline of Palpa's importance within the geo-political system of the local Himalayan region from this point onwards, as the security of Nepal was achieved through Jang's diplomacy rather than military might.

The hundred years from 1850 to 1950 are somewhat paradoxical when we consider the continuing growth and development of Tansen. From the middle of the Nineteenth Century, the district of Palpa retained its status as an important region within Nepal, but this was a status assured by its past glory and former strategic value rather than any continuing importance within the politics of the Nepali state. Indeed, it was now the relative remoteness of Palpa from the centre of power, the court in Kathmandu, which was to suggest a new role for the district and Tansen town during the time of the Rana regime. During the next hundred years, the governors who came to administer Palpa district came as exiles from the Durbar in Kathmandu with almost no exception. With them came other people, Newar and Parbatiya servants, artists, artisans and, aristocratic members of their clique all of whom would contribute to the life of Tansen and many of whose ancestors continue to do so today.[8]

This practice of 'rewarding' members of the court who rivaled the Prime Minister or his closest allies for ultimate power with the prestigious governorship of Palpa had begun in what has been described by Ludwig Stiller (1976) as "the time of troubles" which immediately preceded the rise to power of Jang Bahadur Rana.[9] Prime minister Bhim Sen Thapa, whose relatives we have already noted for their role in the annexation of Palpa and the Anglo-Nepali war sent his younger brother and rival, Rana Bir Singh Thapa, to control the Palpa garrison as *baṛā hākim* (magistrate or governor) in 1833, replacing one of Bhim Sen's other brothers, Bakhtawar Singh Thapa, who had been governor of Palpa since 1824. Bhim Sen had reason to believe that Rana Bir Singh had been plotting with King Rajendra's senior queen, Samrajya Laxmi Devi, to replace him as *mukhtiyār* (chief minister) after appropriating the powers of the regency for herself (King Rajendra still being a child at this time). Confirmation of these suspicions came in January 1833 when Bhim Sen had to wait over a week before being reconfirmed as *mukhtiyār* at the annual *pajani* (the ceremony at which all the servants of the king were appointed or re-appointed).

> The durbar had clearly indicated its displeasure. Bhim Sen was determined not to put Rana Bir back into the palace, where his now open ambition could do further mischief, but he had to find some alternative employment for this man who was so well known and evidently so well liked in the palace. The post of governor of Palpa might do. Sending Rana Bir there as governor might prove less than an ideal solution to Bhim Sen Thapa's problem, but it would remove Rana Bir from the palace and at the same time relieve some of the pressure Bhim Sen was under to restore Rana Bir to his post. Bhim Sen argued with some success that the governorship of Palpa was an especially sensitive post and that it required a person of Rana Bir Singh's talent (Stiller 1976: 261–262, see also comments p. 269).

Stiller goes on to argue that this action, along with the reward of other provincial commands to Bhim Sen Thapa's inner circle, led, somewhat ironically, to the weakening of his control at the centre of power in the Kathmandu durbar and thus his fall from power in 1839 (ibid: 264).

During the following period of Rana rule, the hereditary prime ministers from Jang Bahadur onwards used Palpa as a convenient sop to those such as Khadga Shamser Rana and Pratap Shamser Rana who were far from the direct accession to the ultimate source of power, the office of Prime Minister, but who wielded considerable influence over the life of the court.[10] In this way, the future of Palpa was just as surely dependent upon developments within the politics of the centre, the court in Kathmandu, as it had been in the decades immediately preceding and post-dating the kingdom's annexation by Gorkha. The maintenance of stable political relations with British-India was an explicit aim of the house of Gorkha and of the unified Nepali state throughout the century of Rana rule. The state struggled to maintain its cohesion, indeed its very existence, in the face of internal difficulties centered on the problems of administering a territory divided by culture and terrain or when faced with the external threat of the British East India Company, and Palpa became an element in this struggle.

Palpa's status during this period from 1804 to 1857 was largely that of a colony of Gorkha, albeit one that existed within the official borders of the Nepali state. The reasons for Palpa's peripheral status changed following the success of Jang Bahadur Rana's intervention in the British-Indian crisis of 1857 and the decline of the region's strategic military importance. In many ways the district's new role as a place of exile made this status quite explicit: now Palpa's precise function within the politics of the nation-state was to be negligible, to be irrelevant, to be an entertaining diversion for those who might find more threatening pastimes should they remain in the capital.

One result of this history of exile that might not have been expected was the comparatively early introduction to Tansen of many of the things normally associated with post-1950s development in Nepal. Exile from the Kathmandu Valley was usually reinforced by restrictions on travel to India or beyond the borders of Palpa district, and in some extreme cases according to some ancestors of these exiles still living in Tansen, a ban on traveling beyond the immediate boundaries of the bazaar, although it is not clear to what extent such bans were enforced. These factors contributed to the development of buildings and infrastructure in Tansen that might otherwise be lacking, because many of the elite residents of the town, who were denied access to the resources of the Kathmandu Valley or India, had to establish all the things they needed in Palpa itself.

'Need' is of course a relative concept and for many of the elite this need extended to the construction of grand neo-classical stuccoed mansions in the style familiar from the Nineteenth Century Durbars of Kathmandu. Khadga Shamser, exiled to Thada near Palpa in 1887 for plotting the overthrow of Prime Minister Bir Shamser Rana and given the governorship of the district two years later (Landon 1993, vol. 2: 76), contributed the *Sital Pati* (literally 'the shady shelter'), the vast folly of *Rani Ghat Mahal* ('the palace at the queen's river bank') on the banks of the Kali Gandaki river below Tansen to the north, and possibly the *Mūl Dhokā* (also known as the *Baggi Dhokā*) (lit. 'main gate' or 'the gate through which a carriage can pass') which forms the ceremonial entrance to the durbar compound (although this attribution is disputed by some of Tansen's citizens today, not least because the information board beside the gate claims that Khadga Shamser Rana built the gate between 1832 and 1837 A.D., dates which are obviously too early for Khadga's governorship but do correspond to the governorship of Rana Bir Singh).[11] Pratap Shamser, exiled in 1924, rebuilt the Tansen Durbar in its present form to be his private residence in Tansen. More creditably, he also started the construction of the gravity-fed water supply system that brought drinking water to the centre of the bazaar for the first time. Countless other mansions dotted around the periphery of the old bazaar area, predominantly to the south and northeast, attest to the wealth of Tansen's elite at this time.[12]

The predilection of the Nepali elite for Western goods during the Rana period of which the architecture of their residences is the main extant evidence is infamous (Liechty 1997; Regmi 1978). Mark Liechty observes that,

> If anything, consumption, and especially the consumption of foreignness became an even greater concern for the Nepali nobility during the era of Rana autocracy. European goods—aside from cotton textiles and a few other consumer items—remained exclusively the province of the elites who increasingly came to draw their identities from their material (in addition to political) alignment with dominant British power to the south. The importance of these goods is not in the quantities consumed—the volume of trade was relatively insignificant— but in the ways they were consumed.

During this period, the gap between commoner and elite became a chasm. Unlike Malla rulers who had split the resources of the Kathmandu valley three ways, the Ranas commanded the resources of the entire country. Rana elites invested (and made) fortunes in India and other foreign countries while almost completely ignoring their own nation. The state treasury became the personal expense account of the Prime Minister; the Ranas spent staggering amounts of money and manpower on imported luxury goods and monumental architecture. They further guaranteed their privilege through a variety of sumptuary laws (1997: 40–41).[13]

For Liechty, echoing the work of Nicholas Thomas (1991) on the consumption of Western goods in the Pacific during the colonial era, the consumption of these goods by the Rana elite was an innovative means through which distinctions between rulers and ruled might be maintained and displayed. It is important in this respect to remember that the Ranas were, for all their power after Jang Bahadur Rana seized control over government, a relatively new branch of the Nepali aristocracy. The Rana family name was itself a recent innovation, replacing their original name, Kunwar, and designed to enhance the prestige of the family by linking it to prestigious *kshatriya* lineages (see also the above comments on the *Sanskritic* renaming of place names in Nepal). Liechty notes that the foreign cultural forms and modes of consumption adopted by the Nepali elite at this time, as with other classic examples of "theatre states" (Geertz 1980), placed great emphasis on display and the 'public' demonstration of status—meaning here the limited public of the elite who took part in the rituals of state, rather than the mass populace. The adoption of Western styles of dress, architecture and martial culture offered the Ranas the prospect of a new cultural field through which the competition over elite distinctions could be played out to their own advantage, precisely because it by-passed older forms of aristocratic cultural distinction. Elite society's reproduction of this new cultural field in Tansen was synchronous with it production in the new salons of Kathmandu; once again, the cultural life of the town followed a template that originated elsewhere.[14]

An increasingly important part of this template from the second quarter of the Twentieth Century onwards was education and literacy. The *Dhawal Pustakālaya* (Dhawal Library), founded in 1946 (2003 VS) by a number of Palpa's literati, was the first library constructed outside of Kathmandu in the west of Nepal. Similarly, educational provision was made for children in Tansen earlier than in any other part of provincial Nepal, with the possible exception of Dhankuta in the east. Indeed, it is the case that by the late-1940s Tansen had a population of sufficient literacy to support not only the Dhawal Library, but also a private reading room, which took subscription of Indian newspapers. Very close proximity to the border with India helped no doubt in fostering these educational and communication links. By the time Rudra Shamser Rana was exiled to Palpa in 1933, distance from Kathmandu was, ironically, serving only to strengthen identification with both local institutions and the 'international' debate fomented by the success of the Quit India Movement led by Mahatma Gandhi and the Indian Congress Party.

The formation of several boys' clubs in Tansen in the 1940s, supposedly as educational and keep-fit organizations, served as a focus for the discussion of growing political opposition to the Rana regime in Kathmandu. The first was the *Dhawal Club*, formed in the 1940s by young men from rich families who had returned to Tansen after their education in India. They were inspired by events in India but could not start an overtly political organization. They instead started a health and sports club, which organized physical exercise sessions on Srinagar Hill amongst other ploys, as a means to meet on a regular basis. They still, however, had to explain the nature of their club to the town's authorities. The Dhawal Club was instrumental in founding the *Dhawal Pustakālaya* in 1946.

Another club that influenced the setting up of the library was the *Pustak Paḍhāi Dalān* (literally 'book reading hall') in Taksar Tol. This was set up by a Newar family who lived in Taksar and had been one of the first families to produce school textbooks in Nepal. Ambica Lakol, who founded this reading hall, was famous as a translator of Hindi and Bengali literature. His son, Nagendra Prasad Lakol was later to become the secretary of the Tribhuvan Multiple Campus and of the Nepali Congress in Tansen during the democratic interregnum of the 1950s. According to one informant in Tansen, the Pustak Paḍhāi Dalān was so influential that during the Second World War two of the town's residents were nicknamed 'Hitler' and 'Churchill' because of their respective political allegiances—when the newspaper arrived at the reading room from India, depending whom the reports of the war favored, one would go to the other's house and declaim the news loudly from outside!

After the Rana era the two earliest influential clubs were called *Dilkhuś* [Happy Heart] and *Dildukh* [Sad Heart]. These were competing song groups formed to compose and perform during Gai Jatra. Gai Jatra serves a role as a commemorative day for recently deceased relatives, but is also a time of carnival during which with criticism of the ruling class is tolerated in song and comic play (Anderson 1988: 103). *Dilkhuś* traditionally took the side of the rulers on this day, praising them, whilst *Dildukh* took the anti-rulers line. It is perhaps not surprising that later the members of *Dilkhuś* were alleged to be Congress supporters, whilst *Dildukh* were supposedly members of 'progressive' parties and factions. Two prominent Nepali poets from Tansen, Kamal Raj Regmi and Kul Mani Devkota were members of *Dildukh* and *Dilkhuś* respectively.

This tradition of the formation of clubs, often with a literary or sociopolitical focus continued into the subsequent decades with a number active during the period of my fieldwork. Sometimes, as in the case of a number of boys clubs, they were focused on particular activities such as sport or the welfare of a particular area. Sometimes, as in the case of the civil servants club, they were based around shared work identities. In other instances, the clubs were more informal gatherings of friends and colleagues meeting regularly to discuss the issues of the day. In each case the clubs produced semi-regular magazines or journals containing non-fiction, fiction and poetry, usually printed using the type of mechanical printing presses that were still active in Tansen in the 1990s. The collections of informants showed that many such publications had come into existence over the previous four decades, often lasting for no more than a single issue depending on the longevity of the associated club. In one case, I was shown a handwritten manuscript dating from the late-1940s produced as a single copy of a club magazine to be read and passed around between members because it contained political material that was too risky to have printed.

To return to the situation at the start of the 1950s, Rudra Shamser, supposedly the representative of the regime in Palpa, ignored the activities of the Dhawal Club and the Pustak Paḍhāi Dalān, actions that prefigure the tacit support received by RCTV from local politicians and government officials forty years later. In 1950, when the flight of King Tribhuvan to India precipitated the start of the revolution in Nepal, he came out in open opposition to the Rana regime. Rudra Shamser was quick to win support from both the military force stationed in Palpa and the force sent from Kathmandu supposedly to suppress this revolt. Rudra Shamser's actions led to a remarkable period of hundred days during which Palpa, under the control of a government made up of Shamser and other members of the elite, declared itself to be an autonomous region within Nepal (Pangeni 1994 [2051 VS]). The possession by organized and armed opponents of an area stretching from the Indian border in the south to Mustang in the north almost certainly contributed to the swift and relatively bloodless capitulation of the Rana government in Kathmandu as they realized that their rule was no longer recognized as legitimate not only by the supporters of the political parties whose goal was revolution, but also by members of the elite who recognized that their own status and authority could no longer be guaranteed by the Rana regime.

Tansen in Recent Times: the Panchayat and Second Democratic Eras (1950–1996)

Local administration was reorganized as part of the post-1950 settlement in Nepal and this led in 1966 to a dramatic reduction of Palpa district to a fraction of its previous size. Under the Local Administration Act of 1966, the number of districts (jilla) in Nepal was increased from thirty five to seventy five, including a total of nine separate districts made out of the original administrative area based on the boundaries of the original Sen Kingdom of Palpa (Palpa, Arghakhanchi, Gulmi, Syngja, Parbat, Baglung, Myagdi, Rupendehi and Nawal Parasi). Tansen retained its position as the district administrative headquarters, but this time of a much less significant area, especially now that the Tarai area had been separated from Palpa. It may be indicative of the district's reduced importance that when the system of zonal (añcal) administration was instituted as an additional part of these reforms, Bhairahawa, one of the Tarai towns in Rupendehi District, was made the centre of the zonal administration containing Palpa, rather than Tansen.

The over-throw of the Rana regime in 1950 also separated the administration of the bazaar more completely from the surrounding district. The 1966 act and its subsequent amendment in 1971 resulted in what Martinussen (1993: 26) refers to as "administrative deconcentration rather than decentralization" due to the fact that authority within the districts was divided between a number of newly created posts (Zonal Commissioner, Chief District Officer, Panchayat Development Officer, etc.) rather than being solely within the official remit of one post (the *baṛā hākim* or magistrate), but appointment to these posts was still largely a prerogative of central government. Tansen was still the site of district level administration, but this was now in the hands of officials and Panchayat politicians who were not directly involved in governance of the town. Whereas the governor of Palpa would have also been the ultimate source of authority in the Tansen, the administration of the town, as with all the places designated as urban in Nepal, was placed in the hands of separate municipal administrations, the *nagar panchayats* (town councils) to differentiate them from the four thousand or more *gāũ panchayats* (village councils) created as part of these reforms.

One result of divorcing the administration and legal authority over the town from that of the district has been in the case of Tansen a further diminution of its status as a major urban centre when Nepal is considered as a whole. Nevertheless, a concomitant of this is the fact that control over the town shifted decisively towards the Newar population, who at that time made up a large majority of the urban population. Although the loss of Tansen's position as the headquarters of a large district area meant that Tansen was no longer "an economic centre of gravity" (Gyawali et al. 1993: 79), the wealth from this economic activity was less likely to be expropriated from the local urban population into the hands of a national elite as it was during the period of the Rana regime. So, despite the relative decline in Tansen's economic position, the wealth generated by the town's industrial and commercial activity was placed more firmly in the hands of the general populace. This allowed the Newar majority to consolidate their grip on authority over the various institutions of the town, including formal political bodies such as the *nagar panchayat*, at a time of considerable political uncertainty in Nepal as a whole.

Despite this realignment of the political-economy of the town, the two events of greatest significance to occur during the period of Panchayat rule continued to reflect the influence of agencies beyond the town. The first was the establishment of a hospital in the late 1950s by a Christian aid organization, the United Mission to Nepal (UMN), and the second was the opening of the Siddhartha Rajmarg (highway) that connected Tansen to the rapidly expanding city of Pokhara in the north and the Tarai towns of Butwal and Bhairahawa (and thence India). Whilst the presence of the UMN hospital has generally been perceived as a great benefit to the town, albeit one which has often been fraught with tension, the Siddhartha Rajmarg is regarded as the single most important factor to have affected Tansen in recent years.

To take the Siddhartha Rajmarg first, Tansen is connected to the highway via a four kilometer branch road that has recently been extended by an unsealed road that reaches into the western districts of Gulmi and Syangja, thereby connecting Tansen to those districts' main settlements, Ridi and Tamghas. Prior to the construction of this road, Tansen had served as an entrepôt for many of the areas that had formed what we might describe as 'Greater Palpa'. This function had continued into the post-revolutionary era and these communities had formed the major market for both the goods produced in Tansen, mainly metal ware, jewelry, secondary products of agriculture (such as *ghee* [clarified butter]) and goods imported into Nepal from India, especially cloth. Although initially an encouragement to commerce, by the early 1970s the opening of the highway had diminished the metal ware industry in the bazaar by enabling the import of Indian goods and the products of the rapidly industrializing towns of the Tarai, and allowed the people of the hill areas surrounding Tansen to travel quickly to the cheaper market places of Butwal, Bhairahawa, or even Gorakhpur across the border in Uttar Pradesh.[15] As well as traveling to buy goods in these markets, they could now also take their own produce down to the Tarai to sell rather than using Tansen bazaar. According to Gyawali et al. (1993: 79):

> The possibilities of more diverse economic activities in Butwal or Kathmandu have also prompted a migration of shopkeepers or the educated elite to these centres taking with them the capital and creativity needed to maintain the cutting edge of economic prominence. Many 'sons of Palpa' are engineers with HMG in the Department of Roads, Nepal Electricity Authority or the Civil Aviation Department who have very little to do with Palpa professionally.

Many of the bazaar's merchants, industrialists and their families have themselves started new businesses in Pokhara, Butwal, Bhairahawa, or Narayanghat. The number of empty or under-occupied residences in the old bazaar attests to this new wave of migration and it seems that in demographic terms at least the heyday of Tansen as a bazaar dominated by a largely Newar population may have come to an end.

Production of the distinctive Palpali '*dhaka*' cloth used to make Nepal's national hat, the *topī*, started in the 1960s in Tansen and is one of the few examples of major innovations in the town's industries in the post-Rana period.[16] But, attempts by several entrepreneurs to increase production of *dhaka* cloth through investment in factories and other forms of industrial capital such as powered looms, have been largely unsuccessful. This has been due in no small part to competition from entrepreneurs who have taken advantage of the opportunity to 'put-out' production to village households by taking hand looms to the producers and thus taking advantage of both improved transport allowing for easy distribution and the lower wages demanded by the largely rural, female workforce (Gyawali et al. 1993: 123–4). It is significant that one of Tansen's most famous weaving entrepreneurs had by the mid-1990s shifted the location of the majority of his family's business to Kathmandu and Narayanghat and diversified from cloth production into other areas of commercial activity, including milling flour on a large scale.

Tansen, in common with many hill towns has failed to function as a regional centre for economic growth and continues to rely on its administrative function to generate service-based income. It is noted by Malla (1987) that from the mid-1980s Tansen Nagar Panchayat was forced to borrow to supplement municipality income. Deep Govind Rajkarnikar, co-author of a report into the organization and financial position of Tansen (Adhikari and Rajkarnikar 1994) observes that this financial position had not improved in the intervening decade (pers. comm. 1996) because the municipality could no longer rely on *octroi* revenue to generate income.[17]

Whilst the development of the road has led to the decline of Tansen's commercial importance, the work of the United Mission to Nepal (UMN) hospital has tended to have the opposite effect, even if the relocation of the hospital from its original position in the bazaar to a purpose built site on the eastern fringes of the municipality has been another factor in attracting habitation and business away from the old bazaar area.[18]

Dr Bob Fleming, one of the founders of the Tansen Mission Hospital, came to Palpa in 1951 and initially set up an ad hoc health post on the Tundikhel. Subsequently, in 1953 he returned to Nepal with Dr Karl Fredricks and obtained permission to start a permanent hospital in Tansen. For the next two decades the Mission Hospital staff struggled to provide a Western standard and style of health care in a community that often, according to the accounts of some of the founding staff, resented their presence (Cundy 1994). Despite this fact, the Tansen Mission Hospital was well enough established by the late-1950s for Fredricks to persuade the authorities of the town to grant the UMN a plot of land in Bysal Danda a few kilometers to the east of the bazaar.

The UMN has invested heavily in a purpose built hospital and since 1959, when the first buildings were opened on this site, the hospital has grown rapidly. In 1963 it had sixty three beds, by 1975 one hundred and two beds, and since 1992 it has had one hundred and twenty nine beds on a small campus, which to all intents and purposes is a self-contained community. The UMN estimates that since 1990 it has had about four hundred outpatient visits per day and sees approximately a hundred thousand patients a year from all areas of western Nepal (85% of all outpatients and 92% of inpatients) and the nearby Indian states of Uttar Pradesh and Bihar (8% of outpatients and 4% of inpatients) (United Mission to Nepal 1993). Not surprisingly, the hospital has become a major employer in the municipality, both directly through its total staff of 315 and through the stimulation of other businesses that cater to the needs of both the staff and patients, for example pharmacies, 'hotels' (usually just small guest houses) and *kirānā* (general goods) shops. It therefore contributes a large and unquantifiable amount of income to the municipality, although some indication of its magnitude can be gauged from the fact that in the fiscal year 1992–93 the total expenditure of the hospital itself was NRs28,579,306, equivalent to US$583,250 (ibid.: 6).[19] The development of a more permanent settlement around the gates of the Mission Hospital has been aided by the Communist Party of Nepal (UML)'s decision whilst it was in power in 1995 to grant the squatters on this land the right to own the land they occupied.

The UMN's work in Tansen is also important because it cleared a path for other international non-governmental organizations that now work in Palpa. These include *Redd Barna* (the Norwegian Save The Children organization), the *Red Cross*, *Helvetas* and many others who work indirectly by funding local NGOs. Communication for Development Palpa's link with the *Asia Foundation* is a perfect example of this sort of involvement, but such relationships and projects have not always proceeded as initially planned, as the following example of the Tinau Watershed Project makes clear.

From 1980 to 1995 (with 4 years prior preparation), Tansen was the centre of operations for this massive development project, which was jointly funded by the Swiss organization *Schweizer Gesellschaft für Internationale Zusammenarbeit* (Swiss Organization for International Cooperation, Helvetas) and the *Gesellschaft für Technische Zusammenarbeit* (German Organization for Technological cooperation, GTZ) from Germany. The project had aimed to stimulate overall development through the coordinated establishment of projects in a variety of development sectors (agriculture, cottage industry, marketing, health care, etc.), but was brought to an abrupt end five years before its scheduled conclusion when GTZ withdrew support. Despite this apparent failure, Helvetas have remained committed to development in Palpa through the retention of their interest in the local bridge building program run by the District Development Committee, a project originally started as part of the Tinau Watershed Project. In the mid-1990s they started a new program in Palpa, the Local Initiative Support Program, but it is significant that the scale of investment and the fundamental methods of involvement and contact with local client communities have greatly altered to focus on a 'bottom-up' approach "since the top-down approach has not worked" (Helvetas 2053 V.S.). Such changes reflect the more general tendency within development theory and practice to reject large-scale, external interventions in favor of more participatory, locally-driven development work (Perrons 2004).

Recognition of these trends in the recent historical reconfiguration of Tansen's role within Palpa district and the Western region of Nepal as a whole has been widespread amongst the population of the town. Research on the local economy has confirmed the commonly perceived shift in competitive advantage towards the growing towns of the Tarai and hill markets along the Siddhartha Rajmarg and Tamghas road and the subsequent loss of Tansen's industrial and commercial function (Tinau Watershed Project 1983; Bajracharya 1985; Gyawali et al. 1993). Consequently, most emphasis in recent years has been on other spheres, such as the already established education, health and development sectors, as well as Palpa's potential as a tourist location (Kasajoo 1994; S. Regmi 1991), although Gyawali et al. (1993) point out that the prospects for the latter are severely curtailed by the fact that water supply remains an issue of major concern.[20]

Water supply in the town of Tansen is a problem because of its hillside location (Kaphle 1994; Gyawali et al. 1993). Several springs lie on the outskirts of the town to the east and west. Despite the construction of a gravity fed water system in the 1930s and an electricity fuelled pumping system in the 1970s, these springs are still used by the vast majority of the population for bathing and washing clothing and for ritual purposes, if no longer for drinking water.[21] Older women in the community still recount how they had to spend many hours each day fetching water to their families' homes and are thankful for their children's and grandchildren's sake that this is no longer necessary.

Nevertheless, two problems with water supply remained for the municipality to solve. The first is that because of Nepali law of land ownership, the rights to the use of this precious spring water is controlled by the owners of the agricultural land below, who rely on the spring water for irrigation. The municipality cannot, therefore, use the most accessible water. This leads to the second problem, which is that water must be brought from a great distance away and sixty two percent of the total cost of the system which supplies much of the town's potable water (a vast expense) went to powering the pumping station at Bulke Danda to the west of the summit of Srinagar hill (Kaphle 1994).[22] The problem has been alleviated to a certain extent by a scheme sponsored by a French INGO (*Solidarite Tiers Monde*) with European Community funding to revitalize the gravity fed water supply system, the source of which is located at Banjha near the village of Baugha a few kilometers to the north-west of Tansen (European Community 1995: 122–123). Even so, fully a third of the total energy consumption of the town is devoted to pumping drinking water into the bazaar (ibid.; Kaphle 1994).

Conclusion

By the time RCTV began to produce video programs for broadcast via the cable television network in 1992, Tansen had experienced almost two centuries of change and significant challenges to its very existence. Although it is correct to say that the exact types of media and activities that RCTV was producing had highly innovative characteristics (Pringle et al. 2004), it is also clearly the case that these were built upon a much longer history of cultural change and transformation. As we saw in chapter 2, the personal histories of many of those involved in the production of the local program, especially Buddha Ratna and Mahesh Shakya, show that they were already involved in creative cultural enterprises and activities long before the technologies required to make the local television program were available to them. It is obvious that the desire or need to articulate a sense of culture and identity preceded any particular medium of its expression. Indeed, as chapter 7 will describe, despite the advent of modern mass media, older technologies and practices still form an important part of the town's public culture. Therefore, the first point we must state in conclusion is that RCTV's work is part of a continuum of developments in media and culture, rather than the start of something wholly new. This would inevitably be the case with regard to any example of media, alternative or otherwise. Nevertheless, it is worthwhile demonstrating that this is the case in detail because such media innovations can often appear to be aberrations or extraordinary variations from the norm, especially in places such as provincial Nepal where their existence might not be expected in advance. Such false expectations are indicative of a tendency in media studies to focus on new technologies at the expense of the study of continuities of form and use.

The second point that we must make is that Tansen and Palpa district have a distinctive history, which partially serves to explain why it was that such innovations in media have occurred where they did and in the way they did. Although the precise circumstances in which earlier developments occurred no longer pertain, such as the role of Tansen as a place of exile, the legacy of this history continued to be felt by those who created and supported alternative media in the town. To be Palpali or a 'child of Palpa', to say that you came from Tansen, meant more than a simple statement of facts about your place of birth or residence. It meant that you felt yourself to have inherited a distinctive identity and a sense of place. It is this sense of distinction that served to legitimate the work of RCTV. If it had been truly innovative in the sense of being utterly without precedent, it would have been much more difficult for the organization to survive. Instead, the legacy of Tansen's history meant that something as ambitious and potentially controversial as the creation of a local television station seemed to many of my informants to be somehow appropriate for this community. The local program could exist because it was seen as an evolutionary rather than a revolutionary development, growing out of what had gone before despite the novelty of the technologies used.

At the same time, the gradually worsening economic and political fortunes of Tansen meant that this sense of place and identity was one that was asserted not with hubris or confidence, but often in terms of anxiety and concern for the future. These anxieties are discussed in further detail in the next chapter. What I wish to emphasize here are the concerns that informants and friends in Tansen often expressed about the loss of their community's economic and political power in recent times. Whereas Tansen had thrived in previous times precisely because of its significance as a place on the periphery of the Nepali state, with the change in the geopolitical situation of the Himalayan region from the 1950s onwards this position had become a problem rather than an advantage. Whilst the peripheral position of Tansen had paradoxically served to help foster the development of public institutions and infrastructure in earlier times, the town was now felt to be increasingly marginalized compared to the rapidity of developments occurring in other urban centers. To borrow Burghart's phrase, Tansen, like Nepal as a whole, has increasingly found itself to be "a peripheral power constantly seeking some measure of autonomy in terms of the hegemonic discourses of others" (1996: 261–2).

Alternative media are often regarded as the distinctive products of people or communities who do not feel that their identities are adequately (if at all) represented in mainstream media content or their production. Indeed, we saw previously that RCTV's work could be seen as 'alternative' in terms of both the provision of Nepali language programming before the advent of Nepal Television broadcasts in Palpa and the dominance of national media. It also provides an example of how state control of media was being challenged following the anti-Panchayat revolution of 1990. In these terms, RCTV provides a fairly conventional example of alternative media.

Placing RCTV into historical context, however, enables us to move beyond this rather static approach to interpretation. Too often the analysis of alternative media begins and ends with the identification of a media activity as such. But, as we noted in chapter 2 (p. 45), we are concerned less with identifying the border line between mainstream and alternative media, and then deciding on what side of the line any particular example lies. Instead, we wish to examine "the forces which generate the borders in the first place" (Shohat and Stam quoted in Ginsburg 1995: 64), which in this case involves an appreciation of how Tansen and Palpa came into being, both materially and in terms of the creation of a distinctive subjectivity. To be a citizen of Tansen or *Palpali* is already to be different from other citizens of Nepal. This is not an ethnic or indigenous identity, but one that is based upon a sense of place and shared historical experience. It is not co-incidental that the most familiar term for the RCTV television program was 'the local program' (*isthaniya karykram*), not withstanding the potential confusions that some might have had about what 'local' connoted in this context, which were noted in chapter 1.

This chapter demonstrates that we can identify Palpali identity as something that is constitutive of the local community, which RCTV itself helps to constitute, both in its content and through its very existence (that is as something that is typical of Palpali innovation). However, what this chapter also shows is that this identity has formed over considerable time, taken various characteristics, and been contributed to by a wide number of different peoples. It still continues to vary and to be the subject of contestation. Just as the notion of national identity and what it means to be Nepali has changed, so too has Palpali identity changed. The objective here is to appreciate how these changes are occurring and to appreciate how the alternative media produced in Tansen do not simply represent processes of cultural change occurring elsewhere, but actively contribute to the manifestation and direction of this history. The existence of RCTV is undoubtedly evidence of the continuing development and modernization of the town and its population, but, as Appadurai and Breckenridge (1995: 16) state,

> What is distinctive about any particular society is not the fact of its modernity, but rather its distinctive debates about modernity, the historical and cultural trajectories that shape its appropriation of the means of modernity, and the cultural sociology (principally of class and state) that determines who gets to play with modernity and what defines the rules of the game.

Therefore, in the next chapter we look in more detail at the sociological and cultural characteristics of the population of Tansen and at the continuing 'game' of identity formation within the community.

Notes

1. In the light of Dirks' (1987) ethnohistorical study of a small Indian principality in Nineteenth Century India, Gledhill (1994: 69) comments that "the distinctive cultural structures of the past leave traces in the present, but the colonial process also produced strong discontinuities in development and a restructuring of established institutions, practices and beliefs." In the case of Tansen we are examining both Nepal's semi-colonial relationship with the British and independent Indian state and Palpa's own semi-colonial status in relation to the dominance of the centralized state apparatus based in Kathmandu.

2. Landon (1993 [1928]: 74) described Prithvi Pal Sen, King of Palpa, as "a distinguished Nepalese of undoubted Rajput descent."

3. Srinivas (1967: 7) notes that "the mobility associated with Sanskritization results only in positional changes in the [social] system and does not lead to any structural change. That is, a caste moves up, above its neighbors, and another comes down, but all this takes place in an essentially stable hierarchical order. The system itself does not change" (emphasis in original).

4. Bahadur Shah was the second son of Prithvi Narayan Shah, who was first exiled by his brother Pratap Singh Shah before returning to Nepal after his brother's death to act as chief minister (*mukhtiyar*) for the Queen Mother Rajendra Laxmi. Upon Rajendra Laxmi's death in July 1785 Bahadur Shah became regent for the infant King Rana Bahadur Shah, a post he fulfilled until 1794 when Rana Bahadur attained his majority. History has judged Bahadur Shah more kindly than his nephew for in 1797 Bahadur Shah was imprisoned and committed suicide after being accused, probably falsely, of treason (Uprety and Acharya 1994).

5. The mask of Bhairab which is kept at the temple of Bhairabsthan just to the west of Tansen is famously believed to have originally come from Kathmandu as a trophy of Mukunda Sen I who raided the Valley in the Sixteenth Century AD (Nyaupani 2049 VS).

6. The changing importance of Tansen as a military station can be gauged by comparing the numbers of military units stationed in Palpa with the number in the Kathmandu Valley. According to Hamilton (1986: 112 and 179) writing in 1819, twenty-five companies were stationed near Kathmandu and fifteen in Tansen—approximately 5700 and 3400 men respectively. Just over a hundred years later, Landon (1993 [1928] Vol. II: 11–12 and 187) reported that between 1500 and 2000 men were stationed in Tansen, three battalions, compared to about 22,500, twenty-six battalions, stationed in the Kathmandu Valley.

7. During the festival day of Chait Dashami [Little Dasain] which fell on the day of 14th Chaitra 2052 VS [27th March 1996] during my fieldwork, the Tansen garrison assembled at the Kali temple in the Durbar compound to carry out a series of blood sacrifices in honor of the goddess Kali. These sacrifices were carried out in front of the company's colors and various pieces of military ordnance and mirrored the similar sacrifices carried out by the military in Kathmandu on the ninth day of Dasain when the blessing of Durga is sought to increase the power of the weaponry of the army (M. Anderson 1988: 150–1; cf. Mason 1974: 67, who comments on the significance of this type of ceremony within the Indian army during the time of the British Empire.)

8. Palpa's role as a place of exile is vividly illustrated in *Prem Pinda* ('Token of Love', 1995) directed by Yadav Kharel, one of the most popular Nepali-made films of the 1990s. The film, based on a story by Bal Krishna Sama, recounts the tragic story of a poet's exile from the court of a Rana aristocrat in Kathmandu to the pilgrimage site of Ridi on the western fringe of present day Palpa and his pursuit by the young dancing girl for whose love the aristocrat and poet had vied. The pursuit emphasizes the distance between Kathmandu and Palpa. The young girl is shown walking for many days in bare feet over the rocks of the hills that lie between the two regions, a trek so arduous that she is left almost crippled. Needless to say, the story does not have a happy ending!

9. Stiller (1993: 134, note 9) says that "exiling a Nepalese to an out-of-the-way place in Nepal was accepted procedure. At times such exiles from Kathmandu were even given official duties in the area and had local authority. The center was apparently never too much concerned by the harm such persons might cause. There is no record that they ever fomented revolution from these remote places. To this day many government employees feel that an assignment anywhere outside the Valley is an exile, separating them from the centre of power and the opportunity to advance their own cause in the capital."

10. Inheritance of the mantle of Prime Minister during the Rana period was always based upon hereditary principles, but changed over time, as the size of the Rana family increased and various political coups shifted the line of succession from 'senior' to 'junior' branches of the dynasty. The principle of inheritance changed from a relatively simple system of passing from father to son (the principle favored by Jang Bahadur), to a system of inheritance passed from brother to brother (the principle favored, not surprisingly, by Jang's own brothers and their sons), to a final compromise situation where proximity to the succession was divided into three divisions according to proximity to senior Rana lineage—'A' class Ranas being legitimate members of the senior line, 'B' class being legitimate members of the junior line, and 'C' class being illegitimate members of the Rana dynasty. Only 'A' class Ranas could hope to inherit the mantel of Prime Minister. Khadga and Pratap Shamser Rana were 'A' class Ranas, but they had little chance of becoming Prime Minister by any legitimate means because their age meant that other 'A' class members of the lineage stood before them in the order of succession.

11. *Ghat* in Nepali has several associated meanings; these range from simply the shore or bank of a river, either naturally formed or amended with man-made structures, to a cremation ground, due to the fact that rivers are considered sacred and therefore an appropriate place within which to deposit human remains after cremation. Both these meanings are appropriate for Rani Ghat Mahal, because after the construction of a path down from Srinagar hill to the Kali Gandaki river by Khadga Shamser's engineers prior to the construction of his palace, the *ghats* here became the main site for the cremation of the town's citizens and the palace itself contains several temples, which are the only part of the building still maintained. This changed in the 1970s after the completion of the Siddhartha Rajmarg made access to the cremation site of Ramdi Ghat by motor transport preferable to the arduous trek on foot to Rani Ghat.

12. Perhaps we should actually say, following the example of M.C. Regmi in *Thatched Huts and Stucco Palaces* (1978), his devastating critique of the Rana misuse of the assets of their country that these buildings attest to the elite's ability to extract wealth from the farmers of Nepal who produced it in the first place. Despite our reference to this chapter as the history of Tansen, the majority of the town and region's residents remain invisible within the historical record, their presence only attested to at present by the 'negative' evidence of the palaces built on the strength of their labor. Further work may improve this lacuna within our understanding of the history of Palpa, but such work is beyond the immediate scope of this study.

13. This last point is interesting with regard to the description of the massive main gate into the Tansen Durbar as the Baggi Dhoka, because *baggi* (a Hobson-Jobson word derived from the English *buggy*) is usually only used to refer to a carriage specifically used by the Prime Minister or his family and the gate is commonly referred to by the people of Tansen as having such large proportions so that an elephant bearing a *howdah* could pass unhindered into the durbar compound. One of the sumptuary laws mentioned by Liechty (1997) is the Ranas' ban on the use of elephants and horses as a form of transport by commoners. Clearly, whichever Rana governor did build the gate, it would have served as a potent symbol of his pre-eminence amongst the population of the town, should any further affirmation of this status be required. Srinivas (1967: 17) notes the use of sumptuary laws to "maintain the structural distance between different castes" and also that increasingly, and in modification of his original (1952) formulation of the idea of Sanskritization, adoption of the habits of non-Brahmanical groups, e.g. the Mughal and British elite, was used to promote individual and collective status. He also pre-empts contemporary arguments regarding globalization by arguing that forms of metropolitan and urban culture originating in Western cultural experience perform a similar function in contemporary India, but emphasizes that the form of urban culture derived from this

process is distinctively Indian. Such cultural experiences also remain limited to the bourgeoisie in India, although one should note that since Srinivas's book was published access to modern, urban 'culture' has become more widespread as levels of commodity consumption have risen in India (Stern 1993).

14. A vivid illustration of the operation of this field was provided by one informant, the descendent of an influential Brahman priest exiled to Palpa with his entire immediate family by Prime Minister Chandra Shamser Rana in 1904. He described how his ancestors had started to build a mansion in an area of land that they had bought on the southern outskirts of the bazaar, but the design of the building had to be altered several times as its planned size and the number of pinnacles that were to have adorned its roof were seen as a challenge and an insult by Chandra Shamser Rana. Arguments over the scale of the building meant that its construction was delayed for fifteen years after the family's exile and arrival in Tansen.

15. Nepal's border with India has always been "a political rather than an economic boundary" (Seddon 1979: 35), but since the liberalization of the Indian economy, which started in the late 1980s, this fact has played an increasingly important role in the political economy of Nepal. The Indian government's trade blockade in 1989 precipitated the political upheaval in Nepal.

16. *Dhaka* cloth is so called because the style was allegedly introduced by a Palpali entrepreneur following his government-sponsored trip to Bangladesh to learn new techniques for cloth production.

17. The *octroi* is a tax on all commodities entering the area of the municipality.

18. The development of the UMN's hospital in Tansen has recently been studied by Ian Harper as part of a PhD thesis examining the various forms of healthcare provision in Palpa carried out under the auspices of the School of Oriental and African Studies, London (Harper 2003).

19. This is a large sum especially in the context of Nepal, but still only equivalent to US$ 5.50 per patient.

20. Tansen's transient student population is estimated by Gyawali et al. (1993: 79) to be somewhere in the region of three thousand people, a factor that they note is profitable for those who have property to rent out in Tansen but less important for the urban economy as a whole because the disposable income and needs of this student population tend to be small.

21. Kaphle's study showed that 89% of the households he surveyed still used both piped and spring water sources (1994: 38).

22. The debt incurred by the Tansen Department of Water Supply and Sewerage at Rs. 2,620,000 in the fiscal year 1991/92 was 53% of the *total* DWSS deficit for *all* of Nepal's 23 municipalities outside of the Kathmandu Valley (Kaphle 1994: 39 and Table 13)! As Kaphle points out this structure of water supply and financing was clearly not financially sustainable (ibid.: 37).

Chapter 5
Diversity and Distinction:
The People of Tansen

Wordsworth saw that when we become uncertain in a world of apparent strangers who yet, decisively, have a common effect on us, and when forces that will alter our lives are moving all around us in apparently external and unrecognizable forms, we can retreat, for security, into deep subjectivity, or we can look around us for social pictures, social signs, social messages, to which, characteristically, we try to relate as individuals but so as to discover, in some form, community.

Raymond Williams (1993: 295)

Introduction

The preceding chapter described the gradual loss of sovereignty experienced by Tansen and the district of Palpa over the past two hundred years. It was argued that this sense of loss contributes to the formation of Palpali identity and subjectivity in the modern world. Although prevalent, such ways of thinking are by no means universal. Inevitably, those who hold or once held power in the town are most likely to be affected by the erosion of local autonomy and the failure of successive governments in Nepal to implement promised programs of decentralization and economic development. It is they who have the greatest capability and reason to influence the envisioning of the town. Modern media provide various means through which such visions can be made manifest.

But the elite of a community, however defined, is only a limited fraction of the community as a whole and this chapter also describes those who lack access to the resources through which power is mediated, including modern communication technologies and skills such as literacy. Just as chapter 3 asked to what extent Nepal's media have been representative of the nation as a whole, this appreciation of the distinctions and divisions that exist in Tansen's population allow us to ask whether the media produced on the town's behalf is representative of the community as a whole. This is an important question because one of the key assumptions of alternative media studies is that a perfect, or nearly perfect, identification often exists between the producers of these media and their audiences and is an integral part of the legitimation of such media activities.

Changes in Tansen's Population and Status as an Urban Place

As the previous chapter made clear, Tansen was from its re-foundation in the Nineteenth Century to the middle of the Twentieth Century one of the few recognizably urban settlements outside of the Kathmandu Valley (Landon 1993 [1928]). Since the 1950s, however, this privileged status has been lost due to the explosive growth of towns in the Tarai, the high rate of urban growth in the Pokhara Valley to the north, and the appearance of a great number of smaller settlements that, if not officially classified as urban in terms of their administrative function are certainly fulfilling many of the commercial functions of a bazaar (Sharma 1989). This fragmented urban growth or rather the lack of it in some cases has created a problem for the government of Nepal (Shah 1987: 11). Previous administrative criteria for the designation of a settlement as urban have relied on population levels within a specific designated area, rather than population density or functional criteria (Sharma 1989: 3; Gyawali et al. 1993: 12). In an effort to restrict the number of areas that claim urban status that would then be allowed to claim tax raising and revenue privileges not allowed to rural communities, successive governments have raised the levels at which an area is officially declared to be urban. What this means, however, is that settlements like Tansen with lower rates of population growth have been in danger of slipping through this urban net (See Table 5.1 *Ranking of Urban Places in Nepal According to Population Size, 1961–1991*). Clearly it would not be expedient given the role that Tansen plays as the location of many educational, local government and development institutions, to declassify an urban centre of such long standing. This has led in recent years to what amounts to demographic gerrymandering to maintain Tansen's population at a level above that of the official cut-off point for urban centers.

The major instances of this process in recent years came in 2032 V.S. (1975–76) when Bartung (Ward Nine), Gahira Gaun (Ward Ten) and Kajipawa (Ward Eleven) were absorbed from Bartung Panchayat.[1] Initially Bartung and Kajipawa were classed as one ward, but after 1990 they were separated into two. Later, in 1990 the areas of Dharampani (Ward Twelve) and Bandipokhara (Ward Thirteen) were annexed to Tansen Municipality from Bandipokhara VDC and Bastari (Ward Fourteen) from Madanpokhara VDC. This is the primary reason for the town's recent population growth (see Table 5.2 *Tansen Population Growth, 1961–91*).[2] As a result of these changes, the municipal area no longer corresponds to the old boundaries of the bazaar, which was the previous focus of urban development in Tansen and the place of highest population density. Such things are obviously recognized by the people of Tansen who make the distinction between rural (*gāūle*, literally 'village-like') wards and urban (*bajār*) wards. These distinctions are obvious if we compare the figures for the population of each ward (Table 5.3 *Population of Tansen's Wards, 1993*) with the extent and area of the wards, something that shows up the massive disparity in population densities throughout the municipal area.

Table 5.1. Ranking of Urban Places in Nepal According to Population Size, 1961–1991

1961	1971	1981	1991
Kathmandu	Kathmandu	Kathmandu	Kathmandu
Lalitpur	Lalitpur	Biratnagar	Biratnagar
Biratnagar	Biratnagar	Lalitpur	Lalitpur
Bhaktapur	Bhaktapur	Bhaktapur	Pokhara
Nepalgang	Nepalganj	Pokhara	Birganj
Dharan	Pokhara	Mahendra Nagar	Dharan
Birganj	Dharan	Birganj	Mahendra Nagar
Thimi	Bhairahawa	Dharan	Bhaktapur
Janakpur	Hetauda	Janakpur	Janakpur
Malangawa	Janakpur	Hetauda	Bharatpur
Kirtipur	Birganj	Nepalganj	Hetauda
Banepa	Butwal	Bhairahawa	Nepalganj
Pokhara	Rajbiraj	Bharatpur	Dhangadi
Rajbiraj	Bhadrapur	Dhangadi	Butwal
Tansen	Ilam	Butwal	Damak
Maithani	*Tansen*	Tribhuvan Nagar	Bhairahawa
		Rajbiraj	Tribhuvan Nagar
		Birendra Nagar	Rajbiraj
		Dhankuta	Birendra Nagar
		Lahan	Lahan
		Tansen	Bidur
		Ilam	Inawura
		Bhadrapur	Kalaiya
			Jaleshwor
			Taulihawa
			Dhankuta
			Bhadrapur
			Malangawa
			Tansen
			Ilam
			Banepa
			Dipayal
			Dhulikhel

Source: Sharma (1989) and HMG, Nepal (1994)

Variations between the wards are not only noticeable at the basic level of population size and density. The separate social and cultural characteristics of the residents of the different wards of Tansen are also highly marked, as are the architectural and material cultural differences between the wards. In the sections that follow, I shall describe these areas using data from the national census and my own survey work in Tansen.[3]

Table 5.2. Tansen Population Growth, 1961–1991

	1952/54	1961	1971	1981	1991	1994
Population	4,705	5,136	6,434	13,125	13,599	16,169
Index	100	109	136	279	289	344

Source: Sharma (1989); HMG, Nepal (1994); Adhikari, G. and Rajkarnikar, D.G. (1994)

Table 5.3. Populations of Tansen's Wards, 1993

Ward Number	Ward Name	Population	Percentage
1	Meheldhara	819	5.1
2	Narayan Tol	634	3.9
3	Bhimsen Tol	1,657	10.2
4	Makhan Tol	1,464	9.1
5	Taksar Tol	771	4.8
6	Basantapur Tol	1,043	6.5
7	Kailash Nagar	598	3.7
8	Bhagwati Tol	1,280	7.9
9	Bartung	1,717	10.6
10	Gahira Gaun	1,572	9.7
11	Kajipawa	1,406	8.7
12	Dharampani	1,105	6.8
13	Bandi Pokhara	733	4.5
14	Bastari	732	4.5
15	Asan Tol	638	3.9
Total	Tansen	16,169	100.0

Source: Adhikari and Rajkarnikar (1994)

Five wards (Dharampani, Bandi Pokhara, Bartung, Kajipawa and Bastari) have been added to the area of Tansen municipality since the mid-1980s. As mentioned, these areas are predominantly 'rural' in character; at their furthest extent, they lay some way beyond the confines of the old bazaar and its suburbs. They extend beyond the limits of my own survey area and I do not have the sorts of descriptive statistical data available to me that have relied on in other parts of this chapter. To make up for this I have resorted to 'secondary' data in the form of municipality records of the registration of citizenship to supplement the general description that follows (see Table 5.4 *Distribution of New Citizens between Wards*).[4] This data also provides additional confirmation of the distribution of different ethnic groups throughout the municipality area. The records consulted by me covered a sixteen-month period from the start of the second month of 2052 VS to the start of the fifth month of 2053 VS (approximately mid-May 1995 to mid-August 1996).[5]

Table 5.4. Distribution of New Citizens between Wards

Ward	Ethnic Group				Total	Total
	Newar %	Parbatiya %	Magar %	Others %	No.	%
Meheldhara	16	60	12	12 [a]	25	5.8
Narayan Tol	75	20	0	5 [b]	40	9.3
Bhimsen Tol	40	45	15	0	33	7.6
Makhan tol	38	50	12	0	26	6.0
Taksar Tol	95	5	0	0	20	4.6
Basantapur	27	58	15	0	26	6.0
Kailash Nagar	43	57	0	0	14	3.2
Bhagwati Tol	62	26	13	0	39	9.0
Bartung	0	84	16	0	32	7.4
Gahira Gaun	22	65	13	0	37	8.6
Kajipawa	4	75	21	0	53	12.3
Dharampani	0	100	0	0	28	6.5
Bandipokhara	3	97	0	0	29	6.7
Bastari	0	75	12.5	12.5 [c]	24	5.6
Asan Tol	33	50	17	0	6	1.4
Tansen	29	59	10	2	432	100.0

Source: Tansen Municipality records for period 15th May 1995 to 16th August 1996
[a] Represents three people whose caste could not be accurately identified from name alone.
[b] Represents two people whose caste could not be accurately identified from name alone.
[c] Represents three people of Kumal caste.

What this data clearly shows is that, although in overall terms the relative size of the Newar population of Tansen *municipality* has fallen in recent years, this can probably be accounted for in no small measure by the annexation of the new 'rural' wards to the area of urban administration and not simply by migration of non-Newars to the municipality from further a field or the out-migration of Newars. If we look at these rural wards (wards 9, 11, 12, 13 and 14) we see that virtually no Newar citizens were registered in these wards and Parbatiya people clearly dominated citizenship registration. The reverse is true for the old bazaar wards, although there are a higher number of Parbatiya people registered in these wards (wards 2, 3, 5, 8 and 15). It is impossible to say from the available records whether new citizenship was registered by established residents of these wards or by newly arrived migrants. As one might expect, 'suburban' and 'new town' wards, represented by places like Meheldhara, Barud Khan, Silkhan Tol, Gahira Gaun and Kailash Nagar (wards 1, 4, 6, 7 and10), show the greatest mixture of people from different ethnic groups registering their citizenship within the municipality.

Characteristics of Tansen's Population

It is difficult to draw any firm conclusions about the changing religious and ethnic composition of Tansen based on census statistics, because of changes in the way these questions have been administered.[6] A specific question on ethnicity was only introduced in the 1991 census. Estimates of Tansen's ethnic composition in previous decades must be based on questions about mother tongue and, notoriously, these are suspect when treated as a simple indicator of ethnic identity. Nevertheless, there can be little doubt that the number of Newars living in the municipality and even in the core bazaar area has been steadily declining as a proportion of the total population, even if in real terms the number may be fairly static. Even so, in comparison to the population of Palpa district, the size of the Newar population is high.[7]

An important consideration is that the 'bazaar-centric' nature of my own survey led to an over representation of Newar people and hence Buddhist religious affiliation as a proportion of the total *municipal* population. Comparison of the survey figures with the 1991 census statistics makes this clear (see Table 5.5 *Distribution of Religious, Ethnic and Caste Groups*).

Tansen's population is divided fairly evenly between men and women, there being approximately 1% more men than women (see Table 5.6 *Sex Distribution of Population*). It should also be noted that the very close correspondence between the figures for the 1991 census, Municipality Organizational Development and Administration Study [MODA] survey (Adhikari and Rajkarnikar 1994) and my study survey indicate that this survey represents a reasonably accurate and valid cross-section of Tansen's population as a whole. It is a relatively young population with two-thirds (68%) of the population being below thirty in age.[8] The population below and above the age of thirty is fairly similar and evenly divided between the sexes with a ratio of 52% to 48% for males to females below thirty years old and 50% to 50% for those above thirty years old (HMG Nepal 1993).

As the next table shows over half of the population is married (Table 5.7 *Marital Status of Survey Respondents and Household Members*) and there is considerable variation in the composition of the households in which people reside, with no one type of household taking precedence (Table 5.8 *Household Sizes and Types*).[9] Three quarters of my respondents owned their homes and the remainder, many of whom were students living in rooms with a host family or artisans and their families living in whole houses in the bazaar, lived in rented accommodation.

Table 5.5. Distribution of Religious, Ethnic and Caste Groups

Religion		Author Survey		1991 Census	
		No.	%	No.	%
	Hindu	146	74.9	12,144	89.3
	Buddhist	35	18.0	1,102	8.1
	Muslim	3	1.5	177	1.3
	Christian	1	0.5	163	1.2
	Other	8	4.1[a]	0	0.0
	None	2	1.0	0	0.0

Caste/Ethnicity		Author Survey		1991 Census	
		No.	%	No.	%
Newar	Total	77	39.4	3,386	24.9[b]
	Vajracharya	14	7.2		
	Shakya	17	8.7		
	Uray	3	1.5		
	Shrestha	21	10.8		
	Other 'Shrestha'[c]	9	4.6		
	Maharjan	4	2.1		
	Other 'Maharjan'[d]	7	3.6		
	Khadgi	2	1.0		
Parbatiya	Total	83	42.6	6,351	46.7
	Bahun	30	15.4	3,726	27.4
	Chetri	33	16.9	2,081	15.3
	Occupational	20	10.3	544	4.0
Magar	Total	21	10.8	2,053	15.1
Muslim	Total	—	—	286	2.1
Others	Total	14	7.2[e]	1,523	11.2

Source: Author Survey and HMG, Nepal (1994)
[a] Instances where the respondent answered "All!"
[b] 1991 Census figures do not distinguish between different Newar castes.
[c] Respondents from Shrestha subdivision of Newar caste hierarchy with alternative caste names (e.g. Amatya, Josi, Malla, Pradhan, Raj Lawat, Vaidya).
[d] Respondents from Maharjan subdivision of Newar caste hierarchy with alternative caste names (e.g. Dungol, Gongal, Lakol, Ligal, Simha).
[e] Includes respondents who described their ethnicity as Indian (9 respondents), Kumal, Gurung and Thakali.

Table 5.6. Sex Distribution of Population

	Male		Female		Total
	No.	%	No.	%	No.
1981 Census	6,941	53.0	6,184	47.0	13,125
1991 Census	6,995	51.0	6,604	49.0	13,599
1993 MODA Study	8,176	50.6	7,993	49.4	16,169
1995 Survey (Respondents)	108	55.4	87	44.6	195
1995 Survey (Household Members)	671	50.4	661	49.6	1,332

Source: HMG, Nepal (1984), HMG, Nepal (1994), Adhikari and Rajkarnikar (1994) and Author Survey

Table 5.7. Marital Status of Survey Respondents and Household Members

Respondents	Male		Female		Total	
	No.	%	No.	%	No.	%
Married	71	65.7	59	67.8	130	66.6
Never Married	34	31.5	17	19.5	51	26.2
Widowed	3	2.8	11	12.6	14	7.2
Total	108	100.0	87	100.0	195	100.0

Household Members	Male		Female		Total	
	No.	%	No.	%	No.	%
Married	268	39.9	296	44.8	564	42.3
Never Married	397	59.2	322	48.7	719	54.0
Widowed	6	0.9	43	6.5	49	3.7
Total	671	100.0	661	100.0	1,332	100.0

Source: Author Survey

As Table 5.8 shows, the distribution of household sizes (speaking here only of the figures for household size excluding 'Others', i.e. servants and unrelated people renting accommodation in the same house) has a positively skewed distribution with a major peak at five members and a minor peak at twelve to fourteen members. Although this distribution can obviously be accounted for by the fact that the sample is divided between those households that contain only one family of reproduction (i.e. nuclear families) and those that are an amalgam of two or more families of reproduction (i.e. joint, extended and joint-extended families), the actual numbers of each of these two main categories of household type does not match what we would expect to see from the numbers shown in this table. Put more simply, there appears to be too many small households (those with five or fewer members) compared to the number of nuclear families in the sample and correspondingly too few larger households for the number of joint and extended families in the sample.[10]

Table 5.8. Household Sizes and Types

Household Size No. of People	Households Including Non-kin		Households Excluding Non-kin	
	No.	%	No.	%
1	1[a]	0.5	4	2.1
2	6	3.1	8	4.1
3	13	6.7	11	5.6
4	21	10.8	26	13.3
5	40	20.5	42	21.5
6	20	10.3	21	10.8
7	26	13.3	24	12.3
8	20	10.3	18	9.2
9	10	5.1	8	4.1
10	4	2.1	4	2.1
11	2	1.0	1	0.5
12	10	5.1	9	4.6
13	5	2.6	4	2.1
14	6	3.1	6	3.1
15	3	1.5	2	1.0
16	1	0.5	1	0.5
17	4	2.1	4	2.1
18	2	1.0	1	0.5
19–25	0	0.0	0	0.0
26	1	0.5	1	0.5
Average Size	7.14		6.81	

Household Types	No.	%
Individual	3	1.5
Primary (Married couple)	3	1.5
Nuclear (Married couple with children)	76	39.0
Joint (Combined nuclear or primary)	50	25.6
Extended (Primary/nuclear plus other kin)	37	19.0
Joint Extended (Joint plus other kin)	24	12.3
Other (Non-relatives cohabiting)	2	1.0

Source: Author Survey
[a] Household consisting of servant looking after property for absent family.

The reasons for this supposed discrepancy are simple to explain but also of some importance, because they illustrate several points of relevance to the sociology of Tansen and the methodology of this study. Part of the explanation is that some extended families are only extended in as much as an elderly relative (usually a widow or widower) or a young relative (e.g. a child of a relative staying in Tansen during a period of study) lives with a household that would otherwise consist of only a nuclear family. As such, this discrepancy is partly an artifact of the typology used in the study. This illustrates the methodological point that we must be careful to distinguish between our discussions of the family and of the household. Whilst the two do tend to correspond, they are by no means the same thing. The main *sociological* reason, however, for this lack of correspondence between family type and household size is that a large number of joint households are, as it were, degraded by the absence of one or more male members, occasionally accompanied by a spouse. Invariably these males are working outside of the municipality, either elsewhere in Nepal (typically in Kathmandu, Pokhara or one of the larger towns of the Tarai), in India, or even further a field in one of the Arabian Gulf States or South East Asia. The table below (5.9 *Number of Households with Married Males Absent*) which looks at the absence of *married males* gives some indication of the extent to which this migration affects household numbers for each of the main ethnic groups in Tansen.[11] These figures probably underrepresented the true extent to which household numbers are affected by this factor, because they only include married males. It is difficult to obtain accurate figures on the economic migration of unmarried kin from households in Tansen from the data that was available to me.

Table 5.9. Number of Households with Married Males Absent

Ethnicity	Caste	Number of Married Males Absent		
		One	Two	Three
Newar	Hindu	4	2	0
	Buddhist	3	0	0
Parbatiya	Bahun	3	0	0
	Chetri	5	1	0
	Occupational	1	1	0
Magar		5	1	1
Total	Households	21	5	1
	Individuals	21	10	3

Source: Author Survey

Kinship remains the basis of household formation in Tansen, but the realities of Nepal's urban economy mean that households often include non-relatives (migrants who have come to work or study) or have significant family members absent. The following methodological point, therefore, bears reiteration. Families and households are analytically distinct entities; the structural relation of both needs to be considered carefully, as it is often around this relationship that some of the effects of the Nepal's changing political-economy are felt most strongly in Tansen (as in urban and rural communities in Nepal more generally).

It is important to realize that the categories of household type used here provide only a snap-shot of the relative numbers of people of various ethnic groups who were domiciled in each type of household at the time in which the survey was completed (November and December 1995). It is obviously the case that if any one individual was tracked through time their household circumstances might change. In particular, joint families may divide into separate nuclear families or older members of extended or joint-extended households will die leaving behind either nuclear or joint families respectively. Equally, children may marry. In the case of male children, brides will probably move into their family home creating joint or joint-extended families. Alternatively, newly married males may move out of the family home to set up new nuclear families. Female children who marry will normally move out to live with their husband either in his family home or in a separate nuclear household.

Given that this is the case it is interesting to note that there are almost equal numbers of each type of household present amongst the Newar population, with slight variation between Hindu and Buddhist Newars (5.10 *Correlation of Ethnicity, Caste and Household Type*). We might expect this to be the case given that the majority of these households have been established in Tansen for several generations. What we observe here is a pattern derived from the constant evolution of individual households from one type into another over the course of several generations. The Newar population has reached what we might describe as an equilibrium state with regard to relative numbers of household types given that the cultural norm amongst the Newars is the joint and/or extended family (Nepali 1965; Quigley 1985 and 1986).

Table 5.10. Correlation of Ethnicity, Caste and Household Type

Ethnicity	Caste		Household Type				
			Nuclear	Joint	Extended	Joint/Ext	Other
		No.	%	%	%	%	%
Newar	Hindu	43	33	23	23	21	0
	Buddhist	34	24	29	15	29	3
	All	77	29	26	19	25	1
Parbatiya	Bahun	30	53	17	20	3	6
	Chetri	33	58	12	18	3	6
	Occup'	20	20	45	20	10	5
	All	83	47	22	19	6	6
Magar		21	29	38	29	0	5
Indian		9	89	11	0	0	0
Others		5	20	40	20	0	20
Total		195	39	25	19	12	4

Source: Author Survey

Table 5.11. Correlation of Ethnicity, Caste and Average Size of Household Types

Ethnicity	Caste	Household Type					
		Total	Nuclear	Joint	Extended	Joint/Ext	Other
Newar	Hindu	8.3	5.6	10.7	5.5	12.7	—
	Buddhist	8.7	5.5	10.4	6.0	11.6	2.0[a]
	All	8.5	5.6	10.6	5.7	12.1	2.0
Parbatiya	Bahun	5.9	5.1	7.0	6.8	7.0	2.0
	Chetri	5.5	4.8	10.0	5.3	8.0	1.5
	Occup'	7.8	5.0	8.4	7.3	14.5	0.5
	All	6.2	5.1	8.4	6.4	10.4	1.75
Magar		6.9	6.8	8.5	5.7	—	2.0
Indian		5.9	5.0	12.0	—	—	—
Others		7.5	8.0	10.5	3.0	—	5.0

Source: Author Survey
[a] Figures in italics indicate examples where only one household is recorded in this category.

Variations on joint and extended family arrangements in households are also the norm for virtually all of the ethnic groups of Nepal (Bista 1967). One might, therefore, expect a similar sort of distribution of household types to that of the Newar population amongst the other ethnic groups, but this is not the case for the survey population. Amongst the Bahun, Chetri and Indian caste groups, for example, there are significantly more households of nuclear type. We can probably ascribe this to the fact that there are a high number of immigrants, who might typically be expected to move from one place of residence to another as individuals or in smaller groups (such as that formed by a nuclear family). This is especially the case with the Indian population, many of who contribute to the maintenance of households and property in their place of origin. It is also the case that, as is shown below, Bahun and Chetri households tend to have an individual (normally male) who is engaged in salaried economic activity (either as a professional, member of the civil service or military). As such, they would then have a regular and relatively substantial income that would make the establishment of a sustainable nuclear household a realistic possibility. It is perhaps significant in this regard that the Parbatiya population of 'Occupational' caste status, who are engaged in no salaried employment (see below), tend to remain within joint households within which the costs of living and risks of economic activity in the market place can be shared between a larger number of economically active individuals.

The relatively smaller size of joint and joint-extended households amongst both the Bahun and Chetri population may also be ascribed to the fact that, as mentioned above, individual members of high caste Parbatiya families are more likely than other castes to have salaried jobs or be involved in further education that both requires and enables them to study elsewhere (Table 5.11 *Correlation of Ethnicity, Caste and Average Size of Household Types*).

Table 5.12. Place of Origin and Length of Residence of Migrants

Place	Number of Migrants
Palpa District	50
Western Development Region: Hill District	17
Western Development Region: Tarai Districts	5
Western Development Region: Mountain Districts	1
Butwal	7
Kathmandu	4
Pokhara	3
Ridi	2
Eastern Development Region: Hill Districts	1
Central Development Region: Hill Districts	1
Central Development Region: Tarai Districts	1
Mid-western Development Region: Hill districts	1
Uttar Pradesh, India	7
Origin not specified	1
Total	101

Length of Residence	No.	%
Since Birth	94	48.2
0–1 Year	11	5.6
2–5 Years	27	13.9
6–10 Years	18	9.2
11–15 Years	12	6.2
16–20 Years	14	7.2
More than 20 Years	19	9.7

Source: Author Survey

Further evidence of these changes can be found in figures relating to migration and residency in Tansen. Just under half of the respondents to my survey reported that they had been resident in Tansen since birth, and of the remainder almost a half had lived in the town for over ten years (see Table 5.12 *Place of Origin and Length of Residence of Migrants*). Those who have emigrated to Tansen tend to come from the surrounding rural areas of Palpa or from adjacent hill districts, but, as Table 5.12 shows, immigrants came to Tansen from locations in the higher Himalayas, the Tarai and from as far away as Simla in India (not to mention the permanent population of Western doctors who work at the United Mission to Nepal Hospital and live in Meheldhara and Gahira Gaun close to the hospital compound).

Table 5.13. Correlation of Ethnicity and Sex with Length of Residence

Ethnicity	Sex	Resident Since Birth	Immigrant	Total No.	Migrants' Average Length of Residence[a]
		%	%		
Newar	Male	89.5	10.5	57	15.8
	Female	55.0	45.0	20	15.4
	All	80.5	19.5	77	15.6
Parbatiya	Male	42.9	57.1	35	9.6
	Female	18.8	81.2	48	9.7
	All	28.9	71.1	83	9.7
Magar	Male	20.0	80.0	10	5.9
	Female	18.2	81.8	11	5.4
	All	19.0	81.0	21	5.7
Others	Male	33.3	66.6	6	16.3
	Female	25.0	75.0	8	12.2
	All	28.6	71.4	14	14.3
Total	Male	64.8	35.2	108	11.9
	Female	27.6	72.4	87	10.7
	All	48.2	51.8	195	11.3

Source: Author Survey
[a] Average (mean) calculated omitting figure for migrant with longest length of residence, as this alters the mean considerably.

It is also the case that we can identify a marked disparity between men and women, this time in the ratio of people resident in Tansen since birth and those who are immigrants. This disparity is not, however, equally distributed between each of the different ethnic groups living in the town. This is illustrated in the above table (5.13 *Correlation of Ethnicity and Sex with Length of Residence*). The ratio of men to women for those who have been resident since birth and immigrants is largest amongst the Newar population with Parbatiya residents second, but amongst the Magar population and those of other ethnicity there is little or no disparity. This would seem to suggest that there might be different patterns of migration between these ethnic groups. The most obvious answer to this is that a high proportion of both Newar and Parbatiya female immigrants come Tansen as the brides of men already resident in the town (patrilocal residence is the norm amongst both ethnic groups). Conversely, it is probably the case that Magar and 'Others' are coming to live in Tansen after marriage. This is not to say, of course, that Newar and Parbatiya men and women do not emigrate to Tansen after marriage from their prior place of residence, but that as a proportion of the total number of immigrants there tend to be more 'brides' amongst the Newar and Parbatiya population. Further research would be needed to confirm this hypothesis.

Table 5.14. Place of Origin of Migrants Correlated with Ethnicity

Place	Newar Hindu	Newar Budd'	Bahun	Chetri	Occup'	Magar	Other	Total No.
	%	%	%	%	%	%	%	
Palpa	10	—	18	28	12	30	2	50
WDR: Hill[a]	12	12	29	23	12	6	6	17
WDR: Tarai	—	—	80	—	—	—	20	5
WDR: Mtn	—	—	—	—	—	—	100	1
Butwal	29	—	14	14	14	14	14	7
Kathmandu	—	—	50	50	—	—	—	4
Pokhara	33	—	33	—	33	—	—	3
Ridi	—	—	—	—	50	50	—	2
EDR: Hill	—	—	—	100	—	—	—	1
CDR: Hill	—	—	100	—	—	—	—	1
CDR: Tarai	100	—	—	—	—	—	—	1
MWDR: Hill	100	—	—	—	—	—	—	1
U.P., India	—	—	—	—	14	—	86	7
Not Specified	100	—	—	—	—	—	—	1
Total	13	2	23	22	13	18	11	101

Source: Author Survey
[a] See Table 5.12 for full name of regions included in this table.

Table 5.15. Correlation of Ethnicity and Sex with Property Ownership

Ethnicity	Sex	Own		Rent	
		No.	%	No.	%
Newar	Male	51	89.5	6	10.5
	Female	16	80.0	4	20.0
	All	67	87.0	10	13.0
Parbatiya	Male	25	71.4	10	28.6
	Female	33	68.8	15	31.2
	All	58	69.9	25	30.1
Magar	Male	9	90.0	1	10.0
	Female	6	54.5	5	45.5
	All	15	71.4	6	28.6
Others	Male	3	50.0	3	50.0
	Female	2	25.0	6	75.0
	All	5	35.7	9	64.3
Total	Male	88	81.5	20	18.5
	Female	57	65.5	30	34.5
	All	145	74.4	50	25.6

Source: Author Survey

The figures relating to the average length of time that immigrants have been resident in Tansen are interesting because they begin to show how the pattern of migration to Tansen is changing and how this is beginning to affect the ethnic composition of the town. It is quite clear from the figures that a new phase of migration to the town has begun. Magar people tend to have arrived on average much more recently than Newar residents to the town. There has been a decline, therefore, in the relative numbers of Newar people coming to live in the town compared to Magar people in recent years. The figures in Table 5.14 (*Place of Origin of Migrants Correlated with Ethnicity*) below show that virtually all of these Magar immigrants have come from villages in Palpa district, whereas there is a more even divide between those who have come from Palpa and those who have come from elsewhere in Nepal amongst the Parbatiya population. The figures for Newar immigrants are almost the reverse of those for Magar immigrants with the majority coming from beyond Palpa district. It is also the case that significant Magar migration to Tansen only began from about 1980 with Parbatiya immigration also increasing overall during this period.

Table 5.15 (*Correlation of Ethnicity and Sex with Property Ownership*) shows, as one might expect from the above, that whereas Newar respondents to the survey tended to live in accommodation that was owned by a related member of their household, this was less likely to be the case with those from other ethnic groups, especially 'Others'. Statistics pertaining to occupation and income are notoriously difficult to interpret and care must be taken because the methods used to administer surveys and censuses can vary greatly (HMG 1984). There are marked differences in the figures for occupation between both of the most recent censuses and my own research data (Table 5.16 *Occupation and Activity Rates of Respondent and Household Main Income Earner*).

The main reason for the differences between my own survey findings and the 1991 census is likely to be the previously mentioned emphasis on the bazaar and immediately adjacent areas in the former and the total coverage of the municipality area in the latter. This is chiefly manifested in the relatively high proportion of respondents to the 1991 census who claimed that farming was their chief occupation. It is also the case that my respondents tended to use the general term 'service' (in its English or 'Neplish' form) to encompass categories of activity that the census divides between the three categories of 'service' (strictly speaking, servant's work), clerical and administrative work. My informants made little distinction between working as the servant of an individual and being in the service of an organization, be it a bank or the civil service.

It is difficult to know what to make of the 1981 census figures for occupations, which seem so bizarre as to be unfathomable. One explanation for the massive number of respondents to the 1981 census who claimed farming to be their occupation could be that this census asked for the respondents' main source of income as opposed to occupation. If this is the case, (and I have no definite proof of this as details of the precise phrasing of questions are not given in the published census) then the figures might make more sense.[12] A very large number of residents in the bazaar wards have multiple sources of income and the ownership of agricultural land is a key component in this. This land is often the legacy of service to the state or the investment of previous generations and is seldom farmed in person by the owner. Instead, the land is rented out to a tenant farmer and the produce of the land is divided fifty/fifty between the two parties (the *adhiya* system) (Miller 1990). These figures may, therefore, show the extent to which the inhabitants of the bazaar relied in the past on 'unearned' income from agricultural rents.

Table 5.16. Occupation and Activity Rates of Respondent and Household Main Income Earner

Occupation	Respondent	Main Earner	1991 Census	1981 Census
	%	%	%	%
Active				
Professional	6.2	8.9	10.9	2.9
Administrative	—[a]	—	1.9	0.5
Clerical	—[a]	—	8.7	2.0
Sales	63.1	53.6	17.2	6.0
Service	6.9	13.3	18.8	0.3
Farming	5.4	6.5	22.6	80.3
Labourer/Production	18.5	17.3	16.7	2.7
Not Stated	0.0	0.4	3.2	5.2
Inactive				
Student	43.1	—	53.8	43.9
Homemaker	47.7	—	34.6	38.4
Aged/Invalid	6.2	—	—	7.6
Unemployed	1.5[b]	—	—	2.5
Not Stated	1.5	—	11.6[d]	7.7

Activity Rates	Respondent		Main Earner		1991 Census		1981 Census	
	No.	%	No.	%	No.	%	No.	%
Total Active	130	66.7	248[c]	100.0	4,135	39.8	6,463	68.0
Total Inactive	65	33.3	—	—	6,243	60.2	3,057	32.0

Source: Author Survey, HMG, Nepal (1984) and HMG, Nepal (1994)

[a] No respondent to the author survey used either the term 'Administrative' or 'Clerical' to describe their own or another household member's activity. These categories appear to be subsumed under the general term 'Service' in everyday discourse (see further discussion in main text).
[b] Respondent described their occupation as "unpaid social work."
[c] Includes five respondents who receive income from rental of rooms to tenants and four receiving a pension from a previous occupation but continuing to do other paid work.
[d] Figure represents total of Aged/Invalid, Unemployed and Not Stated categories.

Table 5.17. Correlation of Ethnicity and Sex with Activity Rates

Ethnicity	Sex	Active		Inactive	
		No.	%	No.	%
Newar	Male	50	87.7	7	12.3
	Female	10	50.0	10	50.0
	All	60	77.9	17	22.1
Parbatiya	Male	27	77.1	8	22.9
	Female	20	41.7	28	58.3
	All	47	56.6	36	43.4
Magar	Male	7	70.0	3	30.0
	Female	6	54.5	5	45.5
	All	13	61.9	8	38.1
Others	Male	5	83.3	1	16.7
	Female	6	75.0	2	25.0
	All	11	78.6	3	21.4
Total	Male	89	82.4	19	17.6
	Female	42	48.3	45	51.7
	All	131	67.2	64	32.8

Source: Author Survey

Table 5.18. Correlation of Ethnicity and Caste with Activity Rates

Ethnicity	Caste	Active		Inactive	
		No.	%	No.	%
Newar	Hindu	31	72.1	12	27.9
	Buddhist	29	85.3	5	14.7
	All	60	77.9	17	22.1
Parbatiya	Bahun	16	53.3	14	46.7
	Chetri	19	57.6	14	42.4
	Occupational	12	60.0	8	40.0
	All	47	56.6	36	43.4
Magar		13	61.9	8	38.1
Indian		8	88.9	1	11.1
Others		3	60.0	2	40.0
Total		131	67.2	64	32.8

Source: Author Survey

Changes in the figures for occupation might then also be partly explained by a shift in the balance of sources of income of Tansen's inhabitants. As the value of agricultural land has fallen in recent decades, alternative sources of income have become more important relative to the income from agricultural rents. This income has come from wages for services or professional jobs based in the bazaar (mainly in the education and health sectors), from petty trading (mainly restaurants and *kirana* goods stores) and from urban rents (either renting out rooms in existing property or in newly built property, a phenomenon which will be discussed below).[13] The relatively high inactivity rates reported in the 1991 census (and to a lesser extent in my own survey, which interviewed a lower proportion of children than the population of Tansen as a whole) reflect the large student population in the town, a factor that will be examined in greater detail below when discussing education. A final factor is the extent to which underemployment, rather than unemployment, is a factor in the lives of Tansen's citizens, especially of young men in their late-teens and twenties.

If we look at variation between the sexes for each of the ethnic groups who live in Tansen, we first notice a predictable difference between declared rates of economic activity for men and women. Statistics relating to what census enumerators call 'economic activity rates' are a notoriously blunt instrument with regard to understanding how patterns of work vary between men and women. It is frequently the case that female work that contributes to the resources of a household is under represented for a variety of reasons (cf. Mies' (1982) discussion of this issue in relation to female lace makers in Narsapur, India). Enumerators frequently ask only for the economic activity of a putative household head and often this is typically regarded as a male figure. Economic activity that is not financially remunerated is also overlooked and work described in the Nepali census as 'homemaking' and described as 'inactivity' covers that sphere of domestic work that is almost impossible to quantify with regard to the contribution it makes to the reproduction of the household.[14] These factors must be taken into account when we consider the figures presented below. I have already mentioned that there is a general tendency for more men than women to be described as economically active. The ratio of active to inactive men and women varies, however, between ethnic groups. Newar and 'Other' women are described as most active, followed by Magar women and, finally, Parbatiya women described as least active.

As Table 5.18 (*Correlation of Ethnicity and Caste with Activity Rates*) shows, there is also some minor variation in activity rates within ethnic groups, which can probably be ascribed to the lesser or greater variation in rates of female economic activity. Some explanations for these general trends can be suggested based on statistics relating to the specific forms of economic activity that the households from different ethnic groups rely upon. These are detailed in Tables 5.19 (*Correlation of Ethnicity and Caste with Primary Activity of Household Main Income Earner*) and 5.20 (*Correlation of Ethnicity and Caste with Main Secondary Activity Contributing to Household Income*), which indicate that there is considerable variation in the patterns of occupation amongst the different ethnic groups living in Tansen. These statistics also reinforce the point that traditional, caste-based employment patterns may be breaking down in some cases, but caste still serves as a good predictor of occupation.

Table 5.19. Correlation of Ethnicity and Caste with Primary Activity of Household Main Income Earner

Ethnicity	Caste	Professional	Service/ Admin and Clerical	Sales	Farming	Labor/ Production	Pension/ Rent	Army/ Police	Total
		%	%	%	%	%	%	%	No.
Newar	Hindu	7.0	7.0	62.8	11.6	11.6			43
	Buddhist	2.9	2.9	64.7		29.4			34
	All	5.2	5.2	63.6	6.5	19.5			77
Parbatiya	Bahun	26.7	29.9	26.7	10.0	6.6			30
	Chetri	15.2	24.2	27.3	12.1	6.1	3.0	12.1	33
	Occupational	5.0	0.0	10.0		85.0			20
	All	16.7	20.4	22.9	8.4	25.3	1.2	4.8	83
Magar		4.8	9.5	23.8	14.3	4.8	14.3	28.6	21
Indian			0.0	88.9		11.1			9
Others			0.0	80.0		20.0			5
Total		9.7	11.8	43.6	7.7	20.0	2.1	5.1	195

Source: Author Survey

Table 5.20. Correlation of Ethnicity and Caste with Main Secondary Activity Contributing to Household Income

Ethnicity	Caste	Professional	Service/Admin and Clerical	Sales	Farming	Labor/Production	Pension/Rent	Army/Police	None	Total
		%	%	%	%	%	%	%	%	No.
Newar	Hindu	7.0	2.3	27.9		7.0	2.3		53.5	43
	Buddhist		5.9	35.3		8.8			50.0	34
	All	3.9	3.9	31.2		7.8	1.3		51.9	77
Parbatiya	Bahun	3.3	3.3	12.1	3.3	3.3	3.3		70.0	30
	Chetri	3.0	15.1	6.0		6.0	9.1		60.6	33
	Occupational					10.0	5.0	5.0	80.0	20
	All	2.4	7.2	7.2	1.2	6.0	6.0	1.5	68.7	83
Magar			4.8	33.3		4.8	9.5	4.8	42.9	21
Indian				44.4					55.6	9
Others									100.0	5
Total		2.6	5.1	21.0	0.5	6.2	4.1	1.0	59.5	195

Source: Author Survey

One obvious feature is the greater number of Parbatiya and Magar respondents who state that their household relies on 'unearned' income sources, such as pensions or rent, for all or part of their income. This accounts in particular for the comparatively low rates of economic activity claimed by Magar men who often rely on army pensions for all or part of their income. The second key feature is the reliance of Newar and 'Other' households on 'sales' as a source of income, whilst Bahun and Chetri Parbatiya households have a greater reliance on fixed salary income from 'professional', 'administration' or 'service' jobs. Parbatiya respondents from 'Occupational' castes groups, however, still show an overwhelming reliance on their traditional caste trades for their primary (often their only) household income and this is reflected in the large number who are described as involved in 'laboring or productive' activity. It is the case that both salaried occupations and the trades engaged in by 'Occupational' castes are highly gendered in Nepal, being almost the exclusive preserves of men.[15] 'Sales' on the other hand tends to involve almost all household members—male and female, young and old—at some point during the course of a working day (although overall control over the business and its revenues may still be in the hands of the senior male members of the household). Households that rely on the former categories of economic activity for their primary source of income might be expected, therefore, to show lower rates of female activity compared to those that rely on 'sales' and this does appear to be the case.

Nevertheless, the major caveat regarding the under-representation of female economic activity rates mentioned above applies particularly strongly here. If we look at the Parbatiya population in particular, we notice that many households even in a supposedly urban area control some land used for agriculture or market gardening or own livestock, either in the municipal area or the surrounding VDCs. This was a factor that was grossly under represented in the initial survey upon which these figures for economic activity are based. The more detailed follow-up survey showed that many of the respondents who made no mention of 'farming' as one of their household's resources did in fact derive at least some income from this source, even if this was not financial but the direct consumption of their land's produce. And it is invariably the case that the main burden for the care of this land falls onto the shoulders of female household members. In this way we may confirm the comment of one informant who described Tansen as "more rurban than urban" and, in doing so, question the capacity of a survey based upon this sort of paradigm to convey accurately the contribution of male and female members to the resources and reproduction of the household.

If we should treat figures for occupation with some caution, then individual and household income is doubly difficult to ascertain. The vast majority of informants claimed not to know what their average household income was, and whilst this might not be a surprise in all cases (in particular younger and older informants who were not economically active), it is probably also a sign of extreme reticence on the part of many people to answer detailed questions on this subject. Of the approximately 25% who were willing to place a figure on their household income, the range of *claimed* incomes went from one thousand rupees per month at lowest to fifty thousand rupees per month at highest. At the time of my fieldwork, the Nepali Rupee was worth approximately US$0.018 (an average exchange rate of US$1: NRs55). These figures give a range of US$18.18 to US$909.09) per month. The average (median) income was in the range between four thousand and five thousand rupees (US$72 to US$90).

Official statistics on the cost of living in hill urban areas issued by Nepal Rastriya Bank show that in the early years of the 1990s with which we are principally concerned here the consumer price index rose from 171.7 in 1989/90 to 242.1 in 1992/93 [base year 1983/84 = 100] (HMG 1994: 199–200). Although this increase compares favorably with that of urban areas in Nepal as a whole (179.9 to 260.3) and Kathmandu (190.0 to 283.0), it gives a clear indication of the inflation that threatened to run out of control throughout this period.[16] Inevitably, during periods of high inflation those with the lowest income are hardest hit, because essential food, clothing and housing items that must be purchased, take up an increasing proportion of income. This is especially the case as certain key items rose by more than the average increase in the Consumer Price Index (average rise for urban hill areas between 1989/90 and 1992/93 = 70.4), for example housing (85.7), meat, fish and eggs (88.3), milk and milk products (79.6) and spices (192.6), although other essential foodstuffs rose by less, for example grains and cereals (66.9), pulses 52.2, oil and ghee (56.6) and sugar (19.6).

The actual prices of some of these essential items give some indication of the purchasing power represented by the incomes given above. In 1992/93 medium quality rice, for example, averaged NRs13.57 per kilo, maize NRs6.96 per kilo, ghee NRs121.12 per kilo, chicken NRs75.48 per kilo and lentils between NRs22.28 and NRs28.02 per kilo depending on their quality. Clearly, those on an income of four to five thousand rupees per month (never mind only a thousand rupees per month) would be increasingly hard-pressed to make ends meet even without taking into account the incidental expenditure incurred at certain times of the year (during the festival of Dasain, for example, when people are expected to visit their family and provide gifts) or if expediency requires additional expenditure (due to medical problems or child birth, for example).

What these figures and the following discussion of access to key commodities and technologies show is that despite the apparent absence of extreme poverty in Tansen, the affluence indicated by the large numbers of consumer goods available in the bazaar's shops is not enjoyed by a wide proportion of the population. The absence of poverty visible to the casual observer in the bazaar can be accounted for by the fact that many of the poorest members of the population are short term residents, often young men and women, who have come from their homes in the neighboring hill areas or the Tarai to work as household servants, laborers and petty traders. If opportunities for employment in Tansen do not materialize then these members of the municipal population move on to other towns, generally in the Tarai or India. Sill and Kirkby (1991: 88) note, however, that in net numerical terms the levels of migration to hill towns like Tansen (both from other towns in Nepal or India and from rural areas) is much lower than migration from rural to rural areas by people searching for increasingly scarce land for cultivation. Even so, the presence of these migrants in Tansen is not so much an indicator of poverty in the town itself, but rather it is a reminder of poverty elsewhere in Nepal (KC 2003; Panta 2004; Thieme and Wyss 2005).

It has been observed that the towns and cities of Nepal are comparatively small compared to those in the neighboring South Asian states of India and Bangladesh (Conway and Shrestha 1980). Similarly, the growth rates of Nepalese towns, whilst high in the case of the cities of the Kathmandu Valley and Tarai, are still less than that of most developing nations. And, as we have seen already in this chapter (Table 5.1 *Ranking of Urban Places in Nepal According to Population Size, 1961–1991*) Tansen has one of the lowest growth rates of all Nepal's towns. This factor coupled with the long-standing wealth of the town's established citizens described in the previous chapter form the context within which the relative affluence of the town can be understood.

Despite the overall decline in the political and economic fortunes of the town the standard of living for a large proportion of the population remains high. This is nowhere more evident than from an examination of the rates of access to public utilities such as piped water and electricity and the ownership of durable commodities that such access enables. Indeed, the provision of electricity is almost ubiquitous throughout the municipality, both in bazaar and rural wards (98% provision according to my survey) and piped water does not lag far behind (87% provision). Table 5.21 (*Household Ownership of Utilities, Media and Communication Items*) details the numbers of households encompassed by my survey who owned consumer durables, such as television, radio, telephones, cameras and cable television.

Table 5.21. Household Ownership of Utilities, Media and Communication Items

Item	Households	
	No.	%
Electricity	191	98.0
Piped Water	169	86.7
Black and White Television	76	39.0
Color Television	60	30.8
Both Types of Television	5	2.6
Satellite Television Receiver	5	2.6
Cable Television	42	21.5
Videotape Recorder	24	12.3
Radio	153	78.5
Telephone (landline)	85	43.6
Computer	0	—
Camera	77	39.5
Audiotape Recorder	115	59.0

Source: Author Survey

Access to education (especially that beyond primary level) and certain forms of employment (especially those requiring capital, both financial and cultural) are largely restricted, as one might expect, to males and to those from the 'higher' caste groups (Buddhist and Hindu Newars, Bahuns and, to a lesser extent, Chetris). That such distinctions inevitably lead to gross inequalities in ownership of and access to certain consumption items can be illustrated statistically. Figures for ownership of certain items of communication technology along with direct access to the home of electricity and drinking water for different ethnic/caste groups are shown in the following table (5.22 *Correlation of Ethnicity and Caste with Ownership of or Direct Access to Utilities, Media and Communication Items*). Access is defined here as either owning an item oneself or living in a household with someone who owns the item. A simple statistical test (χ^2) shows that this variation is significant, but as we have noted above, these statistics serve to hide considerable variation within these groups.[17] Kaphle's (1994) study of water supply in Tansen notes that only 11% of households rely on piped water alone, because the inadequacies of the supply system make it unreliable. About 89% of household rely on a combination of both piped and spring water. This figure is close to this study's survey result for piped water, but Kaphle's comments do place this high percentage in its proper context; a better question would be to ask who has regular and reliable access to piped water. Likewise, Sharma (1988: 52) notes that in Kathmandu, where access to electricity is also virtually ubiquitous the key difference between poorer and richer households tends to be greater "end use multiplicity." Whereas poorer households use electricity only for lighting, richer households not surprisingly use electric power for cooking, refrigeration, heating and powering consumer durables such as televisions and video recorders.

Left at this Sharma's observations are something of a truism; those who can afford commodities such as refrigerators and televisions obviously need electricity to power them. However, there is a serious point to be made here. The pattern of inequalities and differential distribution of resources that we see in Tansen is very real and partially reflects the underlying structure of relations between the different caste and class groups that make up the population. Increasingly, divisions within Nepal's urban communities are manifested not only through the structures of caste and kinship, but also through the differential consumption of goods and services (Liechty 2003) amongst which media commodities are often most prominent.

Education is another key indicator of the relative affluence of a significant proportion of Tansen's population. In recent years, those with sufficient income and other resources have been able to purchase private education for their children. The ability of families to send their children to school, even a supposedly free state-school, relies both upon their ability to purchase certain essential supplies (books, pens and a basic uniform, for example) and, especially when the children reach secondary or even upper primary school age, upon the need for their children's labor in agricultural production. The increasing ability of families in Tansen to educate their children is reflected through a number of statistics.

Table 5.22. Correlation of Ethnicity and Caste with Ownership of or Direct Access to Utilities, Media and Communication Items

Ethnicity	Caste	Television	Cable Television	Radio	Audiotape Recorder	Videotape Recorder	Telephone (landline)	Camera	Water	Electricity
		%	%	%	%	%	%	%	%	%
Newar	Hindu	94	47	94	85	26	71	59	100	100
	Buddhist	84	28	91	70	16	63	49	98	100
Parbatiya	Bahun	77	13	93	57		50	37	87	100
	Chetri	67	12	70	55	9	30	27	85	100
	Occupational	45		45	25		10	25	50	95
Magar		62	29	71	43	19	24	43	81	100
Others		29		47	47		16		85	79
Total		71	22	78	58	12	44	39	87	98

Source: Author Survey

Recent censuses have shown a rapid rise in levels of adult literacy in Tansen, from 51.1% of the population in 1981 to 77.6% in 1991. This last census figure closely matches that of my own survey, which showed a literacy level of 79.9%. We may presume that this is in most cases more than functional literacy (the ability to at best 'get by' in a literate, urban society), because questions about newspaper readership in my survey found that 66.1% of people claimed to regularly read newspapers or magazines. This last figure closely matches that for the number of people who had completed at least the primary level of education in Tansen. In actual fact, as the following table 5.23 (*Education of Population*) shows, more people claimed to have had at least some experience of secondary education than had been only to primary school or had no formal education combined. Increasing levels of literacy are, as one might expect, matched by increasing levels of educational experience as demonstrated by the comparison of the 1981 and 1991 census figures given in the following table.

Table 5.23. Education of Population

Level of Education	1981		1991	
	No.	%	No.	%
None	6,596	59.6	1,508	16.1
Primary	1,628	14.7	2,501	26.8
Secondary	2,207	19.9	4,272	45.7
College	644	5.81	1,066	11.4
Total Population	11,075[a]	100.0	9,347[b]	100.0

Source: HMG, Nepal (1984) and HMG, Nepal (1994)
[a] 1981 census figures are for population five years old and over.
[b] 1991 census figures are for population six years old and over.

It is of little surprise that levels of educational attainment and, therefore, literacy are unevenly distributed throughout the survey population, which, as previously noted, gives a reasonably comprehensive sample of the bazaar population as a whole. Tables 5.24 (*Correlation of Ethnicity and Sex with Literacy*) and 5.25 (*Correlation of Ethnicity and Sex with Highest Level of Educational Experience*) give some indication of the extent of this uneven distribution. These figures show that literacy levels in Tansen are relatively high compared to the urban average in Nepal (79.9% in the survey sample and 77.6% in the 1991 census, compared to the national urban average of 66.9% in the 1991 census). Levels of literacy amongst both the male and female population also show figures that are well above the national urban average in the case of males and just above average in the case of females (males equal 78% and females equal 54.8% in the 1991 census). As Table 5.24 shows, however, the population in Tansen does not differ from the national trend for a marked disparity in the ratio of male to female literacy considered as a proportion of the urban population as a whole. So, whilst there are roughly twice as many literate males as females as a percentage of the total population, there are over nine times as many illiterate women as men living in the Tansen bazaar area. It is notable that this trend is more pronounced amongst the non-Newar female population. 25% of Newar women are illiterate compared to 41.7% of Parbatiya, 36.4% of Magar and 100% of 'Other' women. Levels of male illiteracy in Tansen bazaar are almost insignificantly small (only 2.1% of the total population).

Table 5.24. Correlation of Ethnicity and Sex with Literacy

Ethnicity	Sex	Literate		Illiterate	
		No.	%	No.	%
Newar	Male	57	100.0	0	0.0
	Female	15	75.0	5	25.0
	All	72	93.5	5	6.5
Parbatiya	Male	34	97.1	1	2.9
	Female	28	58.3	20	41.7
	All	62	74.7	21	25.3
Magar	Male	10	100.0	0	0.0
	Female	7	63.6	4	36.4
	All	17	81.0	4	19.0
Others	Male	3	50.0	3	50.0
	Female	0	0.0	8	100.0
	All	3	21.4	11	78.6
Total	Male	104	96.3	4	3.7
	Female	50	57.8	37	42.2
	All	154	78.5	41	21.5

Source: Author Survey

Table 5.24 reinforces the obvious point that access to education is very important by showing a fairly strong inverse relationship between education and literacy correlated with sex for the survey population. As we noted above, just over twice as many men as women are literate in Tansen and more than twice as many women as men have received no education at all. But we should also note that, whereas lack of education is not a barrier to literacy for most men (only 4 out of 19 uneducated men claimed to be unable to read and write), women seem to be much less likely to be taught to read and write informally within the home or other non-school environment; the comparable figure for women is thirty seven out of forty one uneducated women (90.2%) claiming to be unable to read or write. Men are also more likely to progress to post-school education than are women. Whilst the figures for attendance at school level are broadly comparable for men and women, more that three times as many men as women have received a post-school education. Once again, variation in educational attainment and sex can be related to ethnicity with by far the most obvious 'anomaly' being the large number of Parbatiya women who have had no formal education.

Table 5.25. Correlation of Ethnicity and Sex with Highest Level of Educational Experience

Ethnicity	Sex	None	Primary	Secondary	College
		%	%	%	%
Newar	Male	14.0	5.3	14.0	66.7
	Female	30.0	20.0	15.0	35.0
	All	18.2	9.1	14.3	58.4
Parbatiya	Male	17.1	20.0	14.3	48.6
	Female	47.9	10.4	20.8	20.8
	All	34.9	14.5	18.1	35.5
Magar	Male	20.0	10.0	50.0	20.0
	Female	54.5	27.3	9.1	9.1
	All	38.1	19.0	28.6	14.3
Others	Male	50.0	16.7	16.7	16.7
	Female	75.0	25.0	0.0	0.0
	All	64.3	21.4	7.1	7.1
Total	Male	17.6	11.1	17.6	53.7
	Female	47.1	16.1	16.1	20.7
	All	30.8	13.3	16.9	39.0

Source: Author Survey

Table 5.26. Correlation of Caste and Sex of Parbatiya Respondents with Highest Level of Educational Experience

Caste	Sex	None	Primary	Secondary	College
		%	%	%	%
Bahun	Male	7.7	15.4	15.4	61.5
	Female	17.6	11.8	29.4	41.2
	All	13.3	13.3	23.3	50.0
Chetri	Male	15.4	7.7	15.4	61.5
	Female	55.0	10.0	20.0	15.0
	All	39.4	9.1	18.2	33.3
Occupational	Male	33.3	44.4	11.1	11.1
	Female	81.8	9.1	9.1	0.0
	All	60.0	25.0	10.0	5.0
Total	Male	17.1	20.0	14.3	48.6
	Female	47.9	10.4	20.8	20.8
	All	34.9	14.4	18.1	32.5

Source: Author Survey

The above table (5.26 *Correlation of Caste and Sex of Parbatiya Respondents with Highest Level of Educational Experience*) shows that there is consid-

erable variation within the Parbatiya ethnic group when we consider the correlation of sex with educational attainment. Whilst Bahun women and men have
records of educational attainment that closely match each other, both Chetri and
'Untouchable' women are far less likely than their male counterparts to either
have any formal education or, if they do enter school, to go on to post-school
education.[18]

Visions of Tansen's Past, Present and Future

The descriptive statistics that form the substance of the first part of this chapter
point to the effects in the present day of the previous two centuries of Tansen's
historical development (remembering that we are here talking of the so-called
'ethnographic present' of the mid-1990s when fieldwork was conducted). The
town's population has been changing rapidly both in terms of the composition of
ethnic groups and the contrasting experiences of intergenerational groups, especially for the female population, even if such changes prevented the continuation
of inequalities in many cases. Nevertheless, Tansen with its streets reminiscent
of "old Kathmandu memories", as a RCTV publicity video has it, may seem to
the eyes of a visitor, especially a foreigner or stranger, to be a remnant of a by-
gone era; unchanging by contrast to the upheavals experienced in other cities
and other countries.

As we shall see in the remainder of this chapter, such discourses are by no
means limited to tourists and their guidebooks, but they are subtly inflected in
the words of Nepali commentators, both current residents of Tansen, migrants
from the town, and others, such as journalists. These form what Raymond Williams calls a distinctive "structure of feeling . . . [which is] the culture of a period: it is the particular living result of all the elements in the general organization [of a society]" (Williams 1965: 64). It is a structure of feeling that shares
much with the evocations of the lost pastoral idylls that Williams so meticu-
lously documents in his work on the relationship between the country and the
city in English literature (1993). The remainder of this chapter, therefore, examines these various comments on Tansen's past, present and future, in order to
describe the essential structural unity that underlies this discourse, a unity that is
mediated through the daily evidence of the "specific forms" (Williams
1993:295) from which social life is made:

> The morning newspaper, the early radio program, the evening television, are in
> this sense forms of orientation in which our central social sense is both sought
> and in specific and limited ways confirmed . . . Much of the content of modern
> communications is this kind of substitute for directly discoverable and transitive
> relations to the world. It can be properly related to the scale and complexity of
> modern society, of which the city is always the most evident example. But it
> has become more general, reaching to the most remote rural regions. It is a form
> of shared consciousness rather than merely a set of techniques. And as a form
> of consciousness it is not to be understood by rhetorical analogies like the
> 'global village'. Nothing could be less like the experience of any kind of village

or settled active community. For in its main uses it is a form of unevenly shared consciousness of persistently external events. It is what appears to happen, in these powerfully transmitted and mediated ways, in a world with which we have no perceptible connections but which we feel is at once central and marginal to our lives (Williams 1993: 295–6).

Discourses centered on the supposed loss of a way of life that was characteristic of Tansen arise therefore out of the material, social and cultural disjunctures that are typical of modernity and which appear to be confirmed by the evident changes in the characteristics of the population that were previously described. But we should not expect such discourses to be accurate in their depiction of the world that once was, for they serve the purposes of the present rather than give voice to the past in any naive sense.

We saw in the previous chapter that modern Tansen was created following the annexation of the kingdom of Palpa by the forces of Gorkha and came to form an architectural and cultural mirror image of the capital city of Kathmandu to the east. Subsequently, it was marginalized as a place of exile. One hundred and fifty years of this experience, however, made it the home of a community with the confidence to carryout an act of great political audacity, the so-called "one hundred days of democratic revolution" (Pangeni 1994) in 1950. These are seen by many in the town as a watershed in the creation of a distinctive Palpali identity, which had been in a process of gestation during this long period.

It is an identification with place that relies for its rhetorical force and the ability to elicit some emotional response upon the paradoxical relationship of the town of Tansen, rather than the district as a whole, with the encompassing body of the Nepali nation-state. As the material and symbolic form of Nepal has changed, so too has Tansen's material form and identity altered in the flux of this history. Umberto Eco claims, echoing the basic tenets of Levi-Strauss's structuralism, that "in any system, whether *geopolitical* or chromatic or lexical, units are defined not in themselves but in terms of opposition and position in relation to other units. There can be no units without a system" (1996: 165; emphasis added). The times of the Anglo-Nepali War of 1814–16 and the hundred days of *de facto* autonomy during the 1950 revolution mark the high points of Palpa's importance in the modern geopolitical system of Nepal, points around which all subsequent developments have been oriented.

Eric von Fürer-Haimendorf (1956: 36) has observed that the architecture of Newar towns embodies their kinship system; a Newar "sees in the precincts of his town the historic limits to the spread of patrilineal exogamous descent groups and considers the citizens of other towns as members of an out-group, even if they should bear a clan name identical with his own." After two centuries of the consolidation of kinship links within Tansen the migration of Newar family members to other towns appears to be placing considerable strain upon this conservative cultural ethos. The difficulty in maintaining functioning *guthi* organisations in Tansen was a common topic of conversation with many of my Newar informants.[19] Mikesell (1988: 218) describes a similar situation in the town of Bandipur where, since the collapse of the cloth trade in the 1970s, over 80% of the Newar population has left.

> [This] meant not only that most of the accumulated mercantile surplus was taken to the lowland, but that landed property around Bandipur has come to be characterized by absentee landlordism . . . Most of the other Newars, even the poorer ones, also wish to abandon Bandipur. Their accumulation of capital and the education of their children are directed towards this purpose.

A closer examination of children's educational experiences can help us to understand better how the town's present identity has been shaped by this history. During our time in Tansen my partner, Harriet, taught English in a local private boarding school. Although in recent years the proliferation of such private schools has reached almost epidemic proportions in the towns and cities of Nepal, this particular school was slightly different. It had been opened as long ago as 1979 during the time when a local weaving entrepreneur who was now its chairman of governors was mayor. Its then Principal explained to me that the school had been financed through a direct grant from the Municipality and charitable donations from wealthy members of the community. The primary motivation in setting up the school was to provide high quality, English-medium teaching in the town to encourage parents to educate their children in Tansen, rather than send them to boarding schools in Kathmandu or India, or migrating as a family to these places in search of better educational prospects. In this way, they hoped to reverse the perceived drain of educated people away from Tansen by preventing their flight at an early age and, perhaps more importantly, by keeping their parents in the town whilst their children studied. Although it was a fee-paying school and almost all revenue came from that source, the Municipality continued to provide some funding for the school.

This combination of fees, historical links to the Panchayat era, and the domination of the first post-1990 Municipality administration by Congress politicians had gained the school a reputation as the school of the elite in the town.[20] This may be one reason why the school was the subject of an arson attack on some of its classrooms in March 1996. Rumors about the identity of the culprits ranged from pupils disaffected by the harsh discipline in the school, to teachers from rival private schools, to Maoist terrorists (the People's War having been declared by the Communist Party of Nepal (Maoist) in the previous month). No one ever admitted responsibility or was charged with this crime.

About one month later Stephen Mikesell, an American anthropologist working in Nepal published an article in a daily newspaper entitled "We are all becoming doctors!" (*Everest Herald* 29th April 1996). In this short article, he described how during a trip to a school in a village north of Kathmandu he found that in answer to his questions all the children declared that they wanted to become doctors after taking their School Leaving Certificate examinations. Given the inadequacy of their education and their background as poor farmers such an aspiration could hardly be realistic and so Mikesell looked for some other explanation for this desire. Mikesell found his answer in the image of a doctor from Kathmandu who visited the village to investigate the land he held there and let to tenant farmers who were in all likelihood the parents of the children in this class.

Rapidly rising land prices meant that this doctor would shortly be selling this land for development further depriving the farmers of their income.

> The young people, sitting raggedly in Spartan, dirt floored classrooms, knew that the only value of farming is being an object of other people's speculation. They see the doctor as one of the speculators, whether as a landlord or indifferent fee collector in the doctor's office, so of course their choice in life is to become a doctor—a speculator with status (ibid.).

I wanted to replicate Mikesell's enquiry and so enlisted the help of my wife's pupils in a class that was just about to embark on their course of SLC studies.[21] They wrote a set of short essays in English entitled "What I am going to do when I am older" from which the following excerpts are taken.[22] They are broadly representative of the twenty seven essays that were completed:

> I'll give SLC examination. I will pass it in first division. I will go to college. I will read subject science. When I'll pass I.Sc. [Intermediate Science] first year I will prepare for medical examination. When I'll give I.Sc. Second year exam I'll give medical exam also. This is because I am going to be a doctor. My aim is to be a doctor if possible. Then when I'll pass the medical exam, I'll give my other exam for being a doctor. All these things I'll do outside of Tansen because science college here is not so good. (Sita Tuladhar)

> When I will pass my SLC exam I will go to university outside country. I will read so hard. When I will come to my motherland I will do a job of Air Hostess. (Menuka Vajracharya)

> When I pass the exam of SLC in first division I will study as an engineer in Britain. (Gajendra Maharjan)

> If I can pass my SLC on good marks I may read maths and science. I will read these subjects out of Tansen somewhere in Nepal. (Shiva Koirala)

> I will study in Tribhuvan University [at Kirtipur in the Kathmandu Valley] and I will study more and more about medicine. I will study in Nepal and I will go to Russia for the study of the doctor. (Rishikesh Chetri)

> I would go to Kathmandu and will start studying at the science campus. After finishing my college life I would start doing a job on in a project. After I built up a strong foundation on this earth to live I will marry a girl from Darjeeling. After being well in my job I will make a house in Kathmandu and I will live there. I will leave the job in the project and start a small hotel. I will gain some money from the hotel which would be enough for me to start a next business. I will take my children in foreign countries for their better knowledge. My next job will be to organize a dyeing factory in Kathmandu itself. (Narayan Sharma)

> When I will finish my education I will plan to go to another civilized country and my best country is India. (Krishna Poudyal)

In Kathmandu I will read B.A. in languages and computing. After finishing my B.A. . . . I am going to the army in USA. I will be in the army in the USA. I will make my home in Kathmandu. Then I will marry one pretty girl. Again I will go to my army job in USA. After completing my army job in USA I will return to Nepal and I will work for developing our society. (Dharam Pandey)

I would like to serve patients being a doctor. I would like to go to the villages where there is lack of education and medicines and serve the people there. I want to serve poor people of my country as our country is known as third poor country in the world. (Radha Shrestha)

This is by no means an exhaustive analysis of these pupils' work but it does seem to confirm Mikesell's observation that becoming a doctor or engineer are common aspirations amongst school children in Nepal and there can be little doubt that the association of these professions with wealth and status play just as important a role here as in the village mentioned in his article. In addition to this, there is the frequently expressed desire to leave Tansen for other places, either in Nepal (invariably Kathmandu) or abroad, where it is perceived that the opportunities for educational and economic advancement are greater. There is, of course, a potentially large gap between the aspirations of children and what they may achieve in practice, but the school did not appear to be generating any strong desire on the part of its pupils to remain in Tansen beyond their studies.

Whilst this particular structure of feeling may not be unique to the citizens of Tansen in contemporary Nepal, it is strongly manifested in the historical experience of the town and its people. It primary manifestation here is the centrifugal, *outward* gaze of these young people and their visions of places beyond Tansen, places where knowledge is located and to which access is achieved by the acquisition of education, specifically the passing of examinations. Whilst this is undoubtedly linked to the development discourse discussed by Pigg (1992; see chapter 6) in that a familiar opposition of *bikasit* (developed) to *abikasit* (undeveloped) places is at work, it is obvious that Tansen is somehow squeezed between, or rather is squeezed out, of this dichotomy. It is a place both with and without the developed or modern characteristics that are privileged in development discourse in Nepal.

It is ironic that the pupils who express these sentiments in their essays are the same ones who are educated in a school set up to counteract some of the disparities that some of their parents' and grandparents' contemporaries perceived in the Nepali landscape of development. For the children of the middle class in Tansen, especially those without any economic capital to tie them to the town or region, educational capital is the key resource upon which they believe that their future will depend (cf. Bourdieu 1988). Believing that no significant material or social concerns tie them to the town, the children are at least free to dream of a future lived elsewhere.

Significantly, the structure of feeling that we can discern in the words and deeds of the older generation is slightly different, although still linked, to many of the same concerns. Williams (1965: 65) claims that a particularly interesting facet of culture is that:

It does not seem to be, in any formal sense, learned. One generation may train its successor, with reasonable success, in the social character or the general cultural pattern, but the new generation will have its own structure of feeling, which will not appear to have come 'from' anywhere. For here, most distinctly, the changing organization is enacted in the organism: the new generation responds in its own ways to the unique world it is inheriting, taking up many continuities, that can be traced, and reproducing many aspects of the organization, which can be separately described, yet feeling its whole life in certain ways differently, and shaping its creative response into a new structure of feeling.

There is great unity between all generations and across almost all social divides in Tansen over the identification of the triumvirate of education, health and tourism as the supposed key to success in the future. The difference lies in the fact that, whereas the most recent generation appears less concerned about whether they have to go elsewhere to seek these icons of the future, for the older generation the direction of their own sentiments seems to be reversed with an emphasis on bringing these developments to Tansen itself, whilst at the same time affirming that this is a *rebirth* of glories that are well within the range of living memory. The town is balanced upon the historical point where past and future meet in the present. As a journalist writing for a weekly news magazine observes, "despite its natural and rich heritage, the beautiful town is gripped in an identity crisis . . . Now most of the residents of Palpa find themselves hard-pressed in their encounter with economic crisis at a time when they have neither new options nor old options" (Devkota 1998: 24).

This point is brought out well in the introduction to a video produced by RCTV to promote both themselves and the town. Amidst a montage of scenes from the bazaar and Srinagar Hill, a female announcer narrates the following in English:

> Tansen: An alluring city just three hundred kilometers to the west of Kathmandu, the capital of Nepal, is situated at 4500 feet on the lap of Srinagar Hill. You will find old Kathmandu memories here in the cobbled stone streets. Old type houses. Temples. Shrines. Stupas. Pleasing weather and beautiful Himalayan panorama. For centuries Tansen has been a leader in different fields; heritage preservation, environment conservation, education, health, and more recently in mass communication.

Old memories are a theme in many pieces of journalism that attempt to evoke the spirit of Tansen. According to Ananda Shrestha (1996), "still unruffled by the arrival of the Twentieth Century and the soon to arrive Twenty First Century, Tansen continues to retain the timeless magic of the centuries." For Dahal (1993: 78), "Tansen is charming because it is unspoiled by modernity, pollution and urban bustle . . . Age-old festivals have yet to be displaced by Hindi cinema here; its people remember the preferences of the gods, and religion has not become solely a product for tourists." Likewise, according to Bhattarai (1996), "the historic city of Tansen is equally rich and famous for its scenic beauty as well as for its natural resources. It geographical location is such that it cannot do without [sic] moving whoever happens to visit the place." The over-whelming sense here is not just of glories from the past but of glories that soon may be a thing of the past if something is not done to arrest the decay and erosion caused by time and neglect. "The ancient, artistic windows have lost their original beauty" (Bhattarai 1996); "Ranighat Durbar loses past glory" (*Everest Herald* 25th June 1996); "Is Tansen dying?" asks Shrish Rana (1994), adding that although "Much of its history is written in . . . the city itself. . . . [T]he glory has gone."[23]

The paradox for Tansen is that in attempting to encourage tourism by representing the history of the town as a heritage resource, the present economic predicament and political marginalization of the town is re-emphasized. Modernization and development, which ordinarily are privileged in cultural discourse, therefore bring not just hope for the future but a threat when placed within the local context of Tansen and Palpa. The dramatic rise and fall of the town's commercial fortunes following the construction of the Siddhartha Rajmarg and the road link into the region to the west are a testament to the fact that these feelings of apprehension are firmly based in and structured by the material history of the town which sees hundreds of tourists pass by on the way to Pokhara and Kathmandu each year, hundreds of people from the hills pass through on buses without stopping each day, and which threatens to send the children of Tansen from the town in increasing numbers in search of a future that the town cannot afford to provide.

Conclusion

Tansen's population has always varied in the social and cultural composition of its population to some extent since its re-foundation in the early decades of the Nineteenth Century. In recent years, however, this variation has become more pronounced as migration from a variety of locations both inside and outside Palpa district, as well as the annexation of rural wards from surrounding VDCs, contributed to a doubling of population size.

In absolute terms the size of the Newar population of the town has risen, but in relative terms the town can no longer be described as a Newar dominated bazaar because of its population alone (cf. Lewis and Shakya 1988). The central market area of Tansen with its historic architecture reminiscent of the cities of the Kathmandu Valley is still dominated by Newar traders and manufacturers, although, as the earlier part of this chapter showed, even this is no longer wholly the case as they have emigrated from the town in increasing numbers. The population has increased due to the arrival of Parbatiya, Magar and Madhesi (Tarai-origin) immigrants and by the expansion of the municipality to surrounding 'rural' wards, which has largely led to an increase in the number of Parbatiya citizens. As the 1991 census figures show, the population of the municipality *as a whole* is divided between Parbatiya, Newar, Magar and 'Others' in an approximate ratio of fifty to twenty-five to fifteen to ten respectively.

The increased diversity in the ethnic composition of Tansen's population does not appear to have been matched by any concomitant shift in the distribution of differing forms of capital within the community. As is the case with Nepal as a whole, Newars (both Hindu and Buddhist) and high caste Parbatiyas (Bahun and Chetri) still hold a dominant position within the town. This dominance rests upon preferential access to key resources such as education (especially beyond primary level), salaried employment within national and local level institutions, and property (both domestic and commercial) from which income can be generated either through productive business or rent. Although the standard of living for Tansen's citizens as a whole is high, even when compared to the most prosperous rural areas in Palpa district, the fortunes of many within the Newar and Parbatiya section of the community are considerably in advance of the general urban population. However, it has been pointed out above that this applies for the most part only to the male segment of this population, as women do not benefit equally from this prosperity, even in a community like Tansen where their situation is better than in many other places.

The owners and producers of Ratna Cable Television's programming, which is the specific focus of this study are drawn from this Newar and high-caste Parbatiya sections of the community. But, we should not assume that this *necessarily* means that the organization and its programming are biased, either consciously or unconsciously, towards the narrow sectional interests of this fraction of the population.

The following chapters look at whether this is actually the case and, if so, how such bias is manifested in practice. They also examine the extent to which local media in Tansen have challenged or contributed to the reproduction of the structures of feeling that have been described in this chapter, since the serious economic problems and social upheaval that the town faces have also caused acute anxiety to many within the same dominant fraction of the town's population.

Notes

1. Village Panchayat is the old designation for the administrative areas now called Village Development Committees (VDCs).

2. In 1994, Wards Nine to Fourteen accounted for 7,265 people out of Tansen's total population of 16,169, or 45% of the total.

3. It must be noted that the ward boundaries within which my survey work was conducted were based on the perceptions of my informants and not those of the precise local government boundaries. Despite this, the following data does serve as a reasonable guide to variations between the different areas of the town. It is also the case that my research confined itself to the most urbanized of the municipality area, as it was within this area that reception of the RCTV local program was possible. Variation in the detail of my own research data should be taken into account because of this factor. I came to know the bazaar and its immediate surroundings much more intimately than the 'rural' wards of the municipality. In retrospect this variation in detail might be regretted, but one mitigating fact is that this variation in contact with and knowledge of the various parts of the mu-

nicipality is not, in my experience, confined to the foreign researcher and is a fact of most bazaar dwellers' lives.

4. See Gaige (1975) and Burghart (1993) for a discussion of the political nature of the official registration of citizenship in Nepal, in particular as it relates to the Tarai region.

5. A period chosen purely on the basis that it extended from the most recent instance of a certificate being issued to the time when a new set of record books were first used.

6. I have decided to disregard the figures for religious affiliation and mother tongue derived from the 1981 census for this reason.

7. According to the 1991 census Palpa's population comprised Magars 116,694 (49.4%), Bahuns 47,911 (20.3%), Chetris 20,150 (8.5%) and 'Others' 51,558 (21.8%) (Gurung 1994). Precisely how many of these 'Others' were Newars is not indicated. Some indication of the differential between Tansen and Palpa as a whole is given by the figures for the 1981 census which list Newari speakers as 21.7% of the town's population but only 2.2% of the total district population (HMG 1984 vol. 3, Tables 9 and 12).

8. We must also contextualize this statement and note that the average life expectancy for Nepal is 55 for males and 53.5 for females, although the life expectancy in urban areas like Tansen is considerably higher than in rural areas and is thus higher than these averages (HMG 1995: 110–112)

9. The classification of household types used here is intended only as a means for presenting an easily quantifiable representation of the various circumstances in which people live. Some informants did refer spontaneously to their household as a 'joint family' but the categories used here are wholly *etic* and do not necessarily correspond to informants' own perceptions.

10. This point can be shown numerically by totaling the number of joint, extended and joint-extended families in the sample (111) and working back through the figures for household size adding them up until this total is reached or surpassed. This does not happen until we reach the point where household size equals 5.

11. In only one case, that of a Thakali hotel owner in Gahira Gaun, did I find an example of a married female who had left her husband's household to work elsewhere ('elsewhere' being in this case Tansen). This is hardly surprising given the patriarchal nature of almost all of Nepal's ethnic groups. My survey sample did include 6 examples of married women who had returned to their natal household in Tansen without their husbands (3 Hindu Newars, 1 Bahun, 1 Chetri and 1 Magar). Given that residence in Nepal is invariably patrilocal after marriage, this would indicate either a breakdown in the marriage or that the woman and her children could not be taken into one of the households of the husband's family during his absence.

12. During my own fieldwork, I discussed the 1991 census of Nepal with a man who was employed as a census enumerator. He stated that during the course of this work, whilst instruction as to the correct question format were given, it was often necessary to improvise question formats in order to elicit a response from his informants, many of whom could not, in his opinion, understand the 'official' form of questions recommended by HMG Central Bureau of Statistics.

13. *Kirana* stores sell a range of everyday goods such as tea, cigarettes, soap and packaged foods like biscuits and noodles.

14. Out of nineteen male respondents who could be described as economically inactive, 84% were students, 16% were retired and none were 'homemakers'. The comparable figures for the forty five 'inactive' female respondents were 29% students, 2% retired and 69% 'homemakers'.

15. A total of four female respondents to the survey regarded their salaried work as their household's primary source of income. Two women regarded their salaried work as

the household's main secondary source of income. These totals represent 21% and 40% respectively of the female survey respondents engaged in salaried work. The figures for female laborers or those engaged in 'productive' activity are seven for primary income and five for secondary representing 18% and 42% of the survey respondents respectively.

16. The increase in the consumer price index for urban areas in the Tarai matched that in hill areas quite closely, rising from 175.0 in 1989/90 to 249.9 in 1992/93.

17. A χ^2 test was carried out on the above figures (excluding those for cable television and video ownership which were too low) to determine whether there was any significant variation between ownership of /direct access to these communication technologies, water and electricity when correlated against ethnicity/caste. $\chi^2 = 66$ and df=36. Critical region at 1% error = 58.6, therefore, the results were significant.

18. No corresponding figures are given for Magar or Newar men and women for several reasons. In the case of the Magar respondents, this research did not consider intra-ethnic variation in sociocultural status, although any study that concentrated solely on Magar communities in Palpa or elsewhere would have to consider this factor. Amongst the Newar community, when compared to the Parbatiya community, there is a far more restricted range of caste groups within the total community. As such, the corresponding figures for educational attainment show little or no significant variation between the men and women of different Newar castes.

19. A similar point is made by Mines (1994) in a study of the southern Indian city of Madras (Chennai), who notes that the association of kinship with locality appears to be weakening. He notes that the failure of sons to return to or migration from their community of origin after education is a major factor in this process.

20. The pupils of the school almost without exception come from high caste Parbatiya and Newar families. Compared to other private schools in Tansen, very few of the pupils came from outside the town and a concomitant of this is that there were few Magar children on the school roll. There were no low caste or Dalit (untouchable) children educated at the school.

21. It is significant that these pupils were about to begin studying for their School Leaving Certificate, because, as Parish (1994) notes, the fact that urban children are educated for considerably longer today than in the past is pushing the rites that traditionally regulated the transition from childhood to adulthood (*kaeta puja*) from puberty into late teenage. One could go further than this and observe that educational institutions and academic culture provides a set of rites of passage that parallel the rites of caste culture.

22. All names are pseudonyms, but reflect the original caste and ethnicity of the student. The syntax is retained from the original essays.

23. Such sentiments will have been felt with terrible force on the night of 1st February 2006 when the Tansen Durbar was destroyed by fire during an attack by Maoist forces on the town (see Wilmore 2008).

Chapter 6
Community, Development and Empowerment

There is no monolithic modernity expanding, inexorably, into new social spaces. To insist on this is not to deny that the social formations we call modern (such as capitalism, bureaucratic rationality, and certain forms of state control) do not have an impact. They do, and their forms and consequences in various societies should be understood. But we should not confuse the label social science uses to signal the complex relation among these forms—modernity—with an essential, immutable, and uniform quality of the social forms themselves . . . Among the simultaneously diverse aspects of modernity is the idea that being modern can be a social identity, distinct from other identities. The idea of the modern posits difference, but it is not the same difference for everyone, everywhere, every time.

Stacy Leigh Pigg (1996: 191–192)

Introduction

This chapter examines the ways in which development (*bikās*) has been manifested in Tansen through the work of various non-governmental and international non-governmental organizations, including *Ratna Cable Television* and its offshoot *Communication for Development Palpa*. 'Development', as chapter 3 explained, has been the predominant form through which modernity has been mediated in the Nepali context, although this should not be taken to imply that such constructions of modernity have not been questioned. This chapter provides evidence for both the adoption and the contestation of development in Tansen, especially as this relates to the work of RCTV/CDP. Such organizations in Nepal work alongside various bodies that are representative of national, district and more local levels of government, as well as individuals and businesses, to bring about material goals that are believed to be congruent with developmental policies. These goals, although often couched in terms of material benefit, also contain within them a significant ideological and normative components that, as indicated earlier, are frequently contradictory in both their rationale and outcome.

Despite this it is not surprising that the norms of development practice and discourse should be so widespread and frequently encountered in Nepal, because they are "ubiquitous", as Laura Ahearn (2001: 178) points out in her study of literacy practices in a Magar village in Palpa. Not only do these discourses appear in magazines explicitly devoted to development, such as *Deurali*, which is published in Tansen, but they are a feature of movies, school text books, on radio, television and, ultimately, even in the private and intimate correspondences studied by Ahearn. "Development projects, many of which have been in existence for half a century or more in Nepal, carry with them not only new agricultural, educational, or social practices; they also disseminate new ways of speaking, thinking, being, and behaving" (Ahearn 2001: 8).

Ubiquity should not, however, be mistaken for uniformity. No discourse can survive without the ability to flex and evolve in the face of repeated use in circumstances that vary from place-to-place, time-to-time and person-to-person. Recognition of this is explicit in the foundational premises of Laura Ahearn's study, which aims to explain the ways in which the multiple ways that "'the idea of development' is taken up, changed, and challenged" (ibid.) by the Magar residents of the village in which she lived and worked, both as a US Peace Corp volunteer and later as an anthropologist. Likewise, Katherine Rankin's (2004) study of Newar merchants in the Kathmandu Valley seeks to explain how the normative assumptions of development, especially the (neo-) liberal assumptions of the economic theories upon which this is premised may be profoundly influenced in practice by the circumstances of the locality in which they are put to work.

However, Rankin does not seek to present a simplistic bi-polar distinction between any pre-existing set of local circumstances, typified by notions of 'tradition' against which the modernizing influence of development can be measured. Working at the intellectual interface of anthropology and geography, she argues that,

> an emphasis on place and scale . . . challenges conventional models of articulation that rely on the notion of 'traditional', 'pre-capitalist', primitive' cultures that once existed autonomously but have now been violated by global capitalism. Traditional articulation models, however much they leave analytical space to explore the unintended consequences of inter-scalar connections, are analogous to discourses of cultural imperialism and homogenization in their treatment of culture as a fixed system of symbols and meanings that structure social life. The geographic intervention calls for historical explorations of the processes that go into place-making in the first instance; as Gupta and Ferguson put it . . . , 'instead of assuming the autonomy of the primeval community, we need to examine how it was formed as a community out of the interconnected space that always already existed'. An historical approach to the construction of place foregrounds changes to the spatial distribution of hierarchical relations over time. It thus offers an antidote to the tendency in much of the critical literature on neoliberalism to essentialize, romanticize and indeed imagine the

lingering existence of autonomous 'remote', 'non-capitalist' cultures that might offer guidelines for constructing an alternative to capitalism (Rankin 2004: 71).

Rankin's work, and particularly this extract from her 2004 book on economic liberalization in Nepal, help to make an analytical connection between development, notions of locality and community and alternative media, although media as such are not discussed by her. We have seen in chapters 4 and 5 that it is possible to find a strongly articulated sense of local, Palpali identity in everyday and mediated discourses, to which RCTV's programming makes a very active contribution, but this should not be viewed as something pre-existing or contrasting to 'modern' discourses of development. Indeed, as we observed in the previous chapters, such notions of locality and community identity may in fact be the product of exactly those historical changes that might otherwise be regarded as typical of modernization. Tansen had a relatively early experience of development and this may account for the fact that we see an equally strong articulation of a local identity that does not appear to be tied to any conventional notions of shared ethnicity but arises out of the particular circumstances of Palpa as a colony of the Gorkhali state with a significant migrant population originating elsewhere.

It will also become clear in this chapter that local articulations of development discourse and practice do not necessarily lead to radically different or oppositional forms of action or media content. Development is adopted and adapted according to the needs of local agents, both individuals and organizations, but this does not entail that these activities are therefore designed to create oppositional or autonomous spaces of action. Rather, the contrary may be the case with local forms of development activity helping to further entrench a people and place within the wider framework of hegemonic development practice. As part of these local development initiatives RCTV provides a unique place in the local cable television schedule for the articulation of voices that cannot be heard in national media, but we should not assume that these will be either alternative to or autonomous of "the development status quo" (Prasain: 1998). The existence of such alternative possibilities should not be assumed in advance of any study or intervention; if they are seen to exist they must be placed in relation to the more conservative tendencies with which they compete. This chapter explains why it is that such conservative tendencies may have strongly influenced the work of RCTV and CDP in their early years, and why normative theories of alternative media should not lead us to make misleading assumptions about small-scale media organizations.

The previous chapters have described the severe economic and political crisis faced by Tansen during the past two decades as its role as a market and administrative centre has been usurped by neighboring urban and peri-urban places. The municipal authorities and many of the town's private citizens have sought to reverse this decline by various means (notably in the fields of health care, education and tourism), and RCTV and CDP are part of this effort. In this respect, RCTV's goals are closely aligned with those of many other producers of 'alternative', 'indigenous', or simply 'local' media (to use the various names under which such media are often discussed). They claim to support the culture and way of life of the producers' community in order to counter the influence of various external forces over which the local community has little or no control. Often described in terms of various theories of globalization, these economic, political, cultural and social forces often seem indifferent, if not actually hostile, to the needs of many communities around the world. To quote Faye Ginsburg's influential article *Indigenous Media: Faustian Contract or Global Village?* (1991: 94):

> When other forms are no longer effective, indigenous media offers a possible means—social, cultural, and political—for reproducing and transforming cultural identity among people who have experienced massive political, geographic and economic disruption. The capabilities of media to transcend boundaries of time, space, and even language are being used effectively to mediate, literally, historically produced social ruptures and to help construct identities that link past and present in ways appropriate to contemporary conditions.

This chapter examines the process of mediation described by Ginsburg within the broader discourse of development culture, and shows how local media activity in Tansen not only manifests and recreates national or international development discourse, but is also influenced by local circumstances. These circumstances have formed the basis upon which certain sections of the community have sought to create a distinctive sense of place and identity that may subsequently be mobilized to create a niche within the wider field of development in Nepal. The term 'field' as it is used here is derived from the work of Bourdieu (1983, 1984 and 1998) and will be discussed further below. The chapter addresses the questions of who influences the field of development in Tansen, how this influence is manifested and how it is maintained in the face of competition from other agents located both in the town and elsewhere.

Whilst it is true that media can be used to challenge the political and economic marginalization of local communities in the face of the dominance of national and international agencies, we must also look at the additional impact that media use has upon power relations within communities. The positive outcomes anticipated by Ginsburg and other advocates of alternative media's potential as means of resistance may only be one possibility; indeed, local media production may serve to reinforce the hegemony of those who dominate in the political and economic spheres of their own communities. In the case study presented here, I show how certain sections of the community that produce and control local media enter into transactions or exchange relations with agencies of the Nepali state and other influential non-state agencies (particularly international non-governmental organizations, INGOs). This contributes to their influence and status within the community, but Tansen can also be described as existing in a doubly dependent position given the economic and political marginality of the town within the nation-state of Nepal, and Nepal's own marginality within the South Asian region and internationally. The strategies of capital accumulation and development activities described here show how the middle class of the town exists within the socio-economic interstices of the modern, nation-state of Nepal. It is coming into being literally as a *middle* class, mediating local, national and even international networks of political and economic relations.

Crucial to this analysis, therefore, is an understanding of who is involved in development work in Tansen. It is clear from the data collected during this research that the leading roles in much development activities were taken by a limited number of people who formed a close-knit network of working relationships via their involvement with various organizations. As such, this study provides a good example of the formation of what has popularly come to be called *social capital*, following the influential work of Robert Putnam (Putnam 2000), from which individual members of the network may benefit in their subsequent encounters with external agencies, such as international non-governmental organizations. However, the substance of this chapter also provides a means through which some of the claims made on behalf of social capital theory may also be evaluated, particularly claims regarding the potential of alternative media as agents of democratization.

Constructions of Tansen's Development

As we saw in chapter 4, due to its location and history Tansen has been a key site for the work of *state modernization* (Liechty 1995) in the west of Nepal. Such modernization has been manifested through the growth of health and educational facilities, a high standard infrastructure of urban utilities and the location of many INGO-led projects within the municipality. Paralleling this 'development', however, has been the decline of many of Tansen's industrial and commercial functions in the face of competition from both the towns of the Tarai to the south (Butwal and Bhairahawa) and smaller market centres in the hills (Tamghas, Galyang, etc.), which is directly related to the construction of the Siddhartha Highway in the 1970s (Gyawali et al. 1993). Even before the opening of the road, fears were expressed in Tansen that, despite the fact that compared to other hill districts Palpa was "potentially pregnant with vast possibility of industries" (Sharma 1967: 143), competition from Butwal would destroy manufacturing industries that did exist in the town. Increasingly, the fame of Tansen's metalworking and weaving industries has remained in name alone as 'Palpali' style *dhaka* cloth used to make the distinctive Nepali *topī* (hat) and brass *karuwā* (a ceremonial drinking vessel) have been manufactured not only in other parts of Nepal but also in India for the Nepali market (Gyawali et al. 1993; Tinau Watershed Project 1983).

According to Ananda Shrestha (a native of Tansen now running an NGO based in Kathmandu providing consultancy services to government agencies and INGOs), Tansen's community could only have a prosperous future if it concentrated on its strengths in education, health and tourism, and came to terms with the fact that it could not have an industrial future.[1] Vinaya Kasajoo (1994 [orig. 1990]: 43) commenting on the rise and fall of industrial and commercial activity in Tansen brought about by the Siddhartha Highway says that:

> Because of the sudden changes in the economic activities, the town turned into an abandoned or dying city—having beautiful and aristocratic-looking buildings but no people to live in them. But those people who could not move to other places and those who loved the healthy climate, calm and quiet nature and sober culture of this town made up their mind to revive it on the basis of the originalities of this place.

Not surprisingly, Kasajoo lists these "originalities" as education, health and tourism. He goes on to urge that "local people, whose traditional business has been ruined, should change their business and shift towards the tourism industry" and that "as a side business to tourism, small scale industries which produce traditional handicraft reflecting Nepalese culture and traditions for which Tansen is renowned has begun to flourish" (ibid.: 45). Despite this, the major investors in Tansen's tourism infrastructure are still found within the state sector because the Municipality, central government line agencies and INGOs continue to take the lead. Private investors have opened several 'quality' hotels in recent years but it is clear that they still rely heavily on the business generated from the 'state' sector, e.g. hosting seminars, conference groups and visiting delegations from government and non-government development agencies (Regmi 1991).

This triumvirate of concerns—education, health and tourism—has become the semi-official motto of Tansen Municipality and a mantra reiterated by almost all politicians, intellectuals and industrialists who are resident or have interests in the town. The Municipality has also enshrined this motto within its own infrastructure through the creation of separate committees to oversee and manage the development of education, health and tourism within the town.[2] Nevertheless, D.G. Rajkarnikar, a freelance management consultant working for UDLE (Urban Development through Local Efforts, a project based in Kathmandu funded by GTZ [German Technical Assistance, a government backed ING]) and author of a report (Adhikari and Rajkarnikar 1994) into the functioning of Tansen Municipality was skeptical of the ability of the municipality to put the principles and ideas of its Board and various sub-committees into practice.[3] He pointed in particular to the problem of chronic over-manning of Tansen Municipality. It employed ninety two members of staff but had an income less than that of some towns with half its number of staff. After paying the wages bill, the Municipality had virtually nothing left to spend on development activity in the town and therefore reproduces in miniature the reliance on foreign development aid that is symptomatic of Nepal as a whole.

Increasingly, such development aid is being mediated via locally-founded non-governmental organizations, rather than through the state or direct INGO interventions. "By the mid-1990s," writes Louise Brown (1996: 260),

> there were literally thousands of NGOs operating in Nepal, of which a significant proportion were operated by individuals seeking personal

advancement through the acquisition of finance from aid donors. Many NGOs were one-man [sic.] operations, run by professional people as a lucrative sideline to their permanent employment. It had become politically fashionable for the upwardly mobile middle class to operate an NGO, especially one concerned with environmental questions or gender issues.

There has been a large increase in the number of NGOs in Palpa in recent years (see Table 6.1 *Foundation of NGOs in Palpa District, 1982–1996*). Between 1982–83 (2039 v.s.) when the district's first NGO was created and 1989–90 (2046 v.s.), the year of the Jana Andolan, seven NGOs were created in Palpa. In the first six years and two months after the Jana Andolan, 114 more NGOs were added (Helvetas 2053 v.s.). All the NGOs registered in Palpa prior to 1990 were located in Tansen. Subsequent to that date and up to June 1996, forty two out of sixty five Village Development Committees [VDCs] in Palpa had at least one officially registered NGO, although Tansen with forty two NGOs still had by far the greatest single number.

Table 6.1. Foundation of NGOs in Palpa District, 1982–1996

Year C.E. (Vikram Samvat)		Number of NGOs Founded	Foundation Percentages
1982–83	(2039 V.S.)	4	3.3
1983–84	(2040 V.S.)	1	0.8
1984–85	(2041 V.S.)	1	0.8
1985–86	(2042 V.S.)	—	—
1986–87	(2043 V.S.)	—	—
1987–88	(2044 V.S.)	1	0.8
1988–89	(2045 V.S.)	—	—
1989–90	(2046 V.S.)	—	—
1990–91	(2047 V.S.)	3	2.5
1991–92	(2048 V.S.)	2	1.7
1992–93	(2049 V.S.)	10	8.3
1993–94	(2050 V.S.)	24	19.8
1994–95	(2051 V.S.)	38	31.4
1995–96	(2052 V.S.)	28	23.1
1996–	(2053 V.S.; First 2 month only)	7	5.9
No date	(No date V.S.)	2	1.7
Total		121	100.0

Source: Helvetas 2053 V.S.

Apart from pointing out the purely quantitative aspects of the growth of NGOs, Brown also makes (but does not subsequently explore in detail) the important qualitative connection that exists between development work, modernity and the formation of a distinctive bourgeoisie in Nepal. Before turning to this more general consideration of development, I shall provide some brief details about the growth of NGO activity in Palpa and look at a case study of how an INGO has operated in the district and fostered local NGOs during the past three decades.

The rapid growth in the number of indigenously created NGOs also coincided with the recognition on the part of international non-governmental organizations that prior approaches to development in Nepal had failed to bring about the level of success that had been hoped for. This was nowhere more apparent than in Palpa where over a decade of work by the German governmental agency GTZ and its Swiss counterpart Helvetas under the auspices of an integrated rural development program known as the *Tinau Watershed Project* (TWP), later re-named the *Palpa Development Project* (PDP), had led to achievements far short of those envisaged in the original project planning (Brandenberg et al. 1979). An anonymously authored report on the work of Helvetas (2053 V.S.) in Nepal notes that,

> It is now clear after many years working with government line agencies in Palpa, Helvetas has to find more effective ways of supporting the people. And since the top-down approach has not worked, it seems sensible to try the bottom-up approach which makes demands on government rather than waiting for development to come to the village.

With this in mind, in January 1996 Helvetas opened a new office—the Local Initiative Support Program (LISP)—in Bishal Bazaar, Tansen, under a director who had had previous experience working for an INGO in Palpa as the director of the United Mission to Nepal's Community Health Project. This director described the aim of this new office as helping NGOs to realize their potential.[4] They tried to target NGOs working with disadvantaged groups, especially the poor, women and children, but he noted that because Helvetas has had fifteen years experience working in Palpa working through the government line agencies this inevitably colors the attitude of the districts new NGOs to them. They have had to try to find groups who do not expect to have the work done for them by a rich client INGO. He explained that another organization, the Rural Self Reliance Development Centre (*Swambalamban*, RSRDC) had been working in conjunction with Helvetas in Palpa since 1984 and they have an office in Tansen near his in Bishal Bazaar. RSRDC works in twenty-six VDCs so they have not covered these. This cut the number of NGOs they would consider down to sixty, which was further reduced by ignoring those NGOs that have already established links with national level NGOs or INGOs.

They carried out an initial survey of these remaining NGOs, questioning them about their previous works and aspirations for the future. Those that were just passively waiting for outside resources were excluded. Many of these were groups that were stressing a prohibitive function, i.e. aiming to stop something happening rather than establishing something new. From this survey, they selected a group of seventeen NGOs from rural VDCs for an initial leadership-training program and five to six groups from this selection for intensive help, although they maintained contact with the other groups. The director stressed during our conversation that what is all-important from Helvetas's point of view is that all parties in the Local Initiative Support Program, both the controlling Swiss INGO and its Nepali NGO partners, should be clear about their joint objectives. They must have self-reliance, self-potential and be aware that development is an action process rather than a static situation that has to be simply rectified. Helvetas would mainly act as a monitor and advisor and would facilitate information exchange between the NGOs in this area and between the NGOs and other agencies that they would need to work with.

In contrast to the staffing levels of the TWP/PDP, they have only three professional staff (the director and two field officers) and three support staff (peon and drivers). The management philosophy of the LISP was that they would use the modern business practice of outsourcing to other organization when they feel that those organizations can perform a better service to their client NGOs than they can. Indeed, they wanted to maintain a discrete distance between themselves and the NGOs to stop them from getting over-reliant on Helvetas.

The example of Helvetas's changing attitude to involvement in development work in Palpa is instructive because it illustrates some of the continuities and changes in development practice in Nepal. Although a so-called 'bottom up' tactical approach has replaced the previous grand strategy of the 'top down' approach exemplified by the TWP/PDP the emphasis is still on finding the right *technical* solution to the problems of rural underdevelopment. Where and when the centralized management of projects has failed the principle of subsidiarity might succeed (Martinussen 1993). Perhaps more significantly for those living and working in Tansen, the changes exemplified by this description of Helvetas's work indicate that increasingly the onus was on 'local' people to demonstrate, often through the formal organization of NGO-based activities, that they were doing work that should be supported by INGOs' resources. Local NGOs and their representative were required to present themselves as active partners in developmental work rather than relatively passive recipients of donor aid.

The importance of the careful cultivation of links with international non-governmental organizations was raised by one of my informants (the president of the local branch of an international organization), who claimed that the active and successful NGOs in Tansen were only those with international connections.[5] Clubs formed both during and after the Panchayat era had, he explained, faced problems due to political splits and financial problems, which restricted the dozens of new clubs (NGOs) that have been founded in the past six years since the advent of democracy. Those with major international connections, such as the *Red Cross, Lions Club, Junior Chamber of Commerce* (JCs) and *Reyukai*, had thrived. This is despite the fact that their membership was diverse in terms of party politics. According to my informant, membership in these organizations included "RPP [*Rastriya Prajatantra Party*], democrats [meaning *Congress Party*], some progressives [meaning Communists] and panchas", but, he added "all work together."

It is by no means easy for individuals and organizations to avoid being drawn into this burgeoning network of development institutions, because government and non-government agencies are both the major provider of capital within Nepal and form the institutional apparatus through which this capital is controlled. As Corrigan and Sayer (1985: 96) observe, "*property* ('owning and being owned') and *propriety* ('correctness or behavior or morals') have the same etymological root. State activities were central to the naturalization of both" (emphasis added). For this reason, we must consider cultural aspects of development, even if our primary concern is with the material results of development that directly affects people's lives (Prasain 1998). We may be able to directly observe only the latter, but we must also understand the how the material world and its transformation are made meaningful and interpreted morally by the people who live in this world.

A key means through which the kinds of "working together" described by my informant above are manifested in practice is through the cultivation of what another informant (a prominent teacher and 'social worker' in Tansen) described as "chain relationships."[6] Almost all development institutions and organizations in the town are linked through a network of common members at committee level. Although each organization has its own set of institutional structures, many of the personnel who take up positions of authority within those structures are often the same and this form of nepotism has led to the formation of a core group of citizens in Tansen who control much development work carried out in the town and surrounding district.[7]

So, for example, a senior teacher (X) at a government high school is also a governor of a local private school set up by the then mayor of the municipality (or town panchayat at that time, the late 1970s) and sits on the municipality education sub-committee. Another governor (Y) of this private school is the owner of a local shop to which all the school's pupils are told to go to buy their textbooks. He is also a senior member of the Palpa Chamber of Commerce and Industry, which provides funds for a scholarship scheme for the school. A teacher (Z) at the private school is also a prominent member of the Junior Chamber of Commerce (the Jaycees) of which the first teacher (X) is a past president. X has recently been involved on a committee organizing the implementation of a major scheme to improve the town's drinking water supply sponsored by a French NGO in conjunction with the European Community Development Fund. Z's brother has recently been on a trip to France sponsored by this NGO.

This process of making close circles of association is often referred to in Nepal as *aphno manche*, meaning 'one's own people'. According to Bista (1991: 97–100), such circles are integral to the ordering and functioning of Nepali society through their role in the creation of distinctions between those with whom one does or does not prefer to make transactions of various sorts. People outside one's own circle are treated almost as non-persons whose needs and requirements will always be disregarded if members of one's own circle are competing for the same resources. Membership is generally *ad hoc,* although Bista (1991) points out the importance that organizations like the *Lions Club, Rotary Club* and *Reyukai* play in the creation of *aphno manche* circles in contemporary Nepal. He mentions this in the context of a wider observation that it is Newars with their long history of compact urban living that have exemplified the *aphno manche* phenomenon. Bista's assertion that such circles and organizations are dominated by groups of homogeneous caste and/or ethnic identity might be true amongst the large Newar populations of the Kathmandu Valley cities, but in Tansen such dominance appears less assured. Membership sometimes does transcend other forms of social identity such as caste, ethnicity, gender or religious identity, but, even so, many of the organizations were still patronized and run by a much larger proportion of Newars relative to their number within the population of the municipality as a whole. It is certainly the case that members of caste groups that are positioned at wide extremes of the caste hierarchy are unlikely to be found within the same circle; the touchable/untouchable divide remains largely impermeable, especially at committee level. However, in the relatively grey, middle areas of the caste hierarchy, especially as found within the complex multi-ethnic, multi-hierarchical context of Nepal, *aphno manche* relationships may serve to create political and economic institutions that are viable, even if they are also socially exclusive.

'Outside' representatives of national and international organizations, whether Nepali or foreigners, appointed to work with, monitor or otherwise account for an organization's activities in Tansen tend to meet only the local branch members of their own organization. Therefore, the monopolization of development activity in the town by a relatively restricted section of the town's population remains hidden from their view. The ultimate results of this could be described as the formation of a parallel structure of authority in Tansen. This structure is linked to the official municipality government by common membership, as those who hold political office are also heavily involved in developmental institutions, but it operates beyond the strictures of democratic accountability (cf. Krämer 2003).[8] There are no organizations or institutions in Tansen that are not directly influenced by this network of politicians, educationalists and industrialists, which in effect forms a corporate group controlling the flow of development resources to and from the municipality. This corporate group is the local manifestation of what Prasain refers to as "the development status quo" (1998), by which he means "the powerful players of development. That includes donors, development 'experts', development consultants, high ranking bureaucrats, politicians, members of the National Planning Commission, powerful people from big NGOs and INGOs, and development managers who are drawn from the politically, economically and culturally elite section of Nepali society" (Prasain 1998: 341, footnote 1).

In the light of this, it is useful to follow Bourdicu and look at the development field, "as a network, or a configuration, of objective relations between positions…in the structure of the distribution of power (or capital) whose possession commands access to the specific profits that are at stake in the field, as well as by their objective relation to other positions" (Bourdieu and Wacquant 1992: 90). Adopting Bourdieu's approach we can understand how it is that some agents are able to act with greater influence within the development field than others due to their ownership of and access to the sorts of capital (economic, educational, political, social and cultural) that are most valued within the field. Increasing and improving one's power depends both upon quantitative factors, the ability to increase one's capital, and also upon qualitative factors, the ability to reconvert capital held in one form to other "more accessible, more profitable or more legitimate form[s]" (Bourdieu 1984: 131).

Ratna Cable Television can be seen as an example of such capital reconversion strategies in operation. In the early years of the Shakya's business, they moved from the manufacture of metal goods, such as the famous brass Palpali water jugs (*karuwa*) that still feature in the logo of both RCTV and the Municipality, to the repair of radios, televisions and, subsequently, the operation of a commercial cable television business. A more decisive break came when they crossed from the strictly commercial field into the development field and formed the NGO, *Communication for Development Palpa*. As was explained in chapter 2, this move was not taken entirely willingly and has placed considerable constraints upon the use of capital generated from within this field. It can only be put to certain legitimate uses and having the power to decide what is regarded as legitimate is one of the essential determinants of who has the greater power within the field as a whole. The state and INGOs are the most powerful agents in this regard and they have exercised this power to control the work of RCTV.

As Prasain suggests, the ability of sections of the Nepali ruling class to engage in strategies of reconversion to accumulate capital within the development field is a crucial factor in the perpetuation of their power and structures of wealth and poverty within the country more generally, given the importance of this field within Nepal. Tansen's elite has, therefore, recognized that it is imperative that they compete within the national development field and can only do so effectively through collective action.

Such collective actions would appear to be an essential component of the formation of social capital as described in the influential work of Robert Putnam (2000), although he points out that he is not the originator of this term and Bourdieu's theorizations of social capital are also a key source for its adoption into regular social scientific discourse, if not in public policy terminology. Social capital, according to Sobel (2002: 139), "describes circumstances in which individuals can use membership in groups and networks to secure benefits . . . [However,] the extent to which an individual has access to resources through social capital depends on the person's connections (whom they know, but also connections through common group membership), the strength of these connections, and the resources available to their connections." Drawing on the analogy with material forms of capital, social capital is regarded as "affect[ing] the productivity of individuals and groups" (Putnam 2000: 19).

Putnam makes a distinction between *bonding* and *bridging* forms of social capital, explaining that the former originates in strongly felt experiences of shared, in-group identity, whilst the latter refers to the weaker, but no less important connections that are formed between the members of different groups. Again, what we observe in Tansen appears to be exemplary of both of these forms of social capital formation, with the creation of bonding capital based on chain relationships serving to enhance the capacity of group members to cultivate links with 'outside' agencies and organizations. The question that must be addressed, however, is whether the existence and utilization of these forms of social capital leads to the sorts of positive externalities that are anticipated by Putnam and other advocates of social capital theory. In other words, whilst it is clear that a limited number of agents (individuals and organizations) form the core group promoting development works in Tansen, does the concomitant formation of bridging capital by this group that links the town and district to the wider resources of both the state and international development agencies prove beneficial to the community as a whole? Does the specific reciprocity of *aphno manche* relationships lead to more generalized reciprocity that enhances the welfare of the community as a whole? In particular, we must ask what kinds of social capital are formed from the media work of RCTV/CDP. For some observers in the town itself, these questions do not lead to positive answers.

The Perceived Political Bias of the RCTV Local Program

As I sat with a member of the RCTV team watching the rapid editing of the news program broadcast on Saturday 25th May 1996, several items caught my attention. The first item that day was the inauguration of the *Small Scale and Cottage Industry Association* seminars held at a local hotel. The commentary was brief, simply outlining the fact of the event's occurrence and listing the names of those shown collecting awards for their work on behalf of the organization from the guests of honor, a prominent local businessman and the Chief District Officer (the highest ranking civil servant and representative of the state at the district level).

Commenting on these kinds of speech program whilst simultaneously editing, the team member voiced the familiar criticism that no effective practical action arises from all this talking. Later, however, he excused RCTV's extensive coverage of these events in its news programs with the observation that their own activities rely on the good will of those who take part in these events. He observed that his main problem in editing these reports was how to ensure that all those involved appear at least once and were thus satisfied by the coverage!

Following this was a story about a truck accident during the previous day, the result of a drunken lorry driver approaching a corner too fast and crashing into a group of young women. One of these women and one of the young male passengers in the truck were killed and several others were injured. The driver was arrested and taken into custody at Tansen police station. The footage included pictures of the two victims lying on the side of the road and there appeared to be no restrictions imposed upon RCTV's video recording of the scene. Graphic scenes of the corpses were included in the finished bulletin .

The story that followed also highlighted this lack of reticence in showing potentially disturbing images with a minimum of censorship. A very badly deformed baby had been delivered, stillborn that week at the UMN Hospital. RCTV had been informed of this birth by some of the staff and had received permission from the director of the hospital to film the corpse of the baby, providing the identity of the mother was not revealed. The footage showed the baby, rather poignantly and pathetically lying on an old copy of a Norwegian newspaper.

I was quite shocked by what I had just seen and asked him whether he had any qualms about showing this footage. Without any hesitation, he said no, explaining that people in Tansen were not squeamish and were more interested than scared or repulsed by such things.[9] I asked him if there was anything that RCTV would not show. "Politics," he said with a smile and a small laugh, which indicated that he recognized the indignation with which some people in Tansen would greet this assertion. Because, for many people in Tansen the political bias of his organization is self-evident and such accusations of bias should come as little surprise given the politically charged atmosphere of life in post-1990 Nepal. Criticisms of RCTV tended to come from those who were members of the then opposition parties, the *Communist Party of Nepal (United Marxist-Leninist)* [UML] and *Rastriya Prajatantra Party* (National Democratic Party) [RPP].

The reasons for the perceived political bias of RCTV's coverage of local politics in Tansen cannot be ascribed to a simplistic conspiracy theory, whereby the organization works actively on behalf of any particular political party as an instrument of propaganda. Rather, as Hall et al. (1999) point out bias in the media arises more usually from the implicit politics of media practices, rather than explicit political or ideological affiliation. Firstly, media organizations rarely create the coverage of news items themselves, but are instead "'cued in' to specific topics by regular and reliable institutional sources" (Hall et al. 1999: 648). Some of the time pressure that the media are under can be alleviated by relying on pre-scheduled events (such as speech programs, seminars and award ceremonies) to provide the bulk of their program content. Secondly, the very notion of 'objectivity' or 'impartiality' leads to biases because only certain 'accredited' sources are regarded as providing 'facts' as opposed to 'opinions'. Accredited sources tend to be those who represent major social institutions (e.g. industrial and development agencies), more broadly the people (e.g. elected politicians), or experts (e.g. doctors and teachers). "Ironically, the very rules which aim to preserve the impartiality of the media, and which grew out of desires for greater professional neutrality, also serve powerfully to orientate the media in the 'definitions of social reality' which their 'accredited sources'—the institutional spokesmen—provide" (Hall et al. 1999: 649). Hall and his co-authors (1999: 649) go on to summarize their argument:

> These two aspects of news production—the practical pressures of constantly working against the clock and the professional demands of impartiality and objectivity—combine to produce a systematically structured *over-accessing* to the media of those in powerful and privileged institutional positions. The media thus tend, faithfully and impartially, to reproduce symbolically the existing structure of power in society's institutional order.

These aspects of media production are seen both in Nepal in general (Brown 1996: 176) and in the specific case of RCTV. Given the small scale of its resources, especially in terms of trained staff, these biases were even more likely to be manifested as the organization's volunteers struggled to maintain its scheduled weekly broadcast. The fact that RCTV's news program showed local civic events inevitably leads to some bias, because the main actors at these events would invariably be the politicians who dominated the municipality at that time, and the district administrators (notably the Chief District Officer), who were appointed by the Nepal Congress central government. Given the small size of the potential audience it is not surprising that these implicit biases were perceived as explicit favoritism towards one political party that is the Nepali Congress, which was then in power in the municipality.[10]

Controlling Ratna Cable Television

It would be easy to end analysis at this point and claim that the members of the CDP organization, in particular those from the family that own RCTV, the private company at the nucleus of the local program, are members of a hegemonic elite and their media work is simply a device to strengthen their position within this elite. This is certainly true to some extent. But to end our analysis here would be to seriously misconstrue the processes through which hegemony operates in such a complex social situation. As Williams (1994) makes clear, hegemony involves reification but should not itself be reified. Rather, it is processual in character, "'a lived system of meanings and values,' which may not consciously be held, in the way a formal ideology is, but rather saturates 'the whole process of living'" (Williams quoted in Parish 1997). To bring our analysis to an abrupt end may prevent us from seeing all the ways through which RCTV/CDP is part of this living hegemony. To quote Prasain (1998: 391):

> Academic analysis must . . . be directed at this process of reification of development theories, taking into account how the specific history, politics, society and culture provide the context for such processes. Before blindly assigning (or accepting) the 'alternative' role of NGOs, attention must be turned to the basic assumptions under which NGOs operate, the foundations from which they have evolved.

The easiest way to convey this process is to consider the full implications of RCTV's adoption of the identity of an NGO, *Communication for Development Palpa*, to legitimate its broadcasting activities. As was explained chapter 2, RCTV did not have an official license to broadcast at its inception and at the time of my fieldwork central government was keeping a very tight control over the granting of such permission to private organizations. The privately-owned *Kantipur* organization, along with several other private businesses had started to buy broadcast time in 1996 on the FM channel (*FM Kathmandu*) that had recently been established by the state broadcaster Radio Nepal. Permission for these organizations to establish their own commercial radio stations was not granted for a further two years. Several cable operators in Kathmandu had also been granted permission to rebroadcast satellite television signals, but no licenses to broadcast either radio or television had been granted outside the capital, although this has greatly changed subsequently with there being approximately fifty FM radio stations on air by 2005 (Pringle 2007).[11]

We have already discussed the political implications of the fact that local politicians and government officials supported RCTV in its early years and how its journalistic 'objectivity' contributes to implicit bias, although whether it is explicitly biased towards a particular political party or individual public figures is open to debate. The reliance of RCTV on so-called accredited sources within the municipality is, however, a means through which the organization is itself controlled as well as articulating its own hegemonic position. The requirement to officially operate as an NGO was a mixed blessing in this regard. Although it allowed the private business RCTV to continue to function as a broadcaster and benefit from the local program (which had attracted subscribers), it enabled the state and other agencies to intervene more easily in the operation of the organization.

In the case of the state, this pressure was most clearly felt through the control of advertising revenue. CDP was a small NGO and did not have sufficient resources to employ a third party to arrange funding on its behalf. It could not afford, for example, hire a commercial marketing company in Kathmandu to seek advertisers for the local television program. Some local businesses and at least two national level companies (a brewery and a food manufacturer) did advertise with RCTV, but the local scale of the RCTV audience meant that revenue from each advertiser was small and the volume of advertising could not rise because of these marketing restrictions. According to Vinaya Kasajoo, speaking of both his own experience as the publisher of *Deurali Rural Newspaper*, also based in Tansen and operating under the auspices of an NGO (*Rural Development Palpa* [RDP]), central government remained the major source of advertising revenue for many media organizations and this could be an extremely effective means of keeping an organization in line or even driving them out of business.[12] Neither CDP nor RDP received government advertising of any substantial size, although both did benefit from a small amount of income derived from Tansen Municipality.

The history of RCTV also shows how it was drawn, almost by accident in some respects, into the network of interconnections that make up the social structure of the development industry in Nepal. As an NGO, CDP was able to seek funding from INGOs and in terms of capital investment this funding was able to transform the technical operation of the organization. There is no suggestion that this has led to any direct censorship or interference in the editorial content of RCTV's programming, but it does mean that the autonomy of the organization was inevitably reduced. RCTV could only produce programs as an NGO geared towards the furtherance of the specific development aims that were tied to the donation of resources and, perhaps more importantly, the general aims of national development (cf. Adhikary 1996). The immediate implication of the patronage of various NGOs meant that access to new equipment and training has to be directed through these organizations. RCTV/CDP's relationship with *The Asia Foundation* provides a good example of this. In an interview at their Nepal headquarters in Patan, one of their assistant directors claimed that they had recently adopted a more rural emphasis in their work with NGOs.[13] They were he said, "moving out of the [Kathmandu] Valley" and away from urban-based projects. The Asia Foundation's donors, including the US government, were also generally not interested in media at that time because they viewed this as a private sector issue.[14] Regarding the media projects that they sponsored in Palpa, CDP and RDP, he said that The Asia Foundation's policy was that they would have to learn to exist on their own following their provision of start-up capital. Accordingly, they needed to place more emphasis on marketing so that they could succeed in the market place where they would have to bid for contracts. Whether the organizations producing media in Tansen were viable as commercial operations given the restricted size of the potential market for their products and the close proximity of competition in the towns of the Tarai is a moot point. The Asia Foundation was also steering clear of broadcasting projects because of the need for the government approval of licenses to broadcast.[15]

The concomitant of this involvement in the development industry is that RCTV/CDP had at all times to be seen to fulfill the official goals of development and was locked into the processes of "state modernization" and pursuit of 'national' development goals (Liechty 1995). Quite apart from the immediate requirement that CDP did not seek commercial sponsorship or finance beyond a certain level, the local perception of people in Tansen was that the programs made by RCTV/CDP should conform to the criteria of what is regarded as the meeting of aims inspired by development goals. One effect of this was that the style of programming produced by RCTV often conformed to didactic formulae that have often been the focus of criticism by viewers of state run television in South Asia (see Liechty 1998 on *Nepal TV* and Ninan 1995 on *Doordarshan*). Equally, however, to step outside the bounds of this formula and produce programs that are perceived as pure entertainment with no 'serious' content ran the risk of being accused of inappropriate behaviour.[16]

The success of this self-censorship is indicated by the fact that these kinds of accusations were seldom leveled at the content of RCTV's programs. For example, I never heard anyone speak of their programming as "indigestible", as one informant put it when registering his disgust of many Indian or 'English' films and television programs. However, entertainment is equated with commercial broadcasting and the appearance of film songs and 'pop' music (*chitragīt*) on the RCTV program did occasionally provoke mildly negative comments from informants, even when these were songs performed by local individuals or groups. Such comments seldom came from ordinary viewers who I interviewed and many expressed their enjoyment of the *chitragīt* segments on the local program. But some who had been involved in the production of CDP's programs in the first few years of the organizations existence accused the cable organization of blatantly using the local program as a vehicle for its own commercial interests. It is difficult to know how seriously one should take such accusations because, as was noted above, it is almost impossible in practice to separate the two arms of the local program, RCTV and CDP. Apart from advertising content, most of the overtly commercial output of RCTV was made and distributed on behalf of organizations such as the Municipality and *Palpa Chamber of Commerce*, and geared towards the encouragement of external investment in the town.[17] Also, anyone who was seriously motivated by the desire to be entertained would be better served by the regular *Star TV* broadcasts that make up the overwhelming majority of the programming available through the RCTV cable system. Even so, these sorts of comments are indicative of the feelings that surround the local program. To refer again to Corrigan and Sayer's (1985) formulation, it is generally accepted that RCTV/CDP is private property, but this does not remove constraints of public propriety from the organization. These constraints are to a large extent structured through the discourse of development (*bikās*) in Nepal which was discussed in chapter 3 because it provides a shared benchmark against which particular ideas, activities or objects may be evaluated.

Language Issues in RCTV's Broadcasts

Another manifestation of the way development discourse acts to control RCTV/CDP's output can be seen if we look at the question of which languages are used in their broadcasts. In the early years of the local program RCTV was the supplier of the only Nepali language television available outside of the Kathmandu Valley area and until 1995 they provided the only Nepali language television broadcasting in Tansen. In the face of the domination of people's television screens by Indian terrestrial broadcasters (*Doordarshan*), satellite broadcasters (*Star TV*) and the products of foreign film industries on video, this represented an attempt to provide broadcasting in an indigenous language. The cultural influence of India has been felt in the media of Nepal for quite some time, either directly through the import of Indian media products or by influencing the format of programs made in Nepal, just as the Indian film industry has provided the standard format for Nepali films. According to Page and Crawley (2001) Nepal has had a longer experience of *Hindigenization*, that is the experience of India's regional dominance of the media culture brought about by globalization, than have other South Asian states. Providing some alternative to this domination through the production of Nepali broadcasting was clearly a strong initial motivation for RCTV's work.

However, the language issue in Tansen is more complex than this simple opposition of Nepali to Hindi implies. At its inception in 1992 the only competition to RCTV in Nepali language broadcasting was *Nepal Radio*, but in 1995 *Nepal TV* broadcasts became available due to the erection of an aerial on the summit of Srinagar hill above the town. As stated in chapter 2, this led to a decline in the popularity of the RCTV broadcast because they no longer had a monopoly over Nepali language broadcasting. Nevertheless, a large proportion of the population of Tansen speak languages other than Nepali, such as Newari (*Nepal bhasa*) and Magar, as their mother tongue and these are largely absent from the national broadcast media available in Tansen.[18] Although the possibility for further linguistic innovation in RCTV's programs existed, this did not occur and it is interesting to consider why this was so in more detail.

Table 6.2. Cable Television Access, 1995

Ethnicity	Caste	Population Distribution 1991 Census	Population Distribution 1996 Survey	Cable TV Owners in All Households	Cable TV Owners in TV Households
		%	%	%	%
Newar	Buddhist	—	17.4	47.0	50.0
	Hindu	—	22.1	28.0	33.3
	All	24.9	39.5	37.5	41.1
Parbatiya	Bahun	27.4	15.4	13.0	17.4
	Chetri	15.3	16.9	12.0	18.2
	Occupational	2.0	10.3	0.0	0.0
Magar		15.1	10.8	29.0	46.1
Others		13.3	7.2	0.0	0.0
Total		100.0	100.0	21.5	30.2

Source: HMG, Nepal (1993) and Author Survey

Table 6.3. Ratna Cable Television Local Program Audience, 1995

Ethnicity	Caste	Population Distribution 1996 Survey	Watch RCTV Local Program		Distribution of Viewers of RCTV Program
		%	No.	%	%
Newar	Buddhist	17.4	25	12.8	28.1
	Hindu	22.1	27	13.8	30.3
	All	39.5	52	26.7	58.4
Parbatiya	Bahun	15.4	8	4.1	9.0
	Chetri	16.9	9	4.6	10.0
	Occupational	10.3	3	1.5	3.4
Magar		10.8	11	5.6	12.4
Others		7.2	6	3.1	6.7
Total		100.0	89	45.6	100.0

Source: Author Survey

Newar viewers form a higher proportion of the RCTV audience than they did of the population as a whole, because of their relatively high levels of affluence and concentration in the areas of the bazaar where cable connections were most easily installed (see Table 6.2 *Cable Television Access, 1995*). 37.5% of Newar household (both Hindu and Buddhist) had a cable television line, with Magar households in second place with 29%. Both Bahun and Chetri households were well below the average of 21.5%. No households of Occupational caste and from other caste/ethnic groups were found to have a cable connection during my survey of Tansen's population.

When we look at the ethnic composition of the RCTV local program's audience (see Table 6.3 *Ratna Cable Television Local Program Audience, 1995*), we see that the deviation from the distribution of caste/ethnic groups within the population as a whole was even more striking than the variation in cable access suggests. Newar viewers formed an even clearer majority. Interestingly, the figure for Magar viewers dipped below their total for the population as a whole. The number of viewers from Occupational caste groups was the only figure higher than their total representation within the population. This was despite the fact that of all the ethnic groups in Tansen, Magars were more likely than other groups to have a cable television link if they owned a television (46.1% of Magar television owners have cable access, higher even than the total for the combined Newar population of 41.1%). In terms of its audience, the local program would appear to have been Newar dominated. It seems strange therefore that little or no Newari broadcasting was transmitted as part of the program.

If we break the figures for Newar viewers down into Buddhist and Hindu sub-groups we see that the relationship between cable connection and actually viewing the local program was less direct than is suggested by the figures in Table 6.2. From Table 6.3 we can see that although 47% of Buddhist Newar households had a cable connection they formed only just over 28% of the audience compared to 30.3% for Hindu Newars. But even so, the proportion of the audience from both groups was much higher than would be suggested by their size as a proportion of the population as a whole.

There were no Newari language programs in the RCTV broadcast, but it is possible that the producers of the program ignored audience demand for these sorts of programs. I found no evidence for such demand, either during participant observation or when I explicitly asked respondents to describe how they would change the local program in the detailed interviews that followed my initial fieldwork survey. No informant ever raised the language question. Another factor is that, although several of the people who produced the local program have Newari as their mother tongue (notably the Shakyas who are Buddhist Newars), many of the other volunteers were Bahun and Chetri and spoke Nepali as their mother tongue. None of the key volunteers, however, were Magar or from Occupational or other Nepali caste/ethnic groups. Therefore, Nepali as the state language and *lingua franca* of the nation appeared to be the logical choice for broadcasts, especially as the initial desire was to counteract the dominance of Indian broadcasting rather than the dominance of state and private media based in Kathmandu. Even so, this is insufficient to explain the total absence of other languages of Nepal, particularly Newari, in the local broadcasts.

The development discourses within which the local program and its producers are enmeshed provide another possible explanation for the absence of greater linguistic diversity in the broadcasts. The financial survival and creation of 'official' legal status of RCTV was achieved through the creation of an NGO, *Communication for Development Palpa*, which served to legitimate RCTV's work. It is important to note that the process of registration as an NGO was administered through the district administration rather than the municipality. The civil servants who are the key decision making figures in the district administration are also appointees of central government and as such would normally be expected to put the orders of government into practice. As we have seen in relation to RCTV, this has not always happened and it was the initial support of the Central District Officer (CDO) and his deputy that gave RCTV the time to negotiate a compromise that would allow broadcasts to continue. However, this compromise locked the organization into a framework that was as much cultural as it was legal and financial. Above all, it meant that the NGO formed to officially produce the local program had to have a district-wide focus and could not just concentrate on the population of Tansen which formed its core audience. It *had* to become Communication for Development *Palpa* to retain widespread legitimacy.

At the same time, the financial restrictions on NGOs' activities and CDP's failure to secure a license to broadcast through any means apart from the cable system meant that the audience was of necessity restricted to the high-density areas of the bazaar.[19] Broadcasting in Newari would then make the bazaar-centric focus of the local program only too obvious and even raise the possibility that accusations of 'communalism' or ethnic bias could be leveled at the organization by the district administration, which oversees the operation of the NGO. INGO donors were also extremely sensitive to the accusation that they might be supporting organizations that had an overtly ethnic political agenda.

These factors (the lack of demand for Newari language programming from the audience, the limited multiethnic/lingual background of the producers of the broadcasts and the institutional framework within which the programs are produced) acted together to prevent the local program from developing either as a medium to express a specific ethnic identity or as a means to give voice to the ethnic and linguistic diversity that exists in Tansen and Palpa district.

Conclusion

The adoption by *Ratna Cable Television* of NGO status provided a legal compromise that allowed the organization to continue broadcasting as *Communication for Development Palpa* and also brought the organization into the network of state and non-state institutions that together make up Nepal's field of development. Development (*bikās*) is probably the dominant discursive idiom through which the material transformation of Nepal has been conceptualized in the Panchayat and post-Panchayat eras (Pigg 1992; Des Chene 1996). However, this discourse has been increasingly challenged, especially since the political freedoms won after the 1990 revolution (not the least of these being freedom of expression in the media) shattered the illusion of consensus that the Panchayat regime had sought to maintain.

Not surprisingly, the question of how the material resources of development have been distributed amongst the people and places of Nepal has been at the forefront of this debate. Claims and counter-claims of nepotism and corruption within government and other agencies are common. But, as the use of the term *status quo* by Prasain (1998) suggests, the development culture of Nepal has retained some degree of legitimacy in the eyes of the population as a whole because a central tenet of *bikās* ideology is the claim that development is a matter beyond politics, or at least beyond party politics. Development, according to this ideological formulation, is a matter of enhancing the commonwealth of the nation. Development may be the province of the elite in Tansen, but they argue that their work constitutes the development *of* Tansen or Palpa *by* the corporate group *for* the citizens of the town or district as a whole and practices such as nepotism or corruption are thereby condoned (cf. Gross 1998). To adopt the language of social capital theory, the negative externalities generated from the dense networks typical of bonding capital are tolerated due to the expectation that that form of capital will lead to positive externalities of greater magnitude generated by bridging capital. According to Putnam (2000: 23), "bonding social capital, by creating strong in-group loyalty, may also create strong out-group antagonism, . . . and for that reason we might expect negative external effects to be common with this form of social capital. Nevertheless, under many circumstances both bridging and bonding social capital can have powerfully positive social effects."

There may be some limited degree of truth in this argument, because by using relatively cohesive 'chain relationships', the local elite of Tansen can work through collective agency to claim a bigger share of national development resources than would otherwise be the case. A provincial town like Tansen is disadvantaged compared to the core region of the Kathmandu Valley where development resources are concentrated (both in terms of expenditure and in the location of the offices through which allocation decisions that affect other places are made). The viability of Tansen as a commercial and industrial centre is also low given the competition from places in the Tarai and India that resulted from the construction of the road system in the past three decades. But the history of Tansen and Palpa has left an indelible mark upon the cultural identity of this region of Nepal. Palpa, at least in the eyes of its inhabitants, is regarded as quite distinctive compared to other provincial regions. This sense of *local* Palpali identity has been mobilized within the *national* development field to lay claim to a share of available resources. RCTV/CDP embodies this strong sense of local identity and place, both in the images of Tansen and Palpa that it produces and in the organization's very existence, which symbolizes the innovation and entrepreneurial spirit of the district.

Similarly Nepal's elite, those whose power is manifested at the level of the national organs of state, may claim that imperfections in their work are justified by the competition they face with other nations when seeking a share of international development resources. However, this is to say nothing about how the benefits of those resources are distributed at the local level once their procurement has been arranged. If on a national or even global scale, nepotistic, *aphno manche*-type relationships enhance the collective agency of Tansen in relation to other regions or places, on a local level they clearly contribute to the reproduction of social and economic inequalities that exist within the community by limiting access to the so-called 'bonding capital' needed to enter into these wider circuits of exchange. Methodologically it then becomes extremely difficult to evaluate whether the negative costs of strong bonding capital formation are outweighed by the positive benefits of the concomitant formation of bridging capital. Empirically and with the benefit of historical hindsight, it is evident that significant benefits do appear to have accrued to the wider community in Tansen because of the development works fostered by the links with a multiplicity of external agencies, not the least being the on-going development of the CDP run Community Media Center (Pringle et al. 2004 and Pringle 2005). Nevertheless, following the collapse of the Panchayat hegemony in the early 1990s (see chapter 3), the development status quo has been radically challenged by a violent Maoist political movement that employs its own aggressive forms of bonding capital in confronting the Nepali state. John Ehrenberg (1999) points out, it is disingenuous of social capital theorists to claim positive outcomes its formation without giving equal weight to what even Putnam admits is "the dark side of social capital" (2000: 350–363). As Ehrenberg notes, "after all, Putnam's healthy civil society was built on the systematic confinement of women in the home, the accompanying construction of mass consumer culture, an institutionalized racial segregation throughout American society, McCarthyism, and a suffocating ideological uniformity—just to name a few elements" (1999: 231). In addition to this, criminal and reactionary organizations, as well as radical political insurgents, are no less indicative of social capital formation than other, more democratic or progressive groupings.

The issue here is that the formation of social capital is not in and of itself an inherent good and we are *not* faced with a choice between the positive results of social capital's existence or the negative results of its absence. Rather, it appears that "the ability to use network relationships to obtain beneficial outcomes need not be good for society or even for the network" (Sobel 2002:146). Perhaps more importantly, the choice is not even between good or bad forms of social capital formation. We cannot simply distinguish groups on the basis of whether they utilize social capital for beneficial or for damaging purposes. Instead we are confronted by situations where particular instances of social capital formation simultaneously produce *both* positive *and* negative outcomes. Social capital should be viewed as less a solution to social crises than a useful, albeit limited way of describing the general processes of the formation of relationships and transactions that are the context for all social action. Identifying social capital formation in any particular place or time cannot, therefore, be the end point of analysis but only its beginning.

Following on from this, it is clear that Stacey Pigg's (1992) analysis of the dichotomy between developed (*bikasit*) and undeveloped (*abikasit*) places is correct in its general outline. Nevertheless, as she indicates in a subsequent paper (1996) attention must also be given to the symbolic, social and material divisions that exist between places in these categories throughout Nepal in order to understand how the landscape of development is internally differentiated within the boundaries of the nation-state. Just as there is no such thing as capitalism—or social capitalism, for that matter—in any abstract sense only various manifestations of capitalism (Corrigan and Sayer 1985), our analyses must recognize that development may take specific, local forms that do not conform to either the ideological or practical norms of *national* development. I would argue that understanding how and why the perceptions and practice of development and underdevelopment vary in different locations (for example, how Palpali *bikās* varies compared to the *bikās* of other places in Nepal) is crucial if we are to understand the internal dynamic of recent changes in Nepali society and avoid reifying the discursive categories used in our analyses (see Onta 1994).

The "failure of *bikās* to achieve its promise in Nepal since the 1950s" has, as Mary Des Chene (1996: 261) points out, been "much lamented." Nevertheless, the case of *Ratna Cable Television* and *Communication for Development Palpa* provides a vivid example of both the factors that underlie this failure and the advantages that accrue to development practitioners despite widespread public recognition of the inadequacies of their development work. Although it is true that "their ability to act is limited by that very position [as practitioner], and the contradictions and compromises it entails" (Des Chene 1996: 262), acquiescence to the institutional arrangements of the development industry is a price that is often willingly paid in Tansen in order to maintain local involvement in national and international spheres of this work. One facet of the operation of local television in Tansen is the construction of mediated forms of cultural identity that allows sections of the community who control local these forms to enter into transactions and exchange relations with the state and other influential non-state agencies (particularly INGOs). The previously mentioned questions regarding the professionalism of RCTV/CDP's output and their use of so-called amateur recording technologies are indicative of anxieties regarding their perception by outsiders and the potential barriers that block access to exchange networks within the mediascape. Such transactions have only been possible within the development field because Ratna Cable Television, particularly in its incarnation as an NGO, has been accepted as a legitimate representative of the town and district by both the local community and the state. This demonstrates an interesting and paradoxical facet of the working of hegemony, because the accumulation of capital by a restricted fraction of the community (in this case through the creation of media that contributes to their power and status) will only be successful if the local community accepts this group as their legitimate representatives.[20]

The question of how this consent is won lies at the heart of any understanding of power and this study demonstrates how the particular cultural discourses at work in a socio-historical situation influence the operation of hegemony. Whilst "it is evident today that those who have access to capital are the 'new Europeans', are more likely to be able to tell their story, and thus become the gatekeepers of cultural memory" (Kuenhast 1992: 186), it is equally the case that the creators of local media in Tansen have been able to gain access to development capital because they have been willingly accepted as the legitimate gatekeepers of the cultural memory of their community. The accumulation of economic and political capital may make them the so-called new Europeans, but only if they are successful in making cultural commodities with the specific imprint of local (Tansen or Palpali) cultural capital that is their own contribution to the network of exchanges operating on a national and even an international scale within the field of development.

Such hegemonic power is bought at a price, however, and Mark Liechty's (1995: 193) observation about the irony of affluence in the developing world as experienced in Kathmandu is apposite here:

> As Kathmandu's middle class situates itself in the global political economy at the terminus of the 'development aid' pipeline it simultaneously secures itself a local position of class dominance (based on its control of local resources), *and* locks itself into a position of dependence and marginality *vis-à-vis* an external cultural metropole. Herein lies the irony of 'affluence' in the 'developing world': the paradox of the experience of modernity in a place like Kathmandu. The new middle class builds a position of *local* power by entering into the ultimately dependent discourses of modernism (progress and development) and commercial modernity (emphasis in original).

Tansen's middle class is in a doubly dependent position given the economic and political marginality of the town within the nation-state of Nepal and Nepal's own marginality within the South Asian region or internationally. However, the existence of Ratna Cable Television demonstrates that this dependency is not necessarily met with acquiescence or fatalism, but can generate vigorous responses as people seek to become effective agents within the field of development in Nepal. Nevertheless, the response to this experience of marginality by other sections of Nepali society has been very different and, in the case of the Maoist People's War, anything but ironic.

Notes

1. Interviewed 12th June 1996.
2. These are sub-committees of the Municipality Board, the sovereign body of the municipality, which is made up of the town's elected councilors (the mayor, deputy mayor and fifteen ward representatives) and a non-elected official (the Executive Officer) appointed by central government. The Municipality Board can decide to do anything to promote the welfare of the Municipality's citizens, the only restriction being that any

decisions have to be ratified by the Executive Officer who sits as an observer without voting rights on the Municipality Board and advises the board on the legality of the policies implemented by the Municipality with reference to the national constitution. The sub-committees do not have the right to implement policy, but were created to examine the running and planning of the various institutions that are involved in the above fields. The members of the sub-committees with voting rights are all ward representatives. They can decide to appoint non-voting observers to the various sub-committees and also call advisors, but cannot compel attendance. Plans formulated by the sub-committees must then be passed on to the Municipality Board to be ratified (cf. Martinussen 1993).

3. Interviewed 5th April 1996.

4. Interviewed 28th July 1996.

5. Interviewed 14th August 1996.

6. Interviewed 27th March 1996. This informant also described such collective work as fostering a "joint family feeling."

7. Relations between the UMN hospital authorities and the Tansen Municipality have on occasion been strained. This led to the creation in 1995 of a committee jointly run by the municipality and hospital to monitor the work of the hospital (for example, discussing any increases in treatment fees or UMN decisions about funding of the hospital). Needless to say, many of the members of this committee are also active in the Municipal and NGO organizations described in this chapter.

8. Concern about the growth in and extent of the operation of INGOs and NGOs in Nepal has been frequently voiced by politicians and in the national media. Chairman of the Public Accounts Committee, Hridayesh Tripathi, for example, received widespread newspaper coverage in April 1996 when he claimed that such non-governmental organizations were "running a parallel government" (*Everest Herald* 30th April 1996). Of particular concern, according to Tripathi was the fact that although more than forty million rupees (about US$725,000) was officially distributed as accounted for per annum by these organizations, "in reality more money than that is allocated toward the well being of the country. However there is no record anywhere of how the money is spent or if it is spent at all" (*Kathmandu Post* 30 April 1996).

9. A fact borne out later that day when I watched the RCTV broadcast with Mahesh and his family (mother and father [Buddha Ratna], wife and children). When the story of the baby appeared, all those present in the room edged forward on their seats as their fascination drew them closer to the screen.

10. An interesting, if somewhat alarming, twist to the subject of perceptions of RCTV's political bias is provided by more recent events. The organization retained its leading market position in the supply of cable television in Tansen following the arrival of a rival commercial organization at the end of the 1990s. In an attempt to wrest control of the market from RCTV, the rival company's agent in Tansen is reported to have presented a compilation of video clips from the RCTV local program to the Ministry of Information and Communications that supposedly demonstrated that RCTV was producing pro-Maoist material. Despite the imposition of a fine of seven thousand rupees and the threat of imprisonment, Mahesh Shakya was able to call on the support of "local protectors" (Edwards n.d.), who ensured that RCTV was able to continue broadcasting in the face of these threats from central government.

11. Page and Crawley (2001) assert that by the time cable television started in Nepal the national government had recognized the potential of the medium from observation of the Indian experience and put a regulatory framework in place. This has allowed for the introduction of a large-scale commercial cable network, owned by an entrepreneur named Jamim Shah, to be launched in Kathmandu in 1998 without any of the problems experienced by similar organizations in India (see Page and Crawley 2001: 89–93 for a

description of the rivalry between small-scale individual cable operators and larger commercial networks in India). Their description of the situation may be correct with regard to the majority of small-scale cable operators in the towns of Nepal, who were simply ignored by the national government prior to the introduction of the National Broadcasting Act in 1992. But this Act, which consolidated the government's control of the state broadcasters Radio Nepal and Nepal Television, whilst allowing private cable *distributors* to operate, prohibited the production of original programming for broadcast through private cable networks. RCTV began operating shortly before this Act came into force; ignoring this restriction forced both national and local level government agencies to seek a compromise with the organization.

12. Interviewed 16th April 1996.

13. Interviewed 8th August 1996.

14. It should be noted that by the decade's end several major development agencies, for example the United States Agency for International Development (USAID 1999) and the UK's Department for International Development (Burke 1999), were reassessing the importance of media to their overall intervention strategies with a view to offer greater support to activities that they saw as strengthening civil society and achieving the United Nation's Millennium Development Goals (DFID 2006; Skuse 2006).

15. The *Asia Foundation's* decision to reverse its policy regarding the support of NGOs producing media at this time can be attributed to the growing controversy surrounding the *Nepal Forum of Environmental Journalists* (NEFEJ) decision to import FM radio transmitters supplied by the *United Nations* (UNDP and UNESCO) into Nepal in January 1996 (*The Kathmandu Post* 11th April 1996). NEFEJ then began to run test transmissions at the beginning of April 1996 despite the fact that Sher Bahadur Deuba's government did not respond to NEFEJ's request for a broadcasting license. At this time, the government had an official policy of opening up radio broadcasting to increased competition, but Nepal's only functioning FM radio station was *FM Kathmandu* owned by the state broadcaster *Radio Nepal* (although, as noted above, some air time on the station was sold to private media organizations). Finally, in May 1997 NEFEJ (in association with three other organizations—*Himal Association*, publisher of the magazine *Himal*, the *Nepal Press Institute* and *Worldview Nepal*) received a license and began broadcasting as *Radio Sagarmatha*. But, as in the case of RCTV/CDP, conditions were placed upon *Radio Sagarmatha* that they broadcast as an NGO with all the restrictions on the use of commercial sponsorship that this entailed (The Independent [Nepal] 3rd September 1997; see Page and Crawley 2001: 330–2).

16. I am grateful to Pratyoush Onta for pointing out in his comments on a draft version of this work that the history of *Himal* magazine, one of the undoubted success stories of Nepali journalism, shows that "the development trajectory is not hegemonic in media production in Nepal." Whereas an NGO, *Himal Association*, previously published *Himal* in its initial incarnation as a magazine covering the Himalayan region, in 1996 the magazine transformed into *Himal South Asia* with a remit to cover the whole region. This magazine is published by a commercial organization, *Himalmedia*, which also publishes several other magazines in Nepal. The reliance of local media in Tansen on the support of development organizations is clearly due in part to the restricted size of the audience and subsequent potential for raising revenue from commercial sources compared to media produced in the densely populated Kathmandu Valley with a potential readership beyond Nepal. This is an important point to consider when examining the potential for the growth of local media in provincial regions of Nepal and elsewhere. However, I would argue that economies of scale alone cannot account for the particular forms that media institutions and their products take. We must consider carefully how people actually conceptualize

economic activity, rather than view it as simply the outcome of decision-making processes motivated by market-based rationality.

17. RCTV/CDP has, for example, made short publicity films about Tansen and Palpa that are used by the *Palpa Chamber of Commerce and Industry* at tourism conferences in Kathmandu.

18. Minority language speakers in Nepal, especially from the Newar community, have frequently demanded that their languages should be recognized in the national media and this has been a particularly controversial issue with regard to the language policy of *Radio Nepal*. Not surprisingly, given their position as a "host tribe" (Gellner 1997a), demand for and active work in print media occurs amongst the Newar population of the Kathmandu Valley. Print media in languages of Nepal other than Nepali are available in Tansen, but they are predominantly publications from the Kathmandu Valley region. Their popularity appears limited compared to publications in Nepali (both national and local publications).

19. Quite apart from the fact that television ownership is virtually non-existent and electricity supply restricted in the rural areas even of a relatively affluent district like Palpa.

20. We have already noted that RCTV's commercial hegemony over the supply of cable television in Tansen has been challenged in recent years. It is also the case that the cultural hegemony of the caste and class groups who receive the majority of coverage in the local program does not go unchallenged. This is hardly surprising given the changing complexities of Tansen's population and is further explored in the following chapter.

Chapter 7
Televising Tradition: The Mediation of Culture

It may very well be interesting and important for us, as anthropologists, to theorize the kinds of shifts that occur in the self-understandings and practices of a particular social group when, for example, a 'traditional' ritual is performed especially for television cameras. But we must also remember that the ritual itself already is a medium, with its own distinctive mechanisms and possibilities of objectification and translation. The problem, then, is less the meeting of 'culture' and 'media,' and more the intersection of two or more systems of mediation.

William Mazzarella (2004: 353)

Introduction

Rather than assume that the existence of new mass media in a community are indicative of radical cultural change, this chapter conceptualizes the introduction of such media as the continuation of ongoing processes of cultural innovation. The ethnographic material features a number of religious festivals celebrated by Hindu and Buddhist members of Tansen's population, and considers the extent to which these are covered by the broadcasts of the local cable television organization. Both forms of cultural activity, festivals and television, can be described as actions that occur within the town's "public arena" (Freitag 1989). Freitag defines the public arena in her work on communalism and nationalism in Nineteenth and early Twentieth Century north India as,

> a world of ritual, theater, and symbol. It is a universe that sometimes reinforces hierarchy, providing roles for those occupying various positions within society, and at other times expresses conflict among unequals; it may even do both simultaneously. Most important, it is a world that is tied closely to the social and

political contexts of its locale and hence accommodates and reflects change
(1989: 19).

Mass media extend the boundaries of this universe in an obvious material
and spatial sense by adding new dimensions to the public arena. An analysis of
mediation draws our attention to distinctions in the different stagings of such
public events and the potential ways that people are socially positioned as the
result of these mediations. This analysis is concerned with mediation as both the
objectification of social relations in practice and, to return to the more familiar
use of the word, the processes of negotiating agreement between opposing parties. Commonly we think of mediation in this latter sense only when disputes
have evidently occurred. But, as Freitag's work demonstrates, one important
facet of action in the public arena is the attempt to achieve a "sense of shared
community" (1989: 91). Here we are concerned less with agreement about political objectives in any simple sense, than with the sharing of a Durkheimian
'conscience collective', that is with "the knowing instrument *and* the known
thing, [with] . . . the process of representation" (Bohannan quoted in Moore
2004: 53–4; emphasis added). This is especially important given the fact that in
any complex society there will often be contradictory perceptions of what such a
community of knowledge might consist of at the levels of local social relations
and "more encompassing ideological constructions" (Freitag 1989: 91).

The construction of ideological identities is in part, but not exclusively, connected to what Nick Couldry (2003: 2) calls "the myth of the mediated centre...The belief, or assumption, that there is a centre to the social world, and that,
in some sense, the media speaks 'for' that centre." Couldry's work demonstrates
that a claim to represent a pre-existing community is itself one of the most powerful ideological constructions of media producers. Whatever the criteria for
defining community identity, such myth-making serves to limit the imagination
of community (Anderson 1991) and the scope for political action. It is not just
that only some representations of community are accepted, but also that some
ways of representing the community are accepted as constructing the public
arena itself. An advantage of anthropology's commitment to comparative and
holistic analyses of social life is that mass media are defetishized and considered
as only one means through which people mediate a sense of their place in the
world, as the quotation from William Mazzarella at the start of this chapter
makes clear.

We should not take it for granted that people will subscribe to this myth of
the mediated centre and necessarily give new mass media a privileged place in
the construction of their social and political relations. We must instead ask
whether such privileging has occurred and, if so, why. Mediation cannot be understood as the simple transmission of culture, unaltered through various communication technologies, because this "presumes that there is a content, notion-
ally separate from, and transcending, the form, the medium, and the
circumstances of communication" (Hobart 2002: 370). The act of mediation
itself changes the possible perceptions of media content. When people see religious rituals on television, for example, they see the content of the program, the

narrated event, and the act of broadcasting itself, the *narrating* event (Oakdale 2004). While the narrated event may speak of tradition, the act of narrating is indicative of modernity.

Towards the end of my fieldwork, I talked with a member of *Communication for Development Palpa* about the organization and town. "Tansen is a traditional not a commercial place", he said. He continued:

> Previously there were only 'middle people' in Tansen who could not afford to invest in business. Then when the road came what investment there was left the town. But there is history here, whereas in Butwal and other growing towns there is no history. Apart from the history in the buildings of the town there is also a 'joint family feeling' fostered by shared traditions [*paramparā*], attitudes, and character. This has been handed down from our forefathers. Gradual change is happening in Tansen, but there is no problem with traditions. Tradition provides the answer to the question of why you belong in Palpa, what is your 'identity' [he used this English word].

His choice of the word *paramparā* for 'tradition' is interesting because it includes connotations of relatedness like that attributed to race or lineage (Turner 1980 [1931]) that are absent in the alternative term *rit* (alternatively *rīt* or *rītithiti*) that refers only to norms, customs or practices.[1] This is noteworthy in the light of the different definitions of community that are described by Freitag (1989), those based on "social bonds—what Sabean calls 'a series of mediated relationships' . . . personalized connections among participants rather than . . . abstracted ideological connections" (ibid.: 88). This comment is also important given the preceding discussion of social capital in the previous chapter. As we noted earlier, it is these latter forms of ideological connections are often central to media constructions of community identity. Analyzing the coherence or incoherence of different articulations of relational and ideological connections is central to studies of the construction of community.

In addition to this, mass media content is always limited with some cultural actors and acts shown, whilst others are ignored or portrayed in a grossly simplified manner. People and things not included within mass mediated forms of representation may be positioned in a disadvantageous location within prevalent discourses of modernity and development (cf. Pigg 1992). It is in this way that the existence of mass media in a place may influence the mediation of social relations and cultural identities *as a whole* despite the fact that mediated representations do not literally encompass the whole population. As Jarman (1997: 11) states, "even when the form [of a ritual] remains stable it does not imply that the meaning is static: in fact discontinuity between form and meaning may contribute to the persistence of a ritual by increasing the multivocality of the event and thereby its ambiguity, and in turn, its vitality." Discourses of tradition and modernity cannot be easily separated and essentialized, but will be actively constructed by the different people of a community engaged in complex processes of positioning in what Bourdieu (1998) describes as fields of power in the places they inhabit. This chapter examines the operation of such "a field of struggles within which agents confront each other, with differentiated means and ends according to their position in the structure of the field of forces, thus contributing to conserving or transforming its structure" (Bourdieu 1998: 32).

Selected Religious Festivals of Tansen

In the following section I present material on three festivals televised by the local cable organization, *Janai Purnima*, the *Bhagwati Jatra* and *Buddha Jayanti*, one festival that receives little or no coverage, *Krishna Jayanti*, and a privately celebrated rite, *Rakhi Purnima*. An important feature of this material is that these festivals are patronized by different sections the town's population. I then analyze how cultural identity is mediated in the public arena through both old and new 'technologies' of mediation. In conclusion, I argue that we can understand the frequently profound transformations of people's lives wrought by mass media through careful attention to the ways that their use articulates with ongoing processes of cultural innovation in other facets of the locality's public arena.

Janai Purnima and *Kumari Puja (televised)*
We can begin this process of understanding the articulation of different mediations of community identity in Tansen through an account of the important events of *Janai Purnima*, that occur in the town's largest temples and the Nineteenth Century palace (*darbār*) that serves as Palpa district's administrative centre. These events were recorded and subsequently televised by RCTV some days later. On this day in the Hindu ritual calendar male Brahmans replace the thread worn over the shoulder, the *janai*, which symbolizes their religious status. The original bestowal of the *janai* thread during the young male Brahman's initiation is "an essential step in the process of socialization" (Toffin 1995: 205). These ceremonies are with some small differences common to both the Newar and Parbatiya communities in Nepal (Nepali 1988: 400). All other high-caste males receive a wrist thread known as a *raksā* (wrist threads) as a symbol of their caste status.

Like most of Tansen's people, I witnessed what occurred in the *darbār* via RCTV's news broadcast several days later. This began with the newsreader explaining how the past week was the occasion of Tansen's "traditional and religious" festival of Janai Purnima. After showing activities at a temple, where the priest was distributing *raksā*, the scene shifted to the throne room of the *darbār* where a senior Brahman priest first gave a *raksā* to the sword of Prithvi Narayan Shah (the founder of the modern state and present King's ancestor) as a symbol of the monarch's authority over this region. He then turned to the Chief District Officer, the most senior district civil servant and his assistants to distribute further *raksā*. All those involved in this part of the ceremony were men from the two highest Parbatiya caste groups, either *Bahun* (Brahman) or *Chetri* (Kshatriya).

This section of the news program ended with another ceremony in the throne room, this time involving a girl from a different ethnic group, a Buddhist from one of the Newar families living in the bazaar. She plays the role of *Ku-*

mari, the virgin goddess, an incarnation of the deity identified as *Maha Devi*, the Mother Goddess, who is more commonly represented in one of her powerful, mature forms (Taleju, Bhagwati, Durga or Kali). As the Kumari she symbolizes purity and asks the officials what vices they harbor, listing five, desire, anger, jealousy, greed and foolishness as the principal causes of bad karma. She then accepts their 'offering' of a vice in exchange for her blessing.

According to Allen (1992), Kumari Puja (worship) should not be seen as directed either towards the girl herself or the virgin goddess she symbolizes. Rather, her purity invokes the presence of mature manifestations of the powerful goddess:

> Virtually every history text-book in the country recounts how, when Prithvi Narayan Shah entered Kathmandu during the annual Kumari festival [this was in 1769 when he finally stormed the city], he first received *prasad* [consecrated offerings] from the goddess and then decreed that the festival should continue. It is this event that above all is represented as conferring legitimacy on the new dynasty—a symbolic act of great importance still repeated annually (Allen 1992: 18).

Taleju, one of the mature manifestations of Kumari, was the chief protective deity of the Newar kings and through continuing patronage this relationship between goddess and monarch continues. Allen also observes that "when new capitals were established the first act of the founder was to build a temple for Taleju" and this phenomenon occurred in Tansen (Baniya 2053 VS [1996]). Following Palpa's annexation in 1806 the governor consecrated a temple to Bhagwati, another incarnation of the Mother Goddess, in the heart of the bazaar. The compact between the local high-caste Hindu representatives of monarchical authority and the power of the local Newar population is manifested through the Janai Purnima and Kumari Puja rites. The *darbār* throne room becomes the holy of holies of the state in Palpa: a sacred space within which the continuation of the rights of those who rule is transformed from a political fact into a cosmological principle (Burghart 1984).

Bhagwati Jatra (televised)

The rituals that occur during Janai Purnima demonstrate the continued alliance between the elites of the community and the kingdom, which legitimates the Shah (Parbatiya) dynasty's rule and ensures the support of the town's Newar leaders (Todd Lewis (1995) discusses analogous rituals that occur in Kathmandu). Although now witnessed on television sets in houses throughout the central bazaar, the reality of this socio-political fact is also demonstrated to the wider community through the events of the Bhagwati Jatra. This festival also receives extensive coverage in the RCTV program and a documentary produced by the organization has even been broadcast by NTV, the state broadcaster. It occurs a week after Janai Purnima and is the culmination of festivities analogous to those celebrated in all the 'Newar' cities of Nepal.

During the Bhagwati festival an image of the goddess is taken from its normal place in the temple and carried around the town. The chariot is circumambulated around the bazaar accompanied by local politicians, 'social workers' and business people. Karna Baniya (2053 VS [1996]), a local historian, notes that the festival was modeled on the Indra Jatra in Kathmandu, which is the main chariot festival of the royal Kumari of the capital city. As Bhagwati is a manifestation of Taleju, local associations with religious and political powers located in the capital are symbolically reinforced. Such associations are further strengthened when the procession stops to receive ritual offerings at key points of political authority and religious power, which include the *darbār*, municipality headquarters and most of the town's main temples.

According to Parish (1994: 32–3), such festivals are "a ritual construction of order...[that] has universal dimensions: it is social and moral, cosmic and sacred. These aspects of order are linked; the ritually declared connection to the cosmos and divinities helps give legitimacy to the royal and caste order." Inscription of a boundary between the bazaar interior, which remains on the ritually-clean, right-hand side of the devotees as they process with the deity, and its exterior, which remains to their left, symbolizes this order. The area within the bazaar is identified as pure and suitable for habitation by the 'clean' upper castes, whilst the exterior is left to the 'unclean' castes (Levy and Rajopadhyaya 1992). This pattern of habitation was enshrined in law during the Nineteenth Century and although officially repudiated still influences the distribution of households in Tansen today.

Buddha Jayanti (televised)

A chariot procession is also used during the festival of Buddha Jayanti, which commemorates the birth of Shakyamuni Buddha, the historical Buddha who was born in Lumbini not far from Palpa. Unsurprisingly, given that RCTV's owners come from the Newar Buddhist community, Buddha Jayanti receives extensive coverage in the local broadcasts. Most of Tansen's Newar Buddhist population is involved in the procession and a chariot bearing an ornate statue of Shakyamuni Buddha, accompanied by an organized *bhajan* (hymn) group leads the participants.

The celebration of Buddha Jayanti is a comparatively recent practice amongst the Newar Buddhists of Nepal having begun in 1926 (Gellner 1992: 215). The festival is Theravadic in origin and reflects that school of Buddhism's emphasis on the life of Shakyamuni Buddha and anniversaries related to his life, in contrast to the Mahayana tradition normally associated with Newar society. Since 1942 this festival has taken on some attributes of these Mahayana traditions, such as becoming the day for the celebration of the Buddha's enlightenment, although Gellner (1992: 97 and 356, note 36) observes that this is still celebrated through the Mahayana festival of Mataya several months later without any concern with the seeming inconsistency of this double celebration.

The adoption of a Theravadic festival by some sections of the Newar Buddhist population may have some political significance. Following the conquest of their kingdoms by the forces of Gorkha in the Eighteenth Century, the status of the Newars within the Nepali state has been ambiguous. Whilst they were absorbed into the official ranking of castes at only a middle level (Höfer 1979), they have maintained an internal hierarchy of castes that classifies high-caste Newars on a par with high-caste Parbatiyas. For Buddhist Newars this complex situation was further exacerbated because their own status within the Newar caste hierarchy is open to dispute with regard to high caste Hindu Newars. Gellner has described the Newar caste hierarchy as a double-headed structure with the precise configuration of the hierarchy dependent upon whom one is dealing with (Gellner 1992; Gellner and Pradhan 1995). For Newar Buddhists "their strong awareness of being Newar is run together with their attachment to Buddhism: they feel disadvantaged on both counts" (Gellner 1997a: 180).

Given the Mahayana traditions of Newar Buddhism it could seem contradictory for them to adopt a Theravadic festival, Buddha Jayanti, as this syncretism might further undermine their cultural status in the eyes of other Nepalis. But, as Parish (1997) points out, culture is a seamless totality only in the eyes of analysts and such a view denies the agency of those we purport to understand. The obvious syncretism of Hinduism and Buddhism in Nepal has often been romanticized in popular literature (Liechty 1996). The widespread influence of Tantric ideology and practices in Nepal has led to similarities between Buddhist and Hindu ritual, but we should be wary of the assumption that this indicates a 'natural' syncretism that is acquiesced to by the entire Buddhist Newar population, as it potentially asserts the dominance of Hinduism at the expense of Buddhism. The incorporation of religion into the ritual life of the state has already been observed in the earlier examples (cf. Kapferer 1988).

Buddha Jayanti, originating in Theravadic tradition, is harder to appropriate by groups who would wish to absorb it into the body of explicitly Hindu customs and beliefs. According to Gellner (1992) and my own observations of Buddha Jayanti in Tansen, it is a festival that does not attract the involvement of high-caste Hindus. This view is particularly expressed by younger members of the Buddhist community, and "in 1984, the appearance of a (Hindu) Krishna Bhajan (Hymn-singing) group in a Buddha Jayanti procession...drew strong protests from those who saw it as a plot to spread the government view of Buddhism" (Gellner 1992: 93). Gellner contrasts this protest with many older Buddhists, who view the appropriation by Hindu groups from the monarchy downwards as an affirmation of their religion.

It is interesting that the only important deviations of this procession from the route of the Bhagwati Jatra in 1996 were its start and end points at a Buddhist monastery and avoidance of the *darbār* and Municipality Headquarters. Most other processions, whether religious or secular (those to celebrate official state holidays or organized by specific institutions such as schools and NGOs), take routes that never venture into the upper reaches of the town. But, Buddha Jayanti goes that far and thereby asserts the importance of the Buddhist community in relation to the town as a whole.

Krishna Jayanti (un-televised)
The only other festival that includes a procession encompassing the whole town is the celebration of Krishna's birth, Krishna Jayanti or Krishna Janmastami. However, this received little or no coverage in RCTV's broadcasts. Although

Krishna is revered in Nepal, this festival does not have the same importance in the Newar cities or throughout Nepal in general as it does in India (Levy and Rajopadhyaya 1992: 452). A local author and newspaper editor, Vinaya Kasajoo makes no reference to a processional festival in his 1988 book about Palpa. Instead, he refers to the night of Krishna Janmastami only in terms of the performance of a *lakhe* (demon) dance at the Bhagwati temple, which symbolizes Krishna's victory over evil at the time of his birth and starts the Bhagwati festival. The absence of any reference to a specific Krishna Jayanti *jatra* in an otherwise comprehensive work suggests it was recently introduced.

This is not to say that Krishna Jayanti has not been celebrated in other Nepali cities. Anderson (1988: 105) describes how in Patan on the evening preceding Krishna's birth "worshippers carry his garlanded and ornately clothed idols in procession through the streets in their arms, on platforms on their shoulders, or in open trucks crowded with revelers" and how at the important Krishna Temple in Patan people gather to sing hymns in the manner of devotion (*bhakti*) associated with the worship of Krishna. It should be noted, however, that Patan's Krishna temple is associated with a minority group, the Tamots, who are said to have migrated from Mathura, the traditional birthplace of Krishna (Nepali 1988: 295). The architecture of this temple is also of a style more commonly found in South India than the Kathmandu Valley. According to Nepali (1988), Krishna Jatra in the Kathmandu Valley accords the peasant (*Jyapu* or *Maharjan*) castes of the Newar prominence during processions. Levy and Rajopadhyaya (1992: 452 and 654) claim that the Krishna Jayanti Jatra in Bhaktapur is a "minor" festival and says that it had "reportedly" been introduced to the town some eight to ten years before he conducted his fieldwork (from 1973 to 1976, giving an approximate date of introduction of 1963 to 1965). Levy does not explain this recent introduction, but, if it is a festival of the Jyapu/Maharjan caste, its introduction does seem congruent with Gellner and Pradhan's (1995) claim that it asserts their agency through the reinvention of religious traditions. Although they are few in number, Maharjans number amongst the wealthiest and most politically influential of Tansen's families. It is significant that notable members of the Newar Maharjan community participated in the Bhagwati Jatra procession, aligning themselves in the public arena with the 'state' festivity.

The lack of any large temple in Tansen devoted to the worship of Krishna meant that the focus of the Krishna Janmastami celebrations in 1996 was the state kindergarten (Bal Mandir) in the *darbār* compound adjacent to the Bhagwati Temple. This was the only public building in the centre of the bazaar with sufficient space for such an event. However, the popularity of the infant (*bal*) Krishna in story and image may have influenced this choice, as could the proximity of the building to the centers of political and religious life in the town, the *darbār* and Bhagwati temple. During the weeks preceding Krishna Janmastami, several groups collected donations to pay for the celebrations, which included manufacture of a *jhanki* (meaning 'glimpse' or 'tableau') by a craftsman from Uttar Pradesh. This is a typically "Vaishnava performance genre...in which persons or images (usually boys, but sometimes [as in the case of Tansen] figures of painted clay) [that] are dressed and made up as divine characters and placed in settings intended to evoke mythic scenes. These tableaux are presented for contemplation by audiences, often to the accompaniment of devotional singing" (Lutgendorf 1995: 330).

The *jhanki* represented all the major gods and goddesses of the Hindu pantheon. They were instantly recognizable, three-dimensional reproductions of the mass-produced posters, which adorned almost every house and shop in Tansen. Electric lights emphasized the visage of these figures inviting *darśan* (the exchange of looks that creates ritual communion) between the viewers and the images of the deities (Eck 1985). Following the *jatra*, the figures would be thrown into the near-by Kali Gandaki River as a sacrifice to the Mother Goddess and to have their power 'cooled' (cf. Pinney 2002).

A stage was set for a Krishna *bhajan* (hymn) group outside the kindergarten. This was electronically amplified and the noise generated by these festivities was considerably greater than that generated by the crowds in the temple complex barely twenty meters away where the Bhagwati Jatra was beginning. The singing and chanting that accompanied the procession of the chariot (*rath*) carrying the image of Krishna on the following day was also amplified. This chariot's appearance could not have contrasted more greatly with that of Bhagwati, which set off at almost the same time from the neighboring temple. Built out of a bamboo framework, covered in posters of the infant Krishna and bright tinsel decorations, with a small, illuminated statue of Krishna inside, this chariot was obviously a temporary construction whose form had resulted from a process of bricolage, making-do with whatever materials were available to the organizers of the Krishna Jatra.[2] After leaving the kindergarten and the *darbār* compound the Krishna chariot made its way into the crowded streets of the bazaar and then around the whole of the town, as was the Bhagwati chariot simultaneously, although they never clashed overtly. As with the Buddha Jayanti Jatra, the Krishna chariot followed a near identical route to the Bhagwati Jatra with the exception of the omission of stops at the *darbār* and municipality headquarters.

The organizers of the Krishna Jayanti festival came from a different sociocultural background to those involved in the Bhagwati Jatra. Krishna Jayanti was primarily celebrated by the portion of Tansen's population who have migrated there in more recent years from the Tarai, a region more heavily influenced culturally by India to the south than by the hill cultures of the north (Gaige 1975). Once again, the absence of any mention of Tarai peoples in Kasajoo's (1988: 114–126) discussion of "the people of Palpa" provides an indication of their recent impact upon the life of the town. It is also significant that the Krishna Jayanti festivities were patronized by members of the Parbatiya Occupational (Hill Untouchable) castes who were excluded from involvement in the Bhagwati Jatra.

It does not appear to be the case that these *jatra* are used to express intracommunity rivalry in an overtly competitive manner, as with the well-known Biska festival of Bhaktapur (Levy and Rajopadhyaya 1992; Parish 1997), or to antagonize rival sections of the population. Rather, the celebration of Krishna Jayanti is another example of how processional festivals manifest the presence of a particular cultural group in the town's public arena, but in such a way as not to alienate that group entirely from the rest of the population. Given the fact that in Tansen many people from the dominant *pahari* (hill) cultures, both Newar and Parbatiya, express doubt about the Nepali identity of those with Tarai ancestry, often referring to them as 'Indian Nepalis' or even just 'Indians', the need for constructing some sense of shared public cultural identity is clear.

In a sense then, the Krishna Jatra performs a similar function for the Tarai immigrants as the Buddha Jatra does for the Buddhist Newar population. The ostensive content of these festivals marks the participants as different to the rest of the population, making it possible for a politically disadvantaged minority to unite around a distinctive religious identity (Whelpton 1997: 47), whilst also using more widely shared processional idioms to enter into the public arena. The possibility remains, of course, that such festivities could become the means through which more overt statements of political opposition and identification could be manifested, even if this did not appear to be the case during the time of my research.

Rakhī Purnima (a private rite)

Nepali (1988: 401) states that one of the main attributes of Janai Purnima in India, the tying of a thread by a sister around the wrist of her brother is not found in Nepal, stating that this type of ceremonial filial worship (*bhai tika*) is reserved for the festival of Tihar (Diwali) in Kartik (October–November) and takes a quite different ritual form. However, this is not the case in contemporary Tansen. During Janai Purnima, as well as the simple thread bestowed by the temple priests to members of the twice-born castes, another type of 'thread' is given by sisters to their brothers. This is referred to as a *rakhī* using the popular form of *raksā* to distinguish these brightly colored, tinsel covered bracelets sold at this time by several shops in the bazaar from the conventional *raksā*. For members of twice-born castes this appears to be little more than an adjunct to the main ceremonials of Janai Purnima, carried out with little formality and often restricted to younger members of the family (i.e. those who have yet to undergo initiation). However, the *rakhī* ceremony has greater importance for other sections of the community, specifically those excluded from the official public ceremonies of Janai Purnima because of their inferior caste status.

During Janai Purnima, I was invited by a friend to his house to receive *rakhī* from his sister. Govinda is a Sunar goldsmith, a member of a Parbatiya Occupational (untouchable) caste, who lives with his wife (Shanti), father, younger sister and two young sons on the Lahare Pipal. This is the area on the lower southern slopes of the town formed by the ring-road from the bus station to the Ridi Road, which is mainly occupied by Parbatiya Occupational caste families and recent Magar immigrants. It stands outside of the processional route of all Tansen's main public festivals.

On the morning of Janai Purnima we were joined by his wife's two brothers, both of whom were working in Tansen (the elder for a metalware business on the Sadak and the younger for Govinda) and his sister, who had traveled to Tansen from Galyang (a nearby village) for the occasion. We gathered in a small room that served as a spare bedroom and informal parlor. Shanti did *puja* (worship) for her brothers and then Govinda's sister did *puja* for his sons and us. This consisted of a short prayer before an altar of Krishna, adorned with flowers and incense, which was positioned in the corner of the room. She then sprinkled red powder (*abir*) and flowers over our shoulders and gave us a dot on the forehead (*tika*) consisting of a mixture of *abir*, curd and rice. Then she gave each of us a gift of a *rakhī* (she had gone to the bazaar as soon as she arrived in Tansen to buy these). She then gave *prasad* of fruit, *pini roti* (a crispy noodle-type bread) and *ladu* (sweets) to us, before we reciprocated by giving money to her (Rs. 50 in this case). The whole ritual was rounded off with Shanti giving *tika* to Govinda's sister and touching her forehead to her feet, then Govinda doing the same to his sister (including touching forehead to feet).

The ritual described here is different from those considered thus far because it is concerned with the internal distinctions that exist within an ethnic group, in this case the place of the so-called Occupational caste groups within the Parbatiya community, rather than the status of an ethnic group within the population or the district or nation as a whole. It is also concerned with domestic ritual rather than the sort of public rites that we have considered so far, although as we shall see, many of the points raised in this section point to the clear relationship that exists between the domestic and public spheres of life in Tansen.

Janai Purnima is the festival that is most often regarded as the festival of Brahmans (Toffin 1995: 204). As we have already discussed, it is the time when all members of high Hindu castes (i.e. those who are regarded as 'twice-born') receive a sacred thread (*rakṣā*) symbolizing this status within the caste hierarchy from a Brahman priest. Male Brahmans also replace the thread (*janai*) that loops over their right shoulder and across the body, which is the key symbol of their status as an adult Brahman. The original bestowal of this thread during the young male Brahman's coming of age ceremony (*vratabandha*) is "an essential step in the process of socialization...However, it is only several months later, on the day of Janai Purnima, that the young man is definitively integrated into his caste" (Toffin 1995: 205). These ceremonies are with some small differences common to members of both the Newar and Parbatiya communities in Nepal (Nepali 1988: 400).

The development of the *Rakhī Purnima* festival, an import from India, by members of the untouchable castes of Tansen might be seen as a means to claim some sort foothold in the ceremonial events of a day that is seen as the definitive statement of hierarchy within the caste system. It also follows the same logic of appropriation and adaptation of rites to assert the right of different sections of the community to make a place within the religious and cultural life of the community as a whole, albeit behind the closed doors of separate households rather than in the shared space of the town's streets.

Public Festivals as Mediation and Their Remediation through New Communication Technologies

It cannot be doubted that the creation of Tansen's cable television program was a remarkable innovation in the field of media in Nepal. The program creators' claim that they offered local people an alternative to national and foreign broadcasting is clearly justified. Nevertheless, the production of RCTV's television programs could also be interpreted as a demonstration of how media representations of religious culture may be used to reproduce the power of local elites. They reproduce hegemonic political order because many of the festivals that they televised are obviously focused upon elite circuits of exchange (i.e. between upper caste members of the Parbatiya and Newar communities, agents of the state and with INGOs that supported the organization). The selection of these events for broadcast by RCTV and their presentation in other mass media, such as the writings of local historians, journalists and tourist brochures, also helps create an image of these festivals as representative of the town and district *as a whole*. The Bhagwati Jatra in particular has found national exposure thanks to the re-broadcasting of RCTV programs about the festival by Nepal Television. It has become "Palpa's Bhagwati Jatra" (Baniya 2053 VS [1996]), so that a ritual dominated by the municipality's elite stands for the whole town and the ritual of the town stands for the entire district. This process is mythic in the sense suggested by Barthes (1973); one semiological system, the (meta)languages of modernity and development (manifested through mass media), overdetermines another system, the languages of ritual, community and tradition. The fact that the Buddha Jayanti receives extensive coverage by RCTV supports this interpretation. It is elevated into the pantheon of festivals that symbolizes Tansen and this contrasts with the previously uncertain status of Buddhist Newars.

Such mythologization may also be reinforced by the conflation of public and the private spaces during the act of watching television, because events such as festival processions are simultaneously dispersed to numerous homes throughout the bazaar (Wilmore 2008). Jatra are viewed not as a circuitous route performed over a particular duration, but as single points of edited action screened within the objective form of the television set. "The 'public'…is experienced in the (private) domestic realm: it is domesticated. But at the same time, the 'private' is thus transformed or 'socialized'. The space (and experience) created is neither 'public' nor private in the traditional senses" (Morley 1992: 285). The home becomes the site where history enters into collective memory, as Dayan and Katz (1992) point out in their study of so-called "media events", not the least because people can now have a dual experience of this history, once 'live' and then again time-shifted to the edited highlights shown on television and potentially stored on tape for future reference.

As we noted above, festivals such as the Bhagwati Jatra have frequently acted as means through which dividing lines between purity and impurity have been inscribed upon the geography of the urban communities. The disruption of this distinction through the introduction of the processional rite into the private space of the home may appear to be lessened by the cable lines' restricted distribution in locations where the physical structure of the streets (terraced, high-density housing) is better suited to their installation. It is not coincidental that these places in the bazaar also correspond to the areas of highest affluence in the community. These conditions are met within the area of the old bazaar and adjacent suburbs (*tol*), and access to cable television matches the area circumscribed by the Bhagwati Jatra. The old pattern of exclusion is recreated as a by-product of the new cable technology's distribution, although conventional broadcasting would obviously add further complexities to the geography of mediation.

Given that the audience for the program does not include many of the excluded sections of the community due to the limited distribution of the cable system, one might question whether the selective televising of festivals patronized by the same social groups that control the local television broadcast and form its core audience can have any lasting hegemonic effect.[3] In response to this one must reiterate the point made previously that such media speak simultaneously of modernity and tradition. Such media activities manifest a nationally shared ideology of development (*bikās*) in this locality, which is both accepted by the populace as a whole but also clearly controlled by particular people and groups within the community (see chapter 6). At the same time, the broadcasts often comprises selected elements of cultural life that are grounded in local social relations and stated to be aspects of local tradition. This accords with Jonathan Parry's observation that the use of mass communication technologies not only heralds movement towards secular modernity, but may also "reinforce 'traditional' religious values" (van der Veer 1994: 79) or rather become "'neo-traditional'...reconstructions; conscious redemptions of folk culture" (Dayan 1998: 108).

A key question, then, for any study of community life is the extent to which "relational forms of community possess the capacity either to enlarge into, or link up with, ideological expressions of community" (Freitag 1989: 89). Festivals have always made such a link through their integration into wider religious ideologies. We have seen that ideological innovations have occurred in each of the examples chosen so that relational forms of community can be reintegrated at the local level on the basis of renewed claims to wider national or 'universal' ideological connections. I would argue that development ideology manifested through modern, *bikasit* technological forms can be seen as a further example of such processes of community formation that are manifested through the interlinking of relational and ideological forms of community (see Pigg 1992). It is important to note that expressions of socio-political identity that empower the local community vis-à-vis other places within the encompassing nation-state of Nepal, such as RCTV or the Bhagwati Jatra, may at the same time serve to perpetuate inequalities within the locality itself. According to Daniel Hallin (1998), such concern with local structures of power is frequently lacking in studies of mass media in the developing world, dominated as they are by studies situated at national or global levels of analysis, and he calls for comparative studies of mediated communication that anthropologists are ideally placed to produce.

All configurations of community identity "obviously have implicit political implications" (Freitag 1989: 89), but do not go unanswered. However, as I have already mentioned, one of the conundrums of my research was the stolid approval of the local television program by almost everyone I questioned.[4] In part this may be a methodological artifact, as people could be reluctant to state exactly what they might feel about this subject in the face of an outsider's questions. Nevertheless, I don't think that these answers necessarily indicate the absence of objections and resistance on the part of those who are evidently excluded from such visions of community, either to this specific example of local television programming or the broader ideologies of development and religious tradition that television narrates. Rather, we need to look for oblique evidence of such resistance at work in the community, evidence that is more obvious if, as I have suggested, we use the great potential of anthropologists' ethnographic perspective and shift our focus from mass media *per se* to mediations of community relations and identity more generally (cf. Nightingale 1993 and Hughes-Freeland 1998: 22, who argue that the use of ethnographic methodologies within media studies has tended to "reify and over privilege the role of media, and need[s] to take on anthropology's broader conception of ethnography"). As we have seen above in the analysis of religious festivals, other 'technologies' (Gell 1992; Pfaffenberger 1992) are available through which sociopolitical agency can be asserted in the public arena (Dayan 1998: 108).

Dirks (1994: 483) argues that "too often the combination of the key terms 'everyday' and 'resistance' leads us to look for new arenas where resistance takes place, rather than also realizing that more 'traditional' arenas are also brimming with resistance." This suggests that conceptualizing the roles that media play in the assertion of domination and resistance is not as simple as it might at first appear. As Dowmunt (1998: 245) states, "any useful definition of alternative media, or of what constitutes resistance to the empires [of transnational media], is bound to be complex, and will need to be informed by detailed investigation of what exactly is being resisted, by whom, in what contexts." Despite the fact that public reaction to the local program is overtly favorable throughout the local population, expressing a need for a local alternative to national and transnational media and genuine pride in RCTV's work, we should not then be led to conclude that everyone agrees that Tansen's television expresses a "common core of characteristics that define [the] public arena" (Freitag 1989: 19), or what Couldry (2003) refers to as the myth of the mediated centre. As we have seen, members of the town's population have regularly added to or transformed its festivities, skillfully integrating cultural innovations with the traditions of existing ritual form, especially processions. These innovations follow a consistent, shared pattern of action and incorporation in processional ritual, which is often effective, as Paul Connerton (1989) explains, due to this being a shared *bodily* practice. This may go some way to explaining why Nepali urban society has not been subject to the same degree of violent communalism seen in India, where the primary religious divide is between Hinduism and Islam with their distinct systems of belief and practice. Having said this, more recent violent assertions of identity will be discussed shortly.

Recent trends in migration to Nepal's urban areas suggest that religious and ethnic minorities who have hitherto played little part in the public culture of urban Nepal, especially as they are manifested in the operation of recognized circuits of ritual exchange between socially and politically dominant groups, will increasingly be in a position, literally, to assert their collective and individual identity. Denied access to modern, mass media technologies, such as video and cable television, either due to their cost or social discrimination, subaltern groups in Tansen continue to make use of alternative representational 'technologies' derived from religious practice to take up a position in the public arena of the town. Whilst this may be interpreted as resistance of a sort, it is clearly neither radical nor overtly critical of the socio-political status quo. The aim does not appear to be the radical transformation of their position in the public arena according to any new set of ideological principles, but the establishment of cultural practices that might be considered to operate on a par with the others that make up the spectrum of the town's cultural life, including that of the local mediascape (Appadurai and Breckenridge 1995). To return to the point made in the introduction of this chapter, new cultural *content* has been added to the public arena, but through *forms* of representation that perpetuate established and shared ways of knowing.

Van der Veer (1994: 83) rightly points out that what works as resistance on one level may work as domination on another; we see this duality at work in both television and ritual activity in Tansen. We should be wary of forms of "cultural romanticism, increasingly prevalent in media and cultural studies, that sees all forms of grass-roots cultural expression as 'resistance'" (Garnham 1992: 373), an observation that applies equally to all technologies of cultural expression considered here, whether predicated upon discourses of modernity and development in the case of television or tradition in the case of religious festivals and ritual. It is important to note in relation to this point that the changing demography and cultural milieu of Tansen may have contributed to an equal desire on the part of some groups to reaffirm the hegemonic status of certain cultural practices and forms through their representation in mass media, such as television, that convey some prestige through connotations of modernity and development. This is especially apparent when we consider the additional fact that the commoditization of cultural content that occurs through its reproduction in mass media form contributes to local elites' ability to enter into national and transnational circuits of exchange, either in the context of capitalist market relations or through involvement in the development economy (see previous chapter).

The socio-political condition of non-Hindus and minority ethnic groups within the world's only Hindu kingdom has been the subject of increased work in recent years (see for example Dastider 1995; Gellner et al. 1997; Fisher 2001). The growth in research on this subject reflects the realities of politics within post-1990 Nepal where ethnic (*janajati*) and religious identity have become the focus for new forms of political organization. This political reality also includes its concomitant, which is the rejection of such 'traditional' forms of cultural identification by radical, Maoist insurgents (Hutt 2004). Dastider (1995: ix) succinctly summarizes this complex situation: "Absolute monarchy...symbolized the fusion of the state with the nation [and] did not allow ethnic tension to surface on the ground. The fragile nature of this harmony came to the surface with the establishment of a more democratic order." Some religious groups, such as Muslims and Christians, have only managed to assert any freedom to associate and worship in the very recent past, although Islam may have been an implicit element in some aspects of Tarai politics in the past (Gaige 1975). The tensions to which Dastider refers have been visible for longer in the Newar Buddhist community than amongst other religious and ethnic groups in Nepal because they have formed a sizeable minority, often an actual majority of the population of the country's most important cities (see Gellner 1986; Quigley 1987).

The crucial, but ultimately simple question we are forced to ask is who can to represent themselves simultaneously as modern *and* traditional when mediating social identity; conversely, who is unable to mobilize such diversity in self-representation. It is this, above all else, that will determine the outcome of the "struggles within which agents confront each other" (Bourdieu 1998: 32) in any particular field of cultural reproduction. The plurality of mediation must be asserted if we are to avoid reifying the dynamic processes involved in people's construction of cultural identity "out of the seemingly contradictory resources of 'tradition' and 'modernity'" (Liechty 2003: 4). Gitlin (1998) acknowledges such contradictions in his discussion of Habermas's classic formulation of the public sphere, which he criticizes for its assumption that only one such arena for political communication can, or indeed should exist at any time, arguing instead for the existence of a multiplicity of interacting "public sphericules" within any complex society.

Conclusion

It may well be that those who control new media technologies seek to position themselves as "the gatekeepers of cultural memory" (Kuenhast 1992: 186), but, whilst undoubtedly conferring great power upon those who control *these* means to make representations of local life and culture, they remain only one of the many acts of mediation that are simultaneously enacted *in* and enactions *of* community life. "The assumption that what is in the media must have higher status than what is not" (Couldry 2003: 48) must be deconstructed rather than naturalized and reproduced in our analysis. Older mediatory 'technologies' are not swept away by the advent of modern media and we may even find that the same historical currents bringing these new media to a community lead to innovation in other spheres of cultural practice (van der Veer 1994; Meyer 2004). Such innovation is a reflection of the fact that people are engaged in an ongoing struggle over both the right to take up a position as gatekeepers of cultural memory and what may count as a legitimate medium for the "performance of memory" (Jarman 1997).

This chapter's examination of local television and the televising of religious ritual in Nepal is by no means comprehensive, not the least because the ethnographic present of the research (the mid-1990s) is just prior to the first escalation in the current Maoist insurgency, the massacre of King Birendra and his imme-

diate family in 2001, the subsequent return of absolute monarchical rule following King Gyanendra in February 2005 and the restitution of democratic rule in
2006. Such events are clearly indicative of violent political resistance to and
reassertions of state power. Nevertheless, it has sought to define an analytical
position through which the precise object of anthropologists' media research
might be reconceptualized. In this particular place one set of community identities enacted through festivals is *re*mediated through the local television program,
to use McLuhan's (1987) term for the embedding of old media forms in the content of new. This is contrasted to those who have a distinctive vision of their
place in the public arena of the town but access only to the older medium of the
festival. "The double signification of media technologies, the fact that viewers
and listeners are addressed by the content of media and at the same time inter-
pellated by the technology itself, which often carries with it the larger ambitions
of the colonial and post-colonial state" (Ginsburg et al. 2002: 20) is clearly apparent in this case. The processes and outcomes of such remediations become a
crucial subject of enquiry both in anthropological studies that have a specific
focus on media and in the wider ethnographic study of all people whose cultural
lives now incorporate multiple forms of mediatory technology.

Postscript

On 2nd February 2006, to mark the first anniversary of his assumption of direct
rule, King Gyanendra appeared on Nepal Television to address the nation. His
claims to have established stability and tackled the Maoist insurgency during
this time were shown to be hollow only a few hours later when news broke of a
large-scale Maoist attack on the town of Tansen. During this attack twenty
members of the security forces were killed, the Chief District Officer plus several other senior civil servants were kidnapped and most dramatically the *darbār*
was destroyed by fire. The symbolism of the attack itself and the destruction of
the seat of royal power in Tansen shattered confidence in Gyanendra's ability to
control the course of events in Nepal, his claims to the contrary during his televised address not withstanding. On 24th April, following weeks of violent protest
in the towns and cities of Nepal King Gyanendra reappeared on NTV to declare
that he had recalled parliament and reinstated government by elected politicians
(see Wilmore 2008).

Notes

1. I am grateful to an anonymous reviewer of this work for drawing attention to this
distinction.
2. One might speculate whether the form of the Krishna chariot, box-like with a
sculpture of Krishna illuminated by an electric light positioned inside, was designed to
explicitly mimic a television set. Many commentators (e.g. Lutgendorf 1995, Mankekar
1999 and Pinney 1997) have made the connection, which is undoubtedly reflected in

everyday practice, between the act of viewing deities in television programs and the conventions of darshan which form an integral component of Hindu devotional practice (see Eck 1985). (Nepal Television and RCTV showed programs based on legends of both Krishna and Rama during the time of my fieldwork.) Such speculation would, of course, require substantiation through further research. Pinney (2002: 365) also comments that "the overlying of a purely visual perception with tactile extensions that feed into a broader haptic field is apparent in other modes of image customization. The application of glitter or *zari* (brocade) or the adhesion of paper surrounds or plastic flowers moves the image closer to the devotee."

3. This is a highly pertinent question noted by one of the anonymous reviewers of this work, whose contribution I wish to acknowledge.

4. The interesting exceptions to this were a few informants who had previously worked as volunteers for the organization producing the local television program but subsequently left after personal disagreements with other members.

Chapter 8
Conclusion: Our People

The concept of a people is not 'given', as an essential, class-determined, unitary, homogeneous part of society *prior to a politics*; 'the people' are there as a process of political articulation and political negotiation across a whole range of contradictory social sites. 'The people' always exist as a multiple form of identification, waiting to be created and constructed.

Homi Bhabha (1990: 220)

Globalization can be said to enmesh particular localities within "a Mobius-like dialectic" (Abramson 1999: 437) through which people's activities in those places are both constituted *by* and constitutive *of* the increasingly dense networks of activity, interaction and power that characterize the phenomenon. The so-called electronic empires (Thussu 1998) of modern mass communications and media have come to symbolize this dialectic, offering unprecedented possibilities for people and communities to become conjoined with the global political, economic and cultural networks that are increasingly the context within which their lives and livelihoods are constituted (Castells 1996). However, the means through which entry to and existence within such global mediascapes are negotiated often remain poorly understood. Debates can easily devolve into contrasts between dichotomous stereotypes based on either the celebration of a coming harmonization of humanity on the one hand (Negroponte 1996: 230) or active resistance to such homogenizing forces on the other (Dagron 2004: 61). In practice, of course, neither ideal is likely to occur due to the complex, dialectical character of the globalization processes that such binary oppositions fail to grasp (Deger 2006: xxiv).

This point is further reinforced by the example of the development of commercial and community media in post-1990 Nepal and the particular case *of Ratna Cable Television/Communication for Development Palpa*. Any attempted understanding of these developments in the national media of Nepal or Tansen's local mediascape predicated on a simple dichotomy between mainstream and non-mainstream activities cannot account for what has happened there in the past two decades. Distinctions that seem logical at one level of abstraction fail to account for the historically constituted experiences of those whose lives are subject to such forms of mediation. As Mark Peterson (2003: 219) observes in relation to the alternative media that he refers to as "cottage culture industries",

> the worlds of the culture industry and other forms of media production are issues of scale, not kind, and . . . the anthropological study of production need not be seen as an ethnography of producers but as the ethnographic study of the ways in which media production technologies are incorporated into and positioned within the social relations of communities. It urges us to consider ways to describe media worlds that encompass parallel modes of media production, that link consumers and producers, and that see mediation as part of a complex of systems for cultural expression and social formation.

Just as networks of relations operating on a global scale are complex, so are local networks of social relations. Localities are bound into the fabric of national, regional and international relations on the basis of the local relations of communities described by Peterson, but such local networks are simultaneously changed in the process of creating links between different positions in the warp and weft of the global mediascape and the imbricated 'scapes' of ethnicity, technology, finance and ideas that media comment upon and thereby help to construct (Appadurai 1990).

It is for this reason that Chris Atton (2002) is drawn to the influential work of the post-colonial theorist Homi Bhabha at the end of his study of alternative media and argues that we must view *hybridization* as their default characteristic. There can be no pure definition of alternative media (or indigenous, or local, or citizens media and so on) because such media forms arise from the intersection of diverse positions in the mediascape. Claims to a pure or essential character for such media may often be encountered because these claims are frequently mobilized during political battles over the legitimacy of such media activities and activism more generally. But we must recognize these claims as part of the very phenomena that we are seeking to understand rather than privilege them as explanatory in their own right. The many different names used to identify the phenomena that we are here studying do not indicate the existence of different things *sui generis*, but are a short-hand way to describe how particular instances of media activity fit into the structure of the mediascape as a whole.

Hybridity in Bhabha's terms does not simply evoke the biological notion of new and novel forms arising from the conjoining of prior entities, although this 'common sense' meaning may have some appeal when attempting to describe the complex, often confusing features of cultural forms in general and media in particular. Bhabha does, in fact, reject this fairly straightforward definition of hybridization on the grounds that it can too quickly be used to imply that past, original forms of culture were in some ways essential or pure, when in fact "all forms of culture are continually in a process of hybridity" (1990: 211). Hybridity is actually a "third space" (ibid.) created in the interstices of relationships but which is not *determined* in its possibilities by the characteristics of the objects or actors that are thereby conjoined.

The importance of hybridity is that it bears traces of those feelings and practices which inform it, just like translation, so that hybridity puts together the traces of certain other meanings or discourses. It does not give them the authority of being prior in the sense of being original: they are prior only in the sense of being anterior. The process of cultural hybridity gives rise to something different, something new and unrecognizable, a new area of negotiation of meaning and representation (ibid.).

Such descriptions of hybridity may obviously be applied to the political circumstances that existed in Nepal at the time when RCTV was created in Tansen. A time of revolution is by definition a period of foment in relationships with new forms of agency, identity and activity being created with great rapidity. But it is equally clear that such changes are predicated on what existed before, as well as a vision of what might come to be in the future, even though they are not determined by history in any straightforward manner. The examples of RCTV and the wider changes in the mediascape of Tansen demonstrate the obvious point that not everything became obsolete or was challenged in the 1990s, but the consideration of such examples helps us to understand what things or practices survived, what things were transformed and what came to be decisively rejected at this time. Even seemingly innovative things like a community-based cable television station were not without precedent and built on what came before. Such constructions are acts of *bricolage* (Levi-Strauss 1972) not just at the level of the technological creativity required to produce programs, but also in terms of the so-called 'soft' technologies of the social, institutional and legal arrangements required to organize production.

The hybrid character of the local cable television program is therefore seen in the merging of private, commercial concerns of RCTV with the public, civic-centered workings of the non-governmental organization CDP. Not only did this help to change many people's perceptions in Tansen and Nepal more generally about what types of organization could produce media and in what locations, it also altered attitudes to the spheres of activity in which NGOs could operate. As stated at the start of this work, RCTV/CDP was not necessarily a direct antecedent of the many other community media organizations that have subsequently been created in Nepal, but it did have the distinction of being one of the first organizations to take advantage of the possibilities opening up in Nepal at that time, the so-called "fissures in the mediascape" (Rodriguez 2001).

The new circumstances and attitudes that informed things such as freedom of speech and information in post-1990 Nepal did not immediately bring about the wholesale rejection of deeply-rooted ideologies that had undergone extensive processes of maturation in the Panchayat era, the foremost being that of development (*bikās*). Equally, the social and cultural bases upon which RTCV/CDP's work was organized, especially the overdetermination of much of this work by entrenched caste, religious and ethnic identities, as well as the presence of Tansen's unique history, gave the organization and its work distinctive qualities that would never be found in another place. It is for this reason that it may be useful to consider their work as a form of indigenous media even though it does not meet the strict requirements for such identification specified by those who pioneered the use of this term. Rather, this is indigenous media because it bears the hallmarks of its people and place of origin throughout, even as it also bears traces of many influences from elsewhere. It is in this sense another example of what Michaels (1986) called the invention of television. Working within an analytical tradition inspired by Raymond Williams, indigenous media researchers have insisted that 'television' as such does not exist: rather, there are a multiplicity of televisions born out of the conjuncture of material, technological forms and the socio-cultural contexts within which these forms are put to use.

> Here I want to emphasize *the continuity of modes of cultural production across media*, something that might be too easily overlooked by an ethnocentric focus on content. My researches identify how Jupurrurla and other Warlpiri videomakers have learned ways of using the medium that conform to the basic premises of their tradition in its essential oral form. They demonstrate that this is possible, but also that their efforts are yet vulnerable, easily jeopardized by the invasion of alien and professional media producers (Michaels 1994: 121; emphasis in original).

The distinction of being one of the first alternative media organizations to be formed in post-1990 Nepal makes the example of RCTV/CDP instructive in relation to the vulnerabilities alluded to by Michaels. This is because it is less a direct antecedent of what followed in the alternative or community media sphere than an indicator of the types of struggles that were ongoing at the time to re-imagine what media could be like in Nepal. Wilson (2004: 59) notes that "regrettably, many analysts miss the problematic nature of institutions in poor countries. Interested mainly in the technology itself, too many analysts overlook the role that institutions play even in advanced countries. The institutions that enabled the information revolution to occur where and when it did are not present in many developing countries." The compromise that was reached to create CDP and allow the continued broadcasting of the local program in Tansen shows how those who were attempting to create new forms of media in Nepal in the early 1990s had to exercise as much creativity in the formation of such enabling institutions as they did in the technical solutions needed to broadcast their program. However, just as such technical solutions also brought with them restrictions (for example, the limitation to cable broadcasting and the use of pre-recorded material only), so to did institutional solutions restrict what was possible for the organization to include in the content of their programming. Understanding how and why such compromises came about are vital if we are to evaluate fully the contributions that the "champions" (Wilson 2004) of media or information and communication technologies make to their implementation and survival.

The championing of new or alternative media in Nepal has often been achieved at huge cost to those who take on such a role. This was brought home to me with great force after I had been living in Tansen for about six months. I received a phone call from Vinaya Kasajoo, the editor of the *Deurali* rural newspaper. He had just returned from a two-day visit to the neighboring VDC of Madan Pokhara and had some exciting news that he wanted to tell me about. Later that day I visited him in the offices of *Deurali* that adjoined his house. During a long conversation that encompassed much, he told me that he had been discussing the likelihood of setting up a community FM radio station with the elected members of the Madan Pokhara VDC council. Training and equipment had been offered by an INGO and the radio station could be fully functional by the end of the year. The only problem was the reluctance of the central government in Kathmandu to grant licenses to potential broadcasters, either commercial or community. The high costs of the licenses that had recently been granted to a few commercial FM radio stations in the Kathmandu Valley effectively barred any community station from operating legally. However, the advocates of community radio in Madan Pokhara and in other parts of Nepal, himself included, felt strongly that broadcasting was both a right granted by the laws covering freedom of speech in the new constitution of Nepal and a crucial element in improving the livelihoods of the people. They would, he said, be willing to face imprisonment to defend these rights.

Vinaya Kasajoo was not speaking about the threat of prison in any abstract or hypothetical sense when he made this claim. He had already been incarcerated when working as the editor of Tansen's old local newspaper, *Satya* (Truth), during the Panchayat era. Although the people of Nepal had by 1996 enjoyed a half a decade of almost unprecedented political freedom, the memories of the oppression of the Panchayat era (Hoftun and Raeper 1992: 19, 59–60) were recent and clearly not forgotten.

In April 1996 when Vinaya and I had this conversation the 'People's War' had been officially declared by the CPN (Maoist)for two months and violence by both Maoist and government security forces was becoming a terrible feature of daily life for a growing number of people living throughout the country. Over the next decade as many as fifteen thousand people were to lose their lives and many more became casualties in other ways, either through injury, the death of family members or friends, the loss of livelihood and forced migration. The destruction of the Tansen *darbār* in 2006 during a Maoist attack in Palpa during which twenty people were killed stands as a dramatic symbol of this experience of suffering in Palpa district (Wilmore 2008).

The state of emergency that was officially declared by the government of Nepal in 2001 and the subsequent period of direct rule by King Gyanendra led to an increase in attacks on media freedoms through the suspension of various articles of the constitution (Bhattarai 2004; Onta 2006). At the same time, journalists became a target of violence by both Maoist cadres and state security forces; in August of 2001 the organization *Reporters Without Frontiers* went so far as to describe Nepal as "the world's biggest prison for journalists" (quoted in Bhattarai 2004: 3). These direct attacks on the media and media workers were paralleled by the wider situation of extreme uncertainty regarding the durability of Nepal's recently established media freedoms and the institutions or individuals that relied upon these in their work. Although, as Onta (2006) has noted, this situation did not prevent the continuation of the rapid development of media institutions in Nepal that had been seen in the first years of the 1990s, it is also the case that the pace of change in Nepal's mediascape generated its own uncertainties (Wilmore 2007). The attempt by a rival commercial cable television organization to exploit the events of the 'People's war' to undermine RCTV's business in Tansen and the threatened imprisonment of Mahesh Shakya in Tansen are indicative of such problems and their potentially dire effect upon individuals.

And yet amidst this uncertainty and suffering more than fifty independent commercial and community radio stations had come exist in Nepal by 2005. The lasting experimentation with television broadcasting in Tansen stands not as the direct originator of these radio stations; they are not the immediate offspring of RCTV/CDP in any straightforward sense. Rather, RCTV was a pioneer in the exploitation of the new possibilities for action in both the commercial and non-profit, public media spheres; subsequently such possibilities were eagerly taken up by others. The full range of types of new electronic media that exist in Nepal has yet to be described, but it can be said without fear of contradiction that there is as much variety as there is similarity between those that do exist. The media activities undertaken in Nepal in the past fifteen years therefore serve as an exemplar of the hybridity described by Atton (2002) due to the varieties of media produced, the different ways that production is organized and in terms of the identification of the sorts of hybrid political circumstances under which such variety can come into being. At the same time, the violence and repression meted out by all sides in the civil conflict of these years demonstrates that just as hybrid spaces open up the possibilities of greater freedom of expression manifested through the increased possibilities of media production, such opportunities may be forcibly curtailed even as they come into being.

In asking how such freedoms can be protected it is important to look not only at the ways in which they may be supported from above, by INGOs or the state for example, but also at the important role that the support of audiences play in sustaining media activities. As the example of RCTV/CDP indicates, the construction of legitimacy in the eyes of the communities within which media are located is crucial to their survival. Laura Kunreuther's (2004 and 2006) recent work provides a very interesting parallel to the present study because it describes the various modes of interpellation through which FM radio programming addresses its audience, especially members of the Nepali diaspora. As she notes, "FM radio is not simply a medium for broadcasting conversations with Nepalis abroad, but it produces, as one of its persuasive effects, the idea that 'urban Nepalis' and the 'Nepali diaspora' are entities that exist prior to their mediation through the telephone or radio" (Kunreuther 2006: 325). Similarly, RCTV/CDP interpellates its audience in such a way as to naturalize particular ways of thinking about what it means to be Palpali and a citizen of Tansen.

Dagron (2004: 44) argues that alternative media are only sustainable if they work to articulate the voices of those engaged in social struggles. It is easy to see how this appears to be borne out by the examples of successful alternative media that are canonical in the literature or in discussions of their potential. But this position tends to see media as only an instrument of prior social struggles or movements. The active role that media play in actually forming the constituencies for such movements may need to be considered in more detail. For example, although Ginsburg (1995: 66) states that the "changing composition of audiences" has contributed to the indigenous media debate and questions the validity of a "static and reified understanding of culture" (ibid.: 68), her own position is predicated upon a normative and somewhat ahistorical understanding of audience composition. She talks of "the importance of indigenous media as an expression of contemporary indigenous sensibilities, part of a desire on the part of Aboriginal people to 'talk back' on their own terms to those who might have presumed to speak for them" (ibid.: 67–8). However, she does not consider the audience at the level of practice, i.e. in the act of consumption, and as a result pays little attention to the extent to which such practices are actually constitutive of identification with "indigenous sensibilities" (cf. Bourdieu 1998).

All studies of media as a matter of course include assumptions about the audience, whether these are made explicitly or not. Indigenous media studies have contained an *implicit* theorization of the audience because ethnicity is regarded as the key factor through which these are media distinguished from other national and transnational media, just as alternative media are often regarded as synonymous with radical political positions or minority identities. Both the producers of these media and researchers argue that the programming made by media producers is accepted as a more legitimate expression of audience identity when such identities are shared. Unlike 'mainstream' media, which frequently attempt with lesser or greater success to impose the widest possible shared experience upon consumers to form a mass audience, it is argued that the circuit of communication within alternative media forms a virtuous circle because both producer (sender) and audience (receiver) supposedly share the same cultural codes for being in the world. No act of translation is required for there to be understanding between producers and consumers of these media. This remains only an assumption if no attempt is made to show why this is the case; it is by no means obvious that indigenously produced media, here meaning media produced by and on behalf of a community in a wider sense rather than the more restricted, 'ethnic' sense of the term, should *inevitably* be regarded as a more, or even the most, legitimate expression of identity (Miller 1992). It is assumed that it is possible to produce a commonly recognized expression of ethnic (or for that matter any other cultural) identity using modern forms of mass media technology.

This position is most clearly articulated by Ginsburg (1994: 6) in the following statement: "Films embody in their own internal structure and meaning the forms and values of the social relations they mediate, making text and context interdependent." It is implied that media that are not produced with a particular community or group in mind are less able to carry the burden of identity construction than specifically 'indigenous' media. It assumes that there is no 'local' conflict over the constitution of identity and that other factors that affect identity cannot be read into indigenous media by audiences, which are diverse in their social composition and subject to fragmentation along multiple lines (Fiske 1999).

The study of Tansen's population conducted in chapters 4 and 5 demonstrates that whilst it has always been varied in its composition, more recent patterns of migration are leading to new cultural, ethnic, religious and class characteristics. In particular there is a changing balance between those who trace their family's origin to other places in Nepal, such as the Newar and many in the elite Parbatiya community, and those who are indigenous to the rural communities of Palpa, such as the many new citizens of Magar and local Parbatiya origin. The increasing presence of permanent and seasonal migrants from the Tarai must also be noted. Efforts to construct an audience for local media confront a fluid situation within which previously established assumptions about what it means to be a citizen of Tansen or Palpali may appear increasingly anachronistic, even if they are not necessarily directly challenged. The journalistic commentary on the situation that Tansen faced in the mid-1990, which was discussed in chapter 5, reflects such uncertainties.

Therefore, we do well to be reminded by Gledhill (1994: 70) that what may appear to be resistance at one level often seems to reproduce the "categorical and institutional structures of domination" at another, which makes it difficult to decide what exactly counts as resistance. Eco (1995: 199–200) also points out that although alternative information is often presented as an alternative because it takes on forms of mediation that are considered to be quite different to those found in "the official circuit of mass communication... ultimately it experiences the same problems as official information, since the transmitter knows what message is being transmitted and by which code he would like it to be decoded, but he doesn't really know whether all the receivers will decode it in the same way." Samina Mishra (1999: 276) echoes this interpretation of alternative media in her study of cable television operators in a suburb of New Delhi and argues that "local cable [programming] continues to mirror national and global media." As with Imparja and RCTV, the cable operators studied by Mishra operate primarily as commercial organizations and therefore mainly exist to rebroadcast mainstream media products, in this case the Star TV satellite network, only occasionally broadcasting their own locally made programming.

The crucial point is that media only obtain the legitimacy required to make warranted statements about the world in which they are situated in so much as they are able to bring an audience into being (Lull 1995: 58–60). The legitimacy of alternative media and their ability to contribute to the political aspirations of a community cannot, therefore, be assumed prior to analysis of the social and political articulation of those who make media within the multiple levels (local, national, transnational, etc.) of which they are a constituent part. Bhabha's point regarding the political character of the construction of 'a People' as a concept, which is quoted at the start of this concluding chapter, is of crucial importance. If the legitimacy of alternative media rests upon the identification of those who we regard as 'our people' the starting point for understanding any particular instance of such media must be the question of exactly who is regarded as 'one of us' and how this may be reflected in the media that are produced.

It is also the case that cultural hegemony seldom goes unchallenged and this is especially so in the complex and rapidly changing ethnic and religious admixture of Tansen's population. We have seen in chapter 7 that religious identity and its practical manifestation in festivals and ritual is one arena in which cultural forms providing an alternative to the dominant cultural perspective portrayed by the local television program are made manifest. The importance of this observation for the present analysis of media use is that it demonstrates that the hegemony of certain cultural forms may be furthered by their mediation (Sullivan 1993), but alternative cultural forms and practices are available through which other identities can be expressed. Religion provides a privileged pathway for such expressions of identity, because as a 'legitimate' and respected part of Nepal's public arena, many religious-based identities cannot be easily suppressed or denied by the state and its representatives at the district or municipal level. Having said this it should be noted that some religions, notably Christianity, remain outside the mainstream of accepted religious practice. Television clearly plays a role here, but it is not a wholly determining role in so much as religious and, potentially, other forms of cultural identities arise as alternatives for (if not in outright opposition to) the representations that are portrayed as legitimate expressions of locality and community by the media (cf. Stolow 2005).

Seen in the context of a society that is still heavily structured according to the ideology and practice of caste, the creation of alternative religious practices is less a challenge to the dominance of Tansen's elite *per se*, than an attempt to open up the boundaries of class membership to those who might be previously have been excluded because of their cultural or religious identity. Religious practices may be used to assert the equal importance of previously marginalized groups' cultural practices and as such this is a political struggle going on within a conservative framework of existing structures of power and hegemony.

Forms of radical ideology and political struggle appear to *totally* reject the legitimacy of the post-Jana Andolan Nepali state and older, traditional cultural practices have risen to prominence since the middle of the 1990s. This study cannot address the exact reasons why a Maoist revolutionary movement has come into being in Nepal or why long-simmering frustrations with political and social marginalization in the Tarai have recently erupted into violence. Nevertheless, the 'traditional' forms of power and hegemony that have been described here represent in microcosm a particular *state of being* in Nepal and, indeed, a way of *being in the nation-state* to which many have become increasingly opposed. As such I hope this study contributes in some small way to understanding the present problems of Nepal and her people through its description of how this state of being, which is now passing into history, was constructed and the role that media have played in this. I argue that such efforts of understanding are vital, because although this may be a world on the wane its presence will continue to influence people's differing dreams of Nepal's future for many years to come.

Bibliography

Abramson, A. 1999. Dialectics of localization: the political articulation of land rites and land rights in the interior of Eastern Fiji (1874–c.1990). *History and Anthropology* 11:437–477.

Adhikari, G., and D. G. Rajkarnikar. 1994. *A Study Report on the Organizational Development and Administration Program of Tansen Municipality.* Pokhara, Nepal: Urban Development Training Centre.

Adhikary, K. 1996. Naming ceremonies as rituals of development. *Studies in Nepali History and Society* 1: 345–364.

Aditya, A. Editor. 1996. *Mass Media and Democratization: A Country Study of Nepal.* Kathmandu: Institute for Integrated Development Studies.

Ahearn, L. M. 2001. *Invitations to Love: Literacy, Love Letters, and Social Change in Nepal.* Ann Arbor: University of Michigan Press.

Allen, M. R. 1992. *The Cult of Kumari Virgin Worship in Nepal*, 3rd edition. Kathmandu: Mandala Book Point.

Anderson, B. 1991. *Imagined Communities: Reflections on the Origins and Spread of Nationalism*, revised edition. London: Verso.

Anderson, M. 1988. *The Festivals of Nepal.* Calcutta: Rupa and Co.

Ang, I. 1996. *Living Room Wars: Rethinking Audiences for a Postmodern World.* London: Routledge.

Appadurai, A. 1990. Disjuncture and difference in the global cultural economy. *Theory, Culture and Society* 7: 295–310.

Appadurai, A., and C. A. Breckenridge. 1995. "Public modernity in India," in *Consuming Modernity Public Culture in a South Asian World.* Edited by C. A. Breckenridge, pp. 1–20. Minneapolis: University of Minnesota Press.

Atton, C. 2002. *Alternative Media.* London: SAGE Publications.

Aufderheide, P. 1993. Latin American grassroots video beyond television. *Public Culture* 5: 579–592.

—. 1995. The Video in the Villages project: video making with and by Brazilian Indians. *Visual Anthropology Review* 11: 82–93.

Bajracharya, B., and C. Shrestha. 1981. *Transport and Communication Linkages in Nepal*. Kirtipur: Tribhuvan University.

Bajracharya, S. L. 1985. *A Study on Cottage and Small Scale Industries of Palpa District [with Special Reference to Metalcraft]*. Unpublished M.A. (Economics) thesis, Tribhuvan University.

Baniya, K. B. 2053 VS [1996]. *Palpako Bhagwati Jatra* [Palpa's Bhagwati Festival]. Tansen: Shrestha Pustak Bhandar.

Barthes, R. 1973. *Mythologies*. London: Paladin.

Benjamin, W. 1992. "The work of art in the age of mechanical reproduction," in *Illuminations*. Edited by H. Arendt, pp. 211–244. London: Fontana Press.

Bhabha, H. 1990. "The third space: interview with Homi Bhabha," in *Identity: Community, Culture and Difference*. Edited by J. Rutherford, pp. 207–221. London: Lawrence and Wishart.

Bhattarai, B. 2004. *Nepal Press Under Emergency*. Lalitpur: Himal Books.

Bhattarai, S. 1996. "Tansen waits to be transformed into a tourism centre," in *Everest Herald*, 18th May. Kathmandu.

Bista, D. B. 1967. *People of Nepal*. Kathmandu: Ratna Pustak Bhandar.

—. 1991. *Fatalism and Development: Nepal's Struggle for Modernization*. Calcutta: Orient Longman Ltd.

Blaikie, P., J. Cameron, and D. Seddon. 1980. *Nepal in Crisis: Growth and Stagnation at the Periphery*. Delhi: Oxford University Press.

Borre, O., S. R. Panday, and C. K. Tiwari. 1994. *Nepalese Political Behavior*. Aarhus, Denmark: Aarhus University Press.

Bourdieu, P. 1983. The field of cultural production, or the economic world reversed. *Poetics* 12: 311–356.

—. 1984. *Distinction: A Social Critique of the Judgment of Taste*. London: Routledge.

—. 1988. *Homo Academicus*. Cambridge: Polity Press.

—. 1998. *Practical Reason: On the Theory of Action*. Cambridge: Polity Press.

Bourdieu, P., and L. J. Wacquant. 1992. *An Invitation to Reflexive Sociology*. Cambridge: Polity Press.

Brown, T. L. 1996. *The Challenge to Democracy in Nepal: A Political History*. London: Routledge.

Burghart, R. 1984. The formation of the concept of the nation-state in Nepal. *Journal of Asian Studies* 44: 101–125.

—. 1993. "The political culture of Panchayat democracy," in *Nepal in the Nineties: Versions of the Past, Visions of the Future*. Edited by M. Hutt, pp. 1–13. Delhi: Oxford University Press.

—. 1996. *The Conditions of Listening: Essays on Religion, History and Politics in South Asia*. Delhi: Oxford University Press.

Burke, A. 1999. *Communications and Development: A Practical Guide*. Social Development Division, DFID.

Castells, M. 1996. *The Rise of the Network Society*. Oxford: Blackwell.

Chalfen, R. 1992. "Picturing culture through indigenous imagery: a telling story," in *Film As Ethnography*. Edited by P. I. Crawford and D. Turton, pp. 222–241. Manchester: Manchester University Press.

Chitrakar, A. 1990. Deepening crisis in Sagarhawa. *Himal* 3(5): 18.

Communications in Nepal. 1988. Kathmandu: Worldview International Foundation.

Connerton, P. 1989. *How Societies Remember*. Cambridge: Cambridge University Press.

Conway, D., and N. Shrestha. 1980. Urban growth and urbanization in least-developed countries: the experience of Nepal. *Asian Profile* 8: 477–495.

Corrigan, P., and D. Sayer. 1985. *The Great Arch: English State Formation as Cultural Revolution*. Oxford: Blackwell.

Couldry, N. 2000. *The Place of Media Power: Pilgrims and Witnesses in the Media Age*. London: Routledge.

—. 2003. *Media Rituals: A Critical Approach*. London: Routledge.

Cundy, M. 1994. *Better Than the Witch Doctor*. Crowborough, U.K.: Monarch Publications.

Curran, J., and M.-J. Park. Editors. 2000. *De-Westernising Media Studies*. London: Routledge.

Dagron, A. G. 2004. "The long and winding road of alternative media," in *The SAGE Handbook of Media Studies*. Edited by J. Downing, D. McQuail, P. Schlesinger, and E. Wartella, pp. 41–63. Thousand Oaks: SAGE Publications.

Dahal, P. 1993. Gods and warriors at the hill station of Tansen. *Nepal Traveler* 10(6): 77–8.

Dastider, M. 1995. *Religious Minorities in Nepal: An Analysis of the State of the Buddhists and Muslims in the Himalayan Kingdom*. New Delhi: Nirala Publications.

Dayan, D. 1998. "Particularistic media and diasporic communications," in *Media, Ritual and Identity*. Edited by T. Liebes and J. Curran, pp. 103–113. London: Routledge.

Dayan, D., and E. Katz. 1992. *Media Events: The Live Broadcasting of History*. Cambridge, Mass: Harvard U.P.

De Folo, K. 1994 [1971]. "Tansen: city in the mist," in *Tansen in Perspective*. Edited by V. P. Shrestha, pp. 11–12. Kathmandu: Tansen Guthi.

Deger, J. 2006. *Shimmering Screens: Making Media in an Aboriginal Community*. Minneapolis: University of Minnesota Press.

Des Chene, M. 1996. Lessons from reading *Rodhi* and other Tamu writings. *Studies in Nepali History and Society* 1: 97–162.

Deurali Rural Newspaper 1995. *Deurali Weekly Rural Newspaper: Sample Issue in English*, p. 16. Tansen: Rural Development Palpa.

Devkota, P. 1998. "Tansen: quest for a new identity," in *Spotlight*, 9th January, p. 24.

DFID. 2006. *Civil Society and Development: How DFID Works in Partnership with Civil Society to Deliver the Millennium Development Goals*. Department for International Development.

Dirks, N. 1987. *The Hollow Crown*. Cambridge: Cambridge University Press.

—. 1994. "Ritual and resistance: subversion as social fact," in *Culture/Power/History*. Edited by N. Dirks, G. Eley, and S. Ortner, pp. 483–503. Princeton: Princeton University Press.

Dixit, K. 2006. *A People War: Images of the Nepal Conflict 1996–2006*. Lalitpur, Nepal: Nepalaya Pvt. Ltd.

Dixit, K. M. 1995. The porter's burden. *Himal* 8(6): 33–38.

Dogra, B. 1990. Tension and conflict in the Western Tarai. *Himal*, 3(5): 17.

Dowmunt, T. 1998. "An alternative globalization: youthful resistance to electronic empires," in *Electronic Empires: Global Media and Local Resistance*. Edited by D. K. Thussu, pp. 243–256. London: Arnold.

Downing, J., and C. Husband. 2005. *Representing 'Race': Racisms, Ethnicities and Media*. London: SAGE Publications.

Eck, D. L. 1985. *Darsan: Seeing the Divine Image in India*. Pennsylvania: Anima.

Eco, U. 1995. *Apocalypse Postponed*. London: Flamingo/Harper Collins.

—. 1996. "How cultures condition the colors we see," in *The Communication Theory Reader*. Edited by P. Cobley, pp. 148–171. London: Routledge.

Edwards, C. n.d. Community television in Nepal. *Nepal Media* http://www.nepalmedia.org/tv/community_tv.htm [accessed 30th October 2002].

Ehrenberg, J. 1999. *Civil Society: The Critical History of an Idea*. New York: New York University Press.

Escobar, A. 1995. *Encountering Development: The Making and Unmaking of the Third World*. Princeton, N.J.: Princeton University Press.

European Community. 1995. *The MECP: A Pilot Municipal Program on Urban Environment Between Europe and Asia*. Levallois-Peret, France: United Towns Development Agency.

Everest Herald 1996. "Ranighat Durbar loses past glory," in *Everest Herald*, 25th June.

Faris, J. C. 1992. "Anthropological transparency: film, representation and politics," in *Film As Ethnography*. Edited by P. I. Crawford and D. Turton, pp. 171–182. Manchester: Manchester University Press.

—. 1993. A response to Terence Turner. *Anthropology Today* 9: 12–13.

Fisher, W. 2001. *Fluid Boundaries: Forming and Transforming Identity in Nepal*. New York: Columbia University Press.

Fiske, J. 1999 [1989]. "Moments of Television: Neither the Text nor the Audience," in *Media Studies: A Reader*. Edited by P. Marris and S. Thornham, pp. 536–546. Edinburgh: University of Edinburgh Press.

Freitag, S. B. 1989. *Collective Action and Community: Public Arenas and the Emergence of Communalism in North India*. Berkeley: University of California Press.

Gaenszle, M. 1997. "Changing concepts of ethnic identity among the Mewahang Rai," in *Nationalism and Ethnicity in a Hindu Kingdom: The Politics of Culture in Contemporary Nepal*. Edited by D. Gellner, J. Pfaff-Czarnecka, and J. Whelpton, pp. 351–373. Amsterdam: Harwood Academic Publishers.

Gaige, F. H. 1975. *Regionalism and National Unity in Nepal*. New Delhi: Vikas Publishing House.

Garnham, N. 1992. "The media and the public sphere," in *Habermas and the Public Sphere*. Edited by C. Calhoun, pp. 359–375. Cambridge, Mass: M.I.T. Press.

Geertz, C. 1980. *Negara: The Theatre State in Nineteenth Century Bali*. Princeton: Princeton University Press.

Gell, A. 1992. "The technology of enchantment and the enchantment of technology," in *Anthropology, Art and Aesthetics*. Edited by J. Coote and T. Shelton, pp. 40–63. Oxford: Clarendon Press.

—. 1998. *Art and Agency : An Anthropological Theory*. Oxford: Clarendon Press.

—. 1999. "On Coote's 'Marvels of Everyday Vision'," in *The Art of Anthropology: Essays and Diagrams*. Edited by E. Hirsch, pp. 215–231. London: The Athlove Press.

Gellner, D. 1986. Language, caste, religion and territory: Newar identity ancient and modern. *Archives Européenes de Sociologie* 27: 102–148.

—. 1988. "Buddhism and Hinduism in the Nepal Valley," in *The World's Religions: The Religions of Asia*. Edited by F. Hardy, pp. 207–223. London: Routledge.

—. 1992. *Monk, Householder, and Tantric Priest: Newar Buddhism and Its Hierarchy of Ritual*. Cambridge: Cambridge University Press.

—. 1997a. "Caste, communalism, and communism: Newars and the Nepalese state," in *Nationalism and Ethnicity in a Hindu Kingdom: The Politics of Culture in Contemporary Nepal*. Edited by D. Gellner, J. Pfaff-Czarnecka, and J. Whelpton, pp. 151–184. Amsterdam: Harwood Academic Publishers.

—. 1997b. "Ethnicity and nationalism in the world's only Hindu state," in *Nationalism and Ethnicity in a Hindu Kingdom: The Politics of Culture in Contemporary Nepal*. Edited by D. Gellner, J. Pfaff-Czarnecka, and J. Whelpton, pp. 3–31. Amsterdam: Harwood Academic Publishers.

Gellner, D., J. Pfaff-Czarnecka, and J. Whelpton. Editors. 1997. *Nationalism and Ethnicity in a Hindu Kingdom: The Politics of Culture in Contemporary Nepal*. Amsterdam: Harwood Academic Publishers.

Gellner, D., and R. P. Pradhan. 1995. "Urban peasants: The Maharjans (Jyapu) of Kathmandu and Lalitpur," in *Contested Hierarchies: A Collaborative Eth-*

nography of Caste among the Newars of the Kathmandu Valley, Nepal. Edited by D. Gellner and D. Quigley, pp. 158–185. Oxford: Clarendon Press.

Gellner, E. 1988. *Plough, Sword and Book: The Structure of Human History*. London: Collins Harvill.

Gewertz, D., and F. Errington. 1991. *Twisted Histories, Altered Contexts: Representing the Chambri in a World System*. Cambridge: Cambridge University Press.

Ghimire, V. 1990. *Palpa Rajyako Itihos* [A History of the Kings of Palpa]. Bharatpur, Nepal: Padma Ghimre.

Ginsburg, F. 1991. Indigenous media: Faustian contract or global village? *Cultural Anthropology* 6: 92–112.

—. 1993. Aboriginal media and the Australian imaginary. *Public Culture* 5:557–578.

—. 1994. Culture/media: a (mild) polemic. *Anthropology Today* 10:5–15.

—. 1995. The parallax effect: the impact of Aboriginal media on ethnographic film. *Visual Anthropology Review* 11: 64–76.

Ginsburg, F., L. Abu-Lughod, and B. Larkin. Editors. 2002. *Media Worlds: Anthropology on New Terrain*. Berkeley: University of California Press.

Gitlin, T. 1998. "Public sphere or public sphericules?," in *Media, Ritual, Identity*. Edited by T. Liebes and J. Curran, pp. 168–175. London: Routledge.

Gledhill, J. 1994. *Power and Its Disguises: Anthropological Perspectives on Politics*. London: Pluto Press.

Graburn, N. 1976. *Ethnic and Tourist Arts: Cultural Expressions of the Fourth World*. Berkeley: University of California Press.

Grandin, I. 1989. *Music and Media in Local Life: Music Practice in a Newar Neighborhood of Nepal*. Linkoping, Sweden: Linkoping University.

—. 1994. "Nepalese urbanism: a musical exploration," in *Anthropology of Nepal: Peoples, Problems and Processes*. Edited by M. R. Allen, pp. 160–175. Kathmandu: Mandala Book Point.

Gross, L. 1998. "Minorities, majorities and the media," in *Media, Ritual and Identity*. Edited by L. T. and J. Curran, pp. 87–102. London: Routledge.

Gurung, H. 1994. *Nepal Main Ethnic/Caste Groups Based on Population Census 1991*. Kathmandu: Harka Gurung.

Gyawali, D., O. Schwank, I. Z. Thappa, D., J. Pfaff, and S. Bajracharya. 1993. *Rural-Urban Interlinkages: A Challenge for Swiss Development Cooperation*. Zurich/Kathmandu: Interdisciplinary Consulting Group for Natural Resources and Infrastructure Management/ Interdisciplinary Analysts.

Habermas, J. 1992. *The Structural Transformation of the Public Sphere: An Inquiry into a Category of Bourgeois Society*. Cambridge: Polity Press.

Hall, S. 1999 [1973]. "Encoding/decoding," in *Media Studies: A Reader*. Edited by P. Marris and S. Thornham, pp. 51–61. Edinburgh: University of Edinburgh Press.

Hall, S., C. Critcher, T. Jefferson, J. Clarke, and B. Roberts. 1999 [1978]. "The so-
    cial production of news," in *Media Studies: A Reader*. Edited by P. Marris
    and S. Thornham, pp. 645–652. Edinburgh: University of Edinburgh Press.
Hall, S., and L. E. Grossberg. 1996. "On postmodernism and articulation: an inter-
    view with Stuart Hall," in *Stuart Hall: Critical Dialogues in Cultural Stud-
    ies*. Edited by D. Morley and K.-H. Chen, pp. 131–150. London: Routledge.
Hallin, D. 1998. "Broadcasting in the Third World: from national development to
    civil society," in *Media, Ritual and Identity*. Edited by T. Liebes and J.
    Curran, pp. 153–167. London: Routledge.
Hamilton, F. B. 1986 [1819]. *An Account of the Kingdom of Nepal*. New Delhi:
    Asian Educational Services.
Hannerz, U. 1992. *Cultural Complexity: Studies in the Social Organization of Mean-
    ing*. New York: Columbia University Press.
Harper, I. 2003. Mission, Magic and Medicalisation: An Anthropological Study into
    Public Health in Contemporary Nepal. School of Oriental and African Stud-
    ies, London: Unpublished PhD Thesis.
Harper, I., and C. Tarnowski. 2003. "A heterotopia of resistance: health, community
    forestry, and the challenges to state centralization in Nepal," in *Resistance
    and the State: Nepalese Experiences*. Edited by D. Gellner, pp. 33–82. New
    Delhi: Social Science Press.
Heaton-Shrestha, C. 2004. The ambiguities of practicing Jat in 1990's Nepal: elites,
    caste and everyday life in development NGOs. *Journal of South Asian Stud-
    ies* 27: 39–63.
Helvetas. 2053 VS. *List of NGOs in Palpa District*. Unpublished document. Tansen:
    Helvetas Nepal.
HMG, Nepal 1984. *National Population Census, 1981*. Kathmandu: Central Bureau
    of Statistics.
—. 1993. *National Population Census, 1991*. Kathmandu: Central Bureau of Statis-
    tics.
—. 1994. *Statistical Pocket Book of Nepal*. Kathmandu: Central Bureau of Statistics.
—. 1995. *Population Monograph of Nepal*. Kathmandu: Central Bureau of Statistics.
Hobart, M. 2002. "Live or dead? Televising theatre in Bali," in *Media Worlds: An-
    thropology on New Terrain*. Edited by F. Ginsburg, L. Abu-Lughod, and B.
    Larkin, pp. 370–382. Berkeley: University of California Press.
Höfer, A. 1979. *The Caste Hierarchy and the State in Nepal: A Study of the Muluki
    Ain of 1854*. Innsbruck: Universitatsverlag Wagner.
Hoftun, M., and W. Raeper. 1992. *Spring Awakening: An Account of the 1990 Revo-
    lution in Nepal*. New Delhi: Penguin Books.
Hughes-Freeland, F. 1998. "Introduction," in *Ritual, Performance, Media*. Edited by
    F. Hughes-Freeland, pp. 1–28. London: Routledge.
Husain, A. 1970. *British India's Relations with the Kingdom of Nepal, 1857–1947: A
    Diplomatic History of Nepal*. London: George Allen and Unwin Ltd.

Hutt, M. 1988. *Nepali: A National Language and Its Literature*. New Delhi: Sterling Publications Ltd.

—. Editor. 1994. *Nepal in the Nineties: Versions of the Past, Visions of the Future*. Delhi: Oxford University Press.

—. 1997. "Being Nepali without Nepal: reflections on a South Asian diaspora," in *Nationalism and Ethnicity in a Hindu Kingdom: The Politics of Culture in Contemporary Nepal*. Edited by D. Gellner, J. Pfaff-Czarnecka, and J. Whelpton, pp. 101–144. Amsterdam: Harwood Academic Publishers.

—. Editor. 2004. *Himalayan People's War: Nepal's Maoist Rebellion*. Bloomington: Indiana University Press.

—. 2006. Things that should not be said: censorship and self-censorship in the Nepali press media, 2001-02. *The Journal of Asian Studies* 65:361-392.

The Independent 1997. "Trying to survive on thin air," in *The Independent* (Kathmandu), 3rd September.

Jarman, N. 1997. *Material Conflicts: Parades and Visual Displays in Northern Ireland*. Oxford: Berg.

Joshi, B. L., and L. Rose. 1966. *Democratic Innovations in Nepal: A Case Study of Political Acculturation*. Berkeley: University of California Press.

Kapferer, B. 1988. *Legends of People, Myths of State: Violence, Intolerance, and Political Culture in Sri Lanka and Australia*. Washington: Smithsonian Institution Press.

Kaphle, K. 1994. *Pricing of Piped Water Supply in Nepal: A Case Study of Tansen*. Unpublished MA (Econ) thesis. Kirtipur: Tribhuvan University.

Kasajoo, V. K. 1988. *Palpa As You Like It*. Tansen: Kumar Press.

—. 1994. "Tansen's new look," in *Tansen in Perspective*. Edited by V. P. Shrestha, pp. 43–45. Kathmandu: Tansen Guthi.

Kathmandu Post 1996. "NGOs, INGOs ignore govt [sic.] laws," in *Kathmandu Post*, 30th April.

KC, B. K. 2003. Migration, poverty and development in Nepal. United Nations Economic and Social Commission for Asia and the Pacific. http://www.unescap.org/esid/psis/meetings/migrationaug2003/Nepal.pdf [Accessed 26th March 2007].

Khatri, T. B. 1976. *Mass Communication in Nepal*. Kathmandu: Dept. of Information, HMG, Nepal.

Kievelitz, U. 1996. Ethnicity and nationalism in the Nepali context: a perspective from Europe. *Occasional Papers in Sociology and Anthropology (Central Dept. of Sociology and Anthropology, Tribhuvan University, Kathmandu)* 5: 1–16.

Krämer, K.-H. 2003. "How representative is the Nepali state?," in *Resistance and the State: Nepalese Experiences*. Edited by D. Gellner, pp. 179–198. New Delhi: Social Sciences Press.

Krauskopff, G. 2003. "An 'indigenous minority' in a border area: Tharu ethnic associations, NGOs, and the Nepalese state," in *Resistance and the State: Nepalese Experiences*. Edited by D. Gellner, pp. 199–243. New Delhi: Social Science Press.

Kuenhast, K. 1992. "Visual imperialism and the export of prejudice: An exploration of ethnographic film," in *Film As Ethnography*. Edited by P. I. Crawford and D. Turton, pp. 183–195. Manchester: Manchester University Press.

Kunreuther, L. 2004. Voiced writing and public intimacy on Kathmandu's FM radio. *Studies in Nepali History and Society* 9:57–95.

—. 2006. Technologies of the Voice: FM Radio, Telephone, and the Nepali Diaspora in Kathmandu. *Cultural Anthropology* 21:323–353.

Landon, P. 1993. *Nepal* (2 Vols). New Delhi: Asian Educational Services.

Levi-Strauss, C. 1972. *The Savage Mind*. London: Weidenfeld and Nicholson.

Levy, R. I., and K. R. Rajopadhyaya. 1992. *Mesocosm: Hinduism and the Organization of a Traditional Newar City in Nepal*. Delhi: Motilal Banarsidass Publications.

Lewis, T. 1995. "Buddhist merchants in Kathmandu: The Asan Twah market and Uray social organization," in *Contested Hierarchies: A Collaborative Ethnography of Caste Among the Newars of the Kathmandu Valley, Nepal*. Edited by D. Gellner and D. Quigley, pp. 38–79. Oxford: Clarendon Press.

Lewis, T., and D. R. Shakya. 1988. Contributions to the history of Nepal: Eastern Newar diaspora settlements. *Contributions to Nepalese Studies* 15(1): 25–65.

Liechty, M. 1994. *Fashioning Modernity in Kathmandu: Mass Media, Consumer Culture, and the Middle Class in Nepal*. Unpublished Ph.D. thesis. University of Pennsylvania.

—. 1995. "Media, markets and modernization: youth identities and the experience of modernity in Kathmandu, Nepal.," in *Youth Cultures: A Cross-Cultural Perspective*. Edited by V. Amit-Talai and H. Wulff, pp. 166–201. London: Routledge.

—. 1996. "Kathmandu as translocality: multiple places in a Nepali space," in *The Geography of Identity*. Edited by P. Yaeger, pp. 98–130. Ann Arbor: University of Michigan Press.

—. 1997. Selective exclusion: foreigners, foreign goods, and foreignness in modern Nepali history. *Studies in Nepali History and Society* 2(1): 5–68.

—. 1998. The social practice of cinema and video viewing in Kathmandu. *Studies in Nepali History and Society* 3(1): 87–126.

—. 2003. *Suitably Modern: Making Middle-Class Culture in a New Consumer Society*. Princeton: Princeton University Press.

Lull, J. 1995. *Media, Communication, Culture: A Global Approach*. Cambridge: Polity Press.

Lutgendorf, S. 1995. "All in the (Raghu) family: a video epic in cultural context," in *To Be Continued? Soap Operas Around the World.* Edited by R. Allen, pp. 321–353. London: Routledge.

MacDougall, D. 1997. "The visual in anthropology," in *Rethinking Visual Anthropology.* Edited by M. Banks and H. Morphy, pp. 276–295. New Haven: Yale University Press.

Macfarlane, A. 1993. "Fatalism and development in Nepal," in *Nepal in the Nineties: Versions of the Past, Visions of the Future.* Edited by M. Hutt, pp. 106–127. Delhi: Oxford University Press.

Malla, B. C. 1982. Mass-media tradition and change (an overview of change in Nepal). *Contributions to Nepalese Studies* 10(1/2): 69–79.

—. 1987. *Nagar Panchayat: The Problem of Development, Institutional Viability and Co-ordination (with reference to Kathmandu).* Kirtipur: Centre for Development Administration, Tribhuvan University.

Mankekar, P. 1999. *Screening Culture, Viewing Politics: An Ethnography of Television, Womanhood, and Nation in Postcolonial India.* Durham: Duke University Press.

Martin, K., D. Koirala, R. Pandey, S. Adhikari, G. P. Acharya, and K. MS. 2007. Finding the local community in community media: some stories from Nepal. *Asia Rights* 8. http://rspas.anu.edu.au/asiarightsjournal/Issue%20Eight_Martin%20et%20a l.htm [Accessed 2nd February 2008].

Martinussen, J. 1993. *Local Authorities in Nepal: An Assessment of their Present Position and Proposals for Strengthening of Democracy at the Local Level.* Kathmandu: Min. of Local Development, National Planning Commission, HMG of Nepal and Danish Min. of Foreign Affairs/DANIDA.

Marx, K. 1972 [1869]. *The Eighteenth Brumaire of Louis Bonaparte.* Moscow: Progress Publishers.

Mason, P. 1974. *A Matter of Honor: An Account of the Indian Army, Its Officers and Men.* London: Jonathan Cape.

Mazzarella, W. 2004. Culture, globalization, mediation. *Annual Review of Anthropology* 33: 345–367.

McCluhan, M. 1987 [1964]. *Understanding Media: The Extension of Man.* London: Ark Paperbacks.

Messerschmidt, D. 1992. *Muktinath Himalayan Pilgrimage: A Cultural and Historical Guide.* Kathmandu: Sahayogi Press.

Meyer, B. 2004. 'Praise the Lord': popular cinema and the Pentecostalite style in Ghana's new public sphere. *American Ethnologist* 31(1): 92–110.

Michaels, E. 1986. *The Aboriginal Invention of Television in Central Australia 1982–1986.* Australian Institute of Aboriginal Studies.

—. 1994. *Bad Aboriginal Art: Tradition, Media, and Technological Horizons.* Minneapolis: University of Minnesota Press.

Mies, M. 1982. *The Lace Makers of Narsapur: Indian Housewives Produce for the World Market. A Report of the International Labor Office World Employment Program*. London: Zed Books.

Mikesell, S. 1988. *Cotton On the Silk Road: Subjection of Labor to the Global Economy in the Shadow of Empire (Or the Dialectic of a Merchant Community in Nepal)*. Unpublished Ph.D. thesis, University of Wisconsin.

—. 1996. "We are all becoming doctors!," in *The Everest Herald*, 29th April. Kathmandu.

Miller, C. 1990. *Decision Making in Village Nepal*. Kathmandu: Sahayogi Press.

Miller, D. 1992. "The Young and the Restless in Trinidad: a case of the local and the global," in *Consuming Technologies: Media and Information in Domestic Space*. Edited by R. Silverstone and E. Hirsch, pp. 163–182. London: Routledge.

—. 2003. "Advertising, production and consumption as cultural economy," in *Advertising Cultures*. Edited by T. D. Malefyt and B. Moeran, pp. 75–89. Oxford: Berg.

Mines, M. 1994. *Public Faces, Private Voices: Community and Individuality in South India*. Berkeley and Los Angeles: University of California Press.

Mishra, S. 1999. "Dish is life: cable operators and the neighborhood," in *Image Journeys: Audio Visual Media and Cultural Change in India*. Edited by C. Brosius and M. Butcher, pp. 261–277. New Delhi: Sage.

Molnar, H., and M. Meadows. 2001. *Songlines to Satellites: Indigenous Communication in Australia, the South Pacific and Canada*. Annandale, NSW: Pluto Press Australia.

Moore, J. D. 2004. *Visions of Culture*, 2nd edition. Walnut Creek, California: Alta Mira Press.

Morley, D. 1992. *Television, Audiences and Cultural Studies*. London: Routledge.

Morley, D., and K.-H. Chen. Editors. 1996. *Stuart Hall: Critical Dialogues in Cultural Studies*. London: Routledge.

Morley, D., and K. Robins. 1995. *Spaces of Identity: Global Media, Electronic Landscapes and Cultural Boundaries*. London: Routledge.

Morphy, H. 1992. "From dull to brilliant: the aesthetics of spiritual power among the Yolngu," in *Anthropology, Art and Aesthetics*. Edited by J. Coote and A. Skelton, pp. 181–208. Oxford: Clarendon Press.

Munn, N. 1973. *Walbiri Iconography: Graphic Representation and Cultural Symbolism in a Central Australian Society*. Ithaca: Cornell University Press.

Myrdal, G. 1977. *Asian Drama: An Enquiry into the Poverty of Nations (An abridgement of the Twentieth Century Fund Study by Seth King)*. London: Penguin Books.

Negroponte, N. 1996. *Being Digital*. Rydalmere, NSW: Hodder and Stoughton.

Nepali, G. S. 1988 [1965]. *The Newars: An Ethno-Sociological Study of a Himalayan Community*. Kathmandu: Himalayan Booksellers.

Nightingale, V. 1993. "What's 'ethnographic' about ethnographic audience research?," in *Australian Cultural Studies: A Reader*. Edited by J. Frow and M. Morris, pp. 149–161. Urbana: University of Illinois Press.

Ninan, S. 1995. *Through the Magic Window: Television and Change in India*. New Delhi: Penguin Books.

Nyaupani. 2049 VS. Palpako Bhairab [Palpa's Bhairab]. *Palpa Darpan* 3: 74–79.

Oakdale, S. 2004. The culture-conscious Brazilian Indian: representing and reworking Indianness in Kayabi political discourse. *American Ethnologist* 31(1): 60–75.

Onta, P. 1994. Rich possibilities: notes on social history in Nepal. *Contributions to Nepalese Studies* 21(1):1–43.

—. 2006. *Mass Media in Post-1990 Nepal*. Kathmandu: Martin Chautari.

Page, D., and W. Crawley. 2001. *Satellites Over South Asia: Broadcasting, Culture and Public Interest*. London Sage Publications.

Pangeni, B. 1994 [2051 VS]. *Palpama Prajatantrik Andolanko Say Din (V.S. 2007)* [One Hundred Days of Democratic Revolution in Palpa (1950)]. Madan Pokhara, Palpa Nima Pangeni.

Panta, P. R. 2004. Nepalese migration: economic savior or abuse? One World UK. http://uk.oneworld.net/article/view/99943/1 [Accessed 27th March 2007].

Parish, S. 1994. *Moral Knowing in a Hindu Sacred City*. New York: Columbia University Press.

—. 1997. *Hierarchy and Its Discontents: Culture and the Politics of Consciousness in Caste Society*. Delhi Oxford University Press.

Perrons, D. 2004. *Globalization and Social Change: People and Places in a Divided World*. London: Routledge.

Peterson, M. A. 2003. *Anthropology and Mass Communication: Media and Myth in the New Millenium*. New York: Berghahn Books.

Pfaff-Czarnecka, J. 1997. "Vestiges and visions: cultural change in the process of nation-building in Nepal," in *Nationalism and Ethnicity in a Hindu Kingdom: The Politics of Culture in Contemporary Nepal*. Edited by D. N. Gellner, J. Pfaff-Czarnecka, and J. Whelpton, pp. 419–470. Amsterdam Harwood Academic Publishers.

Pfaffenberger, B. 1992. Social anthropology of technology. *Annual Review of Anthropology* 21: 491–516.

Pieper, J. 1975. "Three cities of Nepal," in *Shelter, Sign and Symbol*. Edited by P. Oliver, pp. 52–69. London: Barrie and Jenkins.

Pigg, S. 1992. Inventing social categories through place: social representations and development in Nepal. *Comparative Studies in Society and History* 34(3): 491–513.

—. 1996. The credible and the credulous: the question of "villager's beliefs" in Nepal. *Cultural Anthropology* 11(2): 160–201.

—. 2001. Languages of sex and AIDS in Nepal: notes on the social production of commensurability. *Cultural Anthropology* 16(4); 481–541.

Pinney, C. 1997. *Camera Indica: The Social Life of Indian Photographs*. London: Reaktion Books.

—. 2002. "The Indian work of art in the age of mechanical reproduction. Or, what happens when peasants 'get hold' of images," in *Media Worlds: Anthropology on New Terrain*. Edited by F. Ginsburg, L. Abu-Lughod, and B. Larkin, pp. 355–369. Berkeley: University of California Press.

Prasain, D. 1998. 'In the name of the People': Writing bikas in post-1990 Nepal. *Studies in Nepali History and Society* 3(2): 341–394.

Pringle, I. 2005. Nepal CMC Recognized for Innovative Use of Cheap and Simple Technologies. *UNESCO News*. Paris: UNESCO. http://portal.unesco.org/ci/en/ev.phpURL_ID=19767&URL_DO=DO_TOPIC&URL_SECTION=201.html [accessed 4th February 2008]

—. 2007. *Ten Years On: The State of Community Radio in Nepal*. Paris: UNESCO.

Pringle, I., U. Bajracharya, and A. Bajracharya. 2004. Innovating multimedia to increase accessibility in the hills of Nepal: The Tansen Community Multimedia Centre (CMC). *Mountain Research and Development* 24: 292–297.

Putnam, R. 2000. *Bowling Alone: The Collapse and Revival of American Community*. New York: Simon and Schuster.

Quigley, D. 1985. Household organization among Newar traders. *Cont. to Nepalese Studies* 12(2): 13–44.

—. 1986. Introversion and isogamy marriage patterns of the Newars of Nepal. *Contributions to Indian Sociology (n.s.)* 20(1): 75–95.

—. 1987. Ethnicity without nationalism. *Archives Européenes de Sociologie* 28: 152–170.

—. 1993. *The Interpretation of Caste*. Oxford: Clarendon Press.

—. 1995. "Śreṣṭhas: heterogeneity among Hindu patron lineages," in *Contested Hierarchies: A Collaborative Ethnography of Caste Among the Newars of the Kathmandu Valley, Nepal*. Edited by D. Gellner and D. Quigley, pp. 80–108. Oxford: Clarendon Press.

Raj, P. A. 1985. *Kathmandu and the Kingdom of Nepal*, 5th edition. South Yarra, Australia: Lonely Planet Publications.

Rana, S. 1994. "Is Tansen dying?," in *Tansen in Perspective*. Edited by V. P. Shrestha, pp. 15–17. Kathmandu: Tansen Guthi.

Rankin, K. 2004. *The Cultural Politics of Markets: Economic Liberalization and Social Change in Nepal*. London: Pluto Press.

Reeves, G. 1993. *Communication and the 'Third World'*. London: Routledge.

Regmi, M. C. 1978. *Thatched Huts and Stucco Palaces Peasants and Landlords in 19th Century Nepal*. New Delhi: Vikas Publishing House Pvt. Ltd.

—. 1984. *The State and Economic Surplus Production, Trade and Resource-mobilization in Early 19th Century Nepal.* Varanasi: Nath Publishing House.

Regmi, S. 1991. *Prospects for tourism development in and around Tansen.* Unpublished B.A. (Hons) thesis, Tribhuvan University.

Rodríguez, C. 2001. *Fissures in the Mediascape: An International Study of Citizens' Media.* Cresskill, N.J.: Hampton Press.

Ruby, J. 2000. *Picturing Culture: Explorations of Film and Anthropology.* Chicago: University of Chicago.

Salter, J., and H. Gurung. 1996. *Faces of Nepal.* Lalitpur, Nepal: Himal Books.

Scannell, P. 2002. "History, media and communication," in *A Handbook of Media and Communication Research: Qualitative and Quantitative Methodologies.* Edited by K. B. Jensen, pp. 191–205. London: Routledge.

Seddon, D. Editor. 1979. *Peasants and Workers in Nepal.* Warminster: Aris and Phillips Ltd.

—. 1987. *Nepal: A State of Poverty.* New Delhi: Vikas Publishing House Pvt. Ltd.

Serle, R., U. Baljet, and R. Snater. 1993. *Communication and Rural Development in Nepal: Planning a National Communication Policy.* Amsterdam: The Authors, University of Amsterdam.

Shah, A. 1987. *Access of Low Income Families to Social Services (A Study in Selected Areas of Kathmandu).* Kirtipur: Tribhuvan University.

Shah, R. 1992. *Ancient and Medieval Nepal.* New Delhi: Manohar Publications.

Shah, S. 1993. Throes of a fledgling nation. *Himal* 6(2): 7–10.

Shakya, R. 1997. "The Gorkhapatra and earlier magazines," in *The Rising Nepal [Gorkhapatra Anniversary Supplement]*, 6th May, p. 3.

Sharma, K. N. 1980. *Nation Building and the role of Communication in Nepal.* Kathmandu: UNESCO.

Sharma, P. 1989. *Urbanization in Nepal.* Honolulu, Hawaii: Papers of the East-West Population Institute.

Sharma, P. R. 1994. "Emergence of a hill-town: urban development in Nepal's rural backhills," in *Anthropology of Nepal: Peoples, Problems and Processes.* Edited by M. Allen, pp. 218–231. Kathmandu: Mandala Book Point.

Sharma, S. P. 1988. *Energy Pricing Policies in Nepal.* Geneva: International Labor Office.

Sharma, V. P. 1967. "Palpa: An economic introduction," in *Palpa Sankalan (Collected Papers)*, pp. 143–150. Tansen: Palpa Sankalan.

Shrestha, A. 1996. "A day in Tansen," in *The Rising Nepal*, 12th July.

Shrestha, M. 1994. Broadcasting tongue twister. *Himal* 7(5): 32.

Shrestha, V. P. Editor. 1994. *Tansen in Perspective.* Kathmandu: Tansen Guthi.

Sill, M., and J. Kirkby. 1991. *Atlas of Nepal in the Modern World.* London: Earthscan Publications Ltd.

Silverstone, R. 1999. *Why Study the Media?* London: SAGE Publications.

Skuse, A. 2006. *Voices of Change: Strategic Radio Support for Achieving the Millennium Development Goals.* Information for Communication and Development, DFID.

Smith, A. Editor. 1995. *Television: An International History.* Oxford: Oxford University Press.

Sobel, J. 2002. Can we trust social capital? *Journal of Economic Literature* 40(1): 139–154.

Spitulnik, D. 1993. Anthropology and mass media. *Annual Review of Anthropology* 22: 293–315.

Srinivas, M. 1952. *Religion and Society Among the Coorgs of South India.* New York: Asia Publishing House.

—. 1967. *Social Change in Modern India.* Berkeley: University of California Press.

Stern, R. 1993. *Changing India: Bourgeois Revolution on the Subcontinent.* Cambridge: Cambridge University Press.

Stiller, L. 1976. *The Silent Cry: The People of Nepal, 1816–1839.* Kathmandu: Sahayogi Prakashan.

—. 1981. *Letters From Kathmandu: The Kot Massacre.* Kirtipur: Nepal Research Centre for Nepal and Asian Studies, Tribhuvan University.

—. 1993. *Nepal: Growth of a Nation.* Kathmandu: Human Resources Development Research Centre.

—. 1995. *The Rise of the House of Gorkha,* 2nd edition. Kathmandu: Human Resources Development Research Centre.

Stolow, J. 2005. Religion and/as media. *Theory, Culture and Society* 22:119–145.

Sullivan, N. 1993. Film and television production in Papua New Guinea: how media became the message. *Public Culture* 5(3): 533–555.

Terkel, S. 2008. "The People's voice," in *The Weekend Australian Magazine,* 5–6th January, pp. 24–25.

Thieme, S., and S. Wyss. 2005. Migration patterns and remittance transfer in Nepal: a case study of Sainik Basti in Western Nepal. *International Migration* 43(5): 59–98.

Thomas, N. 1991. *Entangled Objects.* Cambridge, Mass.: Harvard University Press.

Thussu, D. K. Editor. 1998. *Electronic Empires: Global Media and Local Resistance.* London: Arnold.

Tinau Watershed Project. 1983. *A Report on the Study of Non-Agricultural Activities in Palpa District.* Unpublished report. Kathmandu: New Era/TWP.

Toffin, G. 1995. "The social organization of Rajopadhyaya Brahmans," in *Contested Hierarchies: A Collaborative Ethnography of Caste among the Newars of the Kathmandu Valley, Nepal.* Edited by D. N. Gellner and D. Quigley, pp. 186–208. Oxford: Clarendon Press.

Turner, R. L. 1980 [1931]. *A Comparative and Etymological Dictionary of the Nepali Language.* New Delhi: Allied Publishers Ltd.

Turner, T. 1991. "Representing, resisting, rethinking: historical transformations of Kayapo culture and anthropological consciousness," in *Colonial Situations: Essays on the Contextualization of Anthropological Knowledge*. Edited by J. G. W. Stocking, pp. 285–313. Wisconsin: The University of Wisconsin Press.

—. 1992. Defiant images: the Kayapo appropriation of video. *Anthropology Today* 8:5–16.

—. 1995a. Representation, collaboration and mediation in contemporary ethnographic and indigenous media. *Visual Anthropology Review* 11: 102–106.

—. 1995b. Social body and embodied subject: bodiliness, subjectivity, and sociality among the Kayapo. *Cultural Anthropology* 10(2): 143–170.

Uprety, N. P., and Y. N. Acharya. 1994. *An Outline History of Nepal*. Kathmandu: R.C. Timothy, Ekta Books Distributors Pvt. Ltd.

USAID. 1999. *The Role of Media in Democracy: A Strategic Approach*. Centre for Democracy and Governance, Bureau for Global Programs, Field Support, and Research, USAID.

Vajracharya, C. L. 2039 VS [1982]. Nepalko bhai Palpa [Palpa Nepal's younger brother]. *Palpa Darpan* 1:15–20.

van der Veer, P. 1994. *Religious Nationalism: Hindus and Muslims in India*. Berkeley: University of California Press.

van Dijk, J. A. G. M. 2006. Digital divide research, achievements and shortcomings. *Poetics* 34(4/5): 221–235.

Vir, D. 1988. *Education and Polity in Nepal: An Asian Experiment*. New Delhi: Northern Book Centre.

von Fürer-Haimendorf, C. 1956. Elements of Newar social structure. *The Journal of the Royal Anthropological Institute of Great Britain and Ireland* 86(2): 15–38.

Weiner, J. 1997. Televisualist anthropology: representation, aesthetics, politics. *Current Anthropology* 38(2): 197–235.

Whelpton, J. 1983. *Jang Bahadur in Europe: The First Nepalese Mission to the West*. Kathmandu: Sahayogi Press.

—. 1994. "The general elections of May 1991," in *Nepal in the Nineties: Versions of the Past, Visions of the Future*. Edited by M. Hutt, pp. 48–81. Delhi: Oxford University Press.

—. 1997. "Political identity in Nepal: state, nation, and community," in *Nationalism and Ethnicity in a Hindu Kingdom: The Politics of Culture in Contemporary Nepal*. Edited by D. N. Gellner, J. Pfaff-Czarnecka, and J. Whelpton, pp. 39–78. Amsterdam: Harwood Academic Publishers.

—. 2005. *A History of Nepal*. Cambridge: Cambridge University Press.

Williams, R. 1965. *The Long Revolution*. London: Penguin Pelican Books.

—. 1993. *The Country and the City*. London: The Hogarth Press.

—. 1994. "Selections from *Marxism and Literature*," in *Culture/Power/History*. Edited by N. Dirks, G. Eley, and S. Ortner, pp. 584–608. Princeton, N.J.: Princeton University Press.

Wilmore, M. 2007. The digital divide and the social divide in new media access and their implications for the development of civil society in Nepal. *Asia Rights* 8. [http://rspas.anu.edu.au/asiarightsjournal/Issue%20Eight_Wilmore.htm].

—. 2008. Urban space and the mediation of political action in Nepal: local television, ritual processions and political violence as technologies of enchantment. *The Australian Journal of Anthropology* 19(1): 17–32.

Wilson III, E. J. 2004. *The Information Revolution and Developing Countries*. Cambridge, Mass.: MIT Press.

Worldview Nepal. 1988. *Communications in Nepal*. Kathmandu: Worldview International Foundation.

Worth, S. 1981. *Studying Visual Communication (edited with an introduction by Larry Gross)*. Philadelphia: University of Pennsylvania Press.

Worth, S., and J. Adair. 1972. *Through Navajo Eyes: An Exploration in Film Communication and Anthropology*. Bloomington: Indiana University Press.

Index